G000256298

URBAN FOX

Memoirs of an Edinburgh Poacher

URBAN FOX

Memoirs of an Edinburgh Poacher

Bob Redwater

Illustrations by Kathleen Lindsley

THE CROWOOD PRESS

First published in 2009 by
The Crowood Press Ltd
Ramsbury, Marlborough
Wiltshire SN8 2HR

www.crowood.com

© Bob Redwater 2009

All rights reserved. No part of this publication may be reproduced or transmitted in any form or by any means, electronic or mechanical, including photocopy, recording, or any information storage and retrieval system, without permission in writing from the publishers.

British Library Cataloguing-in-Publication Data
A catalogue record for this book is available from the British Library.

ISBN 978 1 84797 087 9

Typeset by Exeter Premedia Services Private Ltd., Chennai, India

Printed and bound in Great Britain by The Cromwell Press Group, Trowbridge

Contents

Dedication

This book is dedicated to the memory of Albert Taylor
aka 'Uncle Bob'

Acknowledgements

I would like to thank the following people for making this book possible, either by their practical help and encouragement or by their inspiration. My early love of nature was inspired by my Uncle Bob who was one of life's gentlemen, an ex-Para, a trout fisherman and a wonderful gardener who understood children and never patronized them. My eldest brother Peter was also someone I looked up to as a child; he was a great tree climber and cross-country runner, and a brave defender of our young family.

Then there is David McCutcheon, my work colleague, who had the patience of a saint in repeatedly instructing a Luddite like me in the basics of computer use. Also Gus McLean, bookseller and eternal optimist who gave me constant encouragement with my early attempts at writing. My friend Lone Eagle Mark Redfox, musician and artist, who gave me my Lakota name and shares my sense of humour. My parents Ruth and Joseph for bringing up six reasonably well balanced children: Peter, Joan, Tom, Ruth, Pauline and baby Francis who all still enjoy the simple things in life. My two talented children Rupert and Rebecca; and last but not least, my long-suffering wife Ellen who has been my constant companion for the last forty years, never batting an eyelid when I staggered into the house with fresh game over my shoulder.

Introduction

I woke at 4am and hit the button on the alarm clock before it went off. I dressed quickly and tiptoed quietly down the stairs without waking my wife and children. I slipped my wellies on in the hallway and put my camouflage jacket on. My old bicycle was leaning against the radiator with a .22 air rifle strapped along the crossbar in a dyed green canvas case. The bike had been painted green to aid invisibility when it was hidden in the woods. I didn't usually bother with breakfast before I left the house, but did take some bread and cheese for later.

Those early morning hunting expeditions were a regular part of my life and I loved being out and about while most law-abiding folk were still fast asleep in their beds. I was living the life of an urban hunter in Scotland's capital and it was very pleasant cycling through the city in the pre-dawn early morning before the stink of traffic polluted the nostrils with petrol and diesel fumes. In the summer months it was possible to smell fragrant flowers when passing by the small city gardens. In the city centre, squabbling seagulls were usually ripping at discarded greasy newspaper chip wrappers that had been dumped at the kerbside by late-night drinkers and slow-moving trucks from the cleansing department patrolled the streets, getting them spic and span for the bright new day ahead. Another familiar sight was the early morning stampede of horse-drawn milk carts from St Cuthbert's dairy beyond Tollcross. It was like a scene from the chariot race in the film *Ben Hur* and impressive to hear so many hoofbeats striking the cobbles. Sean Connery had started his working life at that depot not long before. While cycling through Edinburgh's business district in the New Town, I could see the office cleaners at work through the lighted windows of the splendid Georgian houses.

It was very enjoyable pedalling through those dark city streets in the early morning to get to my hunting grounds within the city limits. As much as I loved the countryside, it was much easier to remain anonymous as a hunter in the city. In a rural environment neighbours noticed things and tales were told. Edinburgh golf courses were always a good source of wild meat: rabbits were plentiful, and brown hares were also a familiar sight on most of the fairways in my youth. The enemy of this city poacher was not the gamekeeper but the occasional pre-breakfast jogger in a pink tracksuit, thumping and gasping his way through the woods, scattering the wildlife ahead of him. I called him the Pink Panter.

1
Growing Up in the City

Public opinion about the status of a person who lives on these islands, owning no land himself but who manages to hunt and fish to feed his own family, is open to debate. Freelance hunters have roamed this land since the beginning of time and there still seems to be a powerful urge for some individuals to continue that tradition into the modern age. Ancient tribes would have protected their hunting domains by force and things are little different today. Landowners still have the backing of the law relating to the ownership of free-ranging wild animals passing through their land. The migrating Atlantic salmon, returning to their birthplaces in our Scottish rivers as wild free fish, are also claimed by the landowner.

In Norman times, when the game laws were at their most severe, a peasant armed with a bow and arrow could be hanged with his own bow string for taking a wild deer from the forest. This capital penalty was later reduced to a lesser punishment to protect the lives of the king's foresters – after all, if a man was going to be killed for feeding his family, then he may as well take a few game-keepers with him in an attempt to escape. But whatever the penalties for poaching game, men have always seemed willing to take the risk and hunt outside the law to provide meat for their families, and the satisfaction of obtaining wild meat by skill and cunning is something very familiar to me because I have done it for most of my life.

Early Childhood

It may be of interest to the reader to hear some-thing of my early life, which might explain how I became a hunter in the city of Edinburgh.

As a child I spent much of my time wandering the countryside on the city outskirts watching birds and animals in the woods and fields. I enjoyed my solitary journeys of discovery because there was always so much more to see when walking alone, silently through the landscape. Egg collecting was very much in vogue during my youth and many boys had modest collections of wild birds' eggs displayed in cottonwool-lined shoeboxes. Those wasted lives, yolks blown through pierced holes in shell ends, were never given a second thought; it was the equivalent of collecting cigarette cards, a passing fad of childhood.

Kim the Crow

I found a fledgling crow on one of my walks, squatting quietly in the long grass under a tall pine tree. The black feathers against the green stems gave no camouflage to the unfortunate creature and a small boy's roving eyes could focus on the smallest detail in the landscape. I picked up the young bird and launched it into the air, expecting to see it fly away, but it parachuted down again on weak wings, landing only a few feet away, croaking indignantly. I lifted the bird and cradled it in my small hands, examining it and placing it gently under my jumper where it settled down after a brief struggle, the sharp black claws on its feet protruding through the knitted navy wool. I could feel the warmth of the bird's body against my stomach. My mother had warned me on more than one occasion about bringing home hungry mouths to feed. I had three sisters and two brothers, Peter,

Joan, Ruth, Pauline and baby Francis, so Ma wasn't overly happy to see the new arrival, especially after receiving a painful peck on that sensitive area of soft skin between her fingers as she tried to stroke the shiny black head.

'Aw Ma, please let me keep it. It'll only eat scraps. It won't cost anything to feed.'

'We'll see what your father has to say about that when he gets home from work.'

That evening the young crow was fed on bread soaked in milk and then stowed in a large cardboard box in the garden shed – out of sight, out of mind – and mother said nothing to my father when he arrived home from work.

In the morning, after my father had left for work, I slipped out to the shed and heard a scratching sound from the bottom of the box. The crow was still very much alive and squawking to be fed, its wide yellow and pink gape fully exposed, waiting for food to be posted in. There were streaks of white droppings lining the box and a musty smell. A bond was quickly formed between myself and the crow, which I christened 'Kim'.

Kim grew quickly on a varied diet, which included food that the family deliberately left over for him. Baked beans and bacon rind were great favourites. The neighbours also saved scraps and enjoyed watching the crow gobble them down. His body grew larger and his feathers grew longer and he began to fly in stages, first flapping to the hand to be fed, then on to the fence, and eventually on to the roof of the house where he was safe from the neighbourhood cats. Kim was gradually becoming a celebrity in the area, although some of his bad habits became quite an irritation to the neighbours. For instance, his early morning visits to the doorsteps, on his milk round, caused much annoyance. The silver foil tops on the milk bottles were stabbed through and the thick cream was siphoned off – and the victims of these visits were unlikely to believe that blue-tits were responsible for the crime.

Kim liked to bathe in a tin bath in the garden and having been raised by a human in place of his mother, his self-preservation skills were limited. One day, a local cat stalked him while he was busy with his ablutions. His feathers were waterlogged and he was unable to fly. The moggie hesitated in its attack and received a stab in the head for its lack of confidence – but the incident fuelled a powerful dislike of felines by Kim.

As Kim grew in size, he also grew in confidence, sitting high on the roof ridge waiting for any unsuspecting cat to follow its regular path through the back gardens. Several unfortunate cats had their wanderings curtailed when they were buzzed by a very angry crow with an old score to settle. The cat's escape route could be monitored by following the crow's progress as it dive-bombed over every garden hedge low-level, sparrowhawk style.

I was able to take my new pet with me to school on account of a sympathetic teacher who shared my fondness for wild birds and Kim was happy to perch on top of the blackboard at the front of the class and doze off. His eyelids would blink slowly and then remain shut while the children got on with their work in silence. When I ran home for dinner, Kim would fly most of the way, occasionally landing on my shoulder for a bumpy ride. My school blazer needed to be sponged down at regular intervals.

For some reason Kim took a dislike to my youngest sister, Pauline. She had always been afraid of the crow and would run away from him at every opportunity. She was low in the pecking order and that bird knew it and would fly after her, landing beside her and pecking her ankles, if he managed to get close enough – and Pauline's fear seemed to encourage the crow's efforts even more.

One of Kim's more endearing habits, while sitting on my shoulder, was to mutter soft sounds in my ear as he attempted to harvest the wax from within. He would also look inquisitively at his own reflection, using my eye as a mirror, and sometimes I would get my eyelashes gently preened. Maybe this was a bonding strategy. The rest of the family looked on in horror at the prospect of a small boy getting his eyes pecked out by a bird with a murderous reputation.

Some years later I did witness a pretty horrific attack, and one that justified the fearful reputation of the carrion crow. I was walking up a steep hill, struggling through deep heather to reach the summit, when I noticed two crows riding the wind against the skyline. They seemed to be making low passes at something on the ground, something I was unable to see until I got a bit nearer to the spot. As I got closer to the top of the hill I saw an old ewe lying on her back, her legs flailing in the air. Her fleece was wet and heavy from the boggy ground she was lying in and her belly was swollen and bloated. I managed to roll her over into an upright position with her legs folded underneath her, satisfied that I had been able to do something to aid the recovery of the poor beast. Ten minutes later, on reaching the top of the hill and turning round, I saw that the ewe was on her back again, her four legs once more in the air. The crows were also back and closing in. One of them landed just a few feet from the sheep's head and stood cautiously for a few seconds before hopping sideways to get nearer and then stabbing the sheep's eye and backing off again. The ewe thrashed about but was unable to rise to defend herself. The second crow landed and they both continued the attack, pecking at the sheep's head and retreating again, backwards and forwards, like some macabre dance. By the time I had run back down to her she had lost both eyes and had stopped breathing. It was a brutal nature lesson for a young boy, which was to haunt me for years.

I continued my hike over the hill and came across a herd of red deer which scattered and ran uphill over a bog. One single hind remained, licking at something in the heather. She moved away reluctantly as I walked towards her but continued to watch me, circling around, keeping the same distance. I found a newborn calf with the afterbirth still on it. It lay still and didn't move. Its fur was still wet and its long legs were folded beneath it. There were fleas all over its nose and its tiny hooves were black at the tips but white halfway up and still soft. It was a beautiful creature. I walked away and watched the mother go straight back to her infant. A couple of hours later, walking past the same hill, I saw the deer herd running with the little one in tow, keeping up with the others.

Anyone who has ever observed the behaviour of crows cannot fail to have been struck by their intelligence. Kim was a skilled thief and not beyond stalking his intended target on foot. He seemed to have quickly realized that he became easier to detect if he was flapping his wings in the vicinity of his intended victim. On one memorable occasion, Kim had observed two neighbourhood women gossiping outside the house just beyond the gate, their full shopping bags beside them. Kim had always had a liking for butter and had been chased from our kitchen table on numerous occasions, in the act of pilfering the golden fat. Kim, up on the roof ridge, watched the gossiping women with interest, then flew down into the garden and approached one of the unguarded shopping bags through a hole in the hedge and along the pavement.

Neither woman noticed the stealthy approach, or saw the crow hopping up on to the bag. There was nothing to Kim's liking on the top of the bag, so he rocked gently back and forth until the bag fell over, spilling the contents on to the ground. A pack of butter toppled on to the pavement and the delinquent bird helped himself to a generous portion before he was spotted and chased away with a slow and clumsily aimed kick. He wiped his greasy bill on the roof gutter where he had made himself comfortable, ready for a well earned snooze.

On windy or rainy nights, Kim would let himself into my bedroom through the window, which was always left open, and his contented muttering could be heard in the darkness from his perch at the end of the bed. Kim became a permanent feature around our house for the next two years until a second crow began to make house calls, sitting in a tall ash tree at the back of the house. The visiting bird was wary, and showed no tameness towards humans. These visits usually lasted only a few minutes but became more frequent as the weeks went by.

I rose one morning to an uncharacteristic silence. There was no squawking crow to meet me in the garden seeking scraps for breakfast. Kim had flown.

I searched the surrounding area, calling my pet's name, and asked all the neighbours to look out for him. This loss was a painful lesson in growing up, and I was devastated by the disappearance of my faithful pet. My mother made every attempt to console me, and told me that birds had to raise families too, but I was not convinced, sobbing for days afterwards and unable to concentrate on anything else.

Rosie the Jay

I was desperate to get another wild bird that I could train, and when spring came around I explored the woods searching for a likely nest that might supply a suitable candidate. I found one, a jay's nest at the top of a tall spindly hawthorn tree. I shinned up to the nest, collecting thorns in both hands and several in my knees. There were three tiny fledglings in the nest that were far too small to remove, so I bided my time and waited for them to grow, and several weeks later returned to the tree to make my selection. The choice was made easier when one of the birds took its maiden flight as my head levelled with the nest.

The bird landed safely in the soft grass below the tree and didn't move. I slid back down the tree as fast as I could go, scooped up my prize and rushed home to show my long-suffering mother the bird that I had 'rescued'. Looking back it is hard to justify stealing a chick from its mother.

The new chick was christened Rosie, on account of her predominant colour. Her squawk was much higher pitched than that of the crow. She had an impressive crest on her head which stood up whenever she squawked and she had the most beautiful blue wing flashes, giving her a very exotic appearance. The gender of the jay had been guessed at, just like the crow's and Rosie's upbringing was a carbon copy of Kim's.

She grew quickly and began to fly free when she was strong enough to look after herself. Her personality was quite different from the crow's. She was a little more timid and lacked the boldness that Kim had demonstrated from an early age. She was smaller than her predecessor and noticeably lighter on my shoulder. Another difference was the slight hook at the tip of her beak, a configuration that was an aid in carrying plundered eggs from other birds' nests.

Rosie became a favourite with the neighbours, being less of a thief than Kim had been and rather more reserved. Unfortunately there was to be a tearful end to this relationship, too.

My family was going on a summer holiday to North Wales for two weeks. I didn't want to go with them if I wasn't able to take Rosie but my father wasn't having any of that nonsense and I was going, whether I liked it or not. A neighbour had agreed to keep an eye on the jay and to feed her each day to ensure that she would stay around the house until we came back but I had a miserable holiday being separated from my pet. I missed her every day and I had a strong sense of foreboding.

When the family returned home, there was no sign of Rosie. Family and friends searched everywhere and once again the neighbours were asked to look out for the missing bird.

After two weeks, there was a breakthrough…great news: the local paperboy had heard a bird squawking in a garden shed nearby. I went round to investigate and was elated when I saw Rosie through the dusty window. She was sitting on a workbench looking dishevelled and unhappy. Her beautiful wings had been clipped and she was squawking, with her crest fully raised.

The shed was padlocked. I was very, very angry. I went round to the front door of the house and knocked as loudly as I could but there was no one at home. I considered breaking the shed window to retrieve my stolen pet but went home to decide what to do next. I made several return trips before someone finally answered the door. A grumpy-looking man came out.

'Please could I have my bird back?' I asked politely.

'It's a wild bird and I'm keeping it,' he told me. I pleaded with him to let the bird decide.

'If you let her out, she'll come to me and I can prove she's mine,' I begged him. I wanted to call her by name – if the man would just open the shed door then I could demonstrate and prove my ownership of the captive bird.

'P— off and don't come back, I don't want you hanging around here thieving,' he told me.

Feeling ready for a good sob, I walked away, completely dejected, and had never felt so depressed in all my young life.

My father went round to speak to the man the following evening but the bird was gone and the shed was empty. God knows what he had done with her. Using hindsight I realized that *I should have broken* into the shed to rescue my wild companion, but breaking and entering wasn't something I would have considered, and my father would have thrashed the living daylights out of me.

This bad experience had a lasting effect on me, and, like many children, I was shocked by the injustice of adults who should have known better. I had expected an entirely different reaction to my heartfelt plea.

The Owl

There were several other wild pets in our household during my childhood, including a tawny owl my big brother brought home one day from the woods. It was another case of rescuing a creature that hadn't been lost and its mother would have known exactly where it was.

On a previous occasion Peter had been very lucky to escape serious injury when he had shinned up to an owl's nest in the top of a pine tree. The bird had been on the nest at the time, about thirty feet up. I watched my brother take a rest when he was half way up, and then an owl's head appeared at the nest hole – but Peter didn't notice as the bird plunged down on to him, feet first. The owl caught him on the top of his head with one of its sharp talons, leaving a deep gash; if Peter had been looking upwards, he would probably have lost an eye.

He lost his grip on the tree and slid down the rough bark, landing on his feet at the bottom. The buttons were ripped off his shirt and his stomach and chest were badly scratched; both his hands were bleeding and blood was dripping down his forehead from the wound in his scalp.

Peter's owlet was kept in the shed and fed frequently on small birds that came within range of his air rifle or catapult. Another source of prey was obtained by the comic book method of using a bin lid, propped up with a stick which was attached to a long piece of string. Bread bait was scattered under the trap and we brothers concealed ourselves inside the house. Very few birds were taken this way, usually starlings. Whenever we approached the shed at feeding time, we could hear the clicking of the owl's beak in anticipation of its meal. Feeding was easy: one sparrow, head first, straight down.

I liked to carry the bird around with me whenever I got the chance and both of my arms were scarred where the owl's talons had pierced my shirt, jumper and blazer. Later I realized that a rolled-up newspaper inside my sleeve provided adequate protection from those needle sharp claws. Raising an owl was not as easy as fostering a member of the crow family. The local butcher saved scraps for the hungry bird and he was well fed. Raw meat was an absolute necessity but owls also need fur and feathers to aid digestion, as we would find out to our cost.

Owlbert, as we called him, was mainly active in the late afternoon and early evening when the shed door would be left open so that he could fly across the garden to the kitchen door to be fed. It was always unnerving when he suddenly appeared close by. His flight was completely silent, unlike other birds, and his movements were ghostlike. Sitting on his perch, his head constantly bobbed from side to side and sometimes swivelled right round so that he could see behind him. The local cats usually avoided him. His large eyes gave him a human appearance.

One morning Owlbert was found dead in his nest box. It was likely that the butcher-meat diet had not provided him with the necessary ingredients for a healthy life. We experienced a sense of guilt when we were made aware that the easy feeding option had probably been responsible for the bird's premature demise.

Other Wild Pets

I came home one day with a wild rabbit, which I had smoked out of its burrow using smoldering grass. I caught it as it bolted into my jacket sleeve, which had been tied at the cuff with a shoelace and placed over the exit hole.

My mother gave me a long-suffering look when I wandered into the house with yet another pet. It was always the same reaction. Yet again she told me she had no intention of looking after my latest pet and that she already had enough to do in the house; but the rabbit settled in nicely and spent the evenings with the family in the living room where it would hop around from person to person before running up my mother's legs and settling on her lap while she knitted. We children teased our mother and called her a big softie.

Feeding a rabbit was the easiest thing in the world, usually with carrots and cabbage leaves. I also collected rose-bay willow-herb and dandelions, which the rabbit was very fond of. This particular pet was one of the more successful members of the family and lived to a respectable old age – although one of its few faults was peeing in the house, and it was remarkable just how much liquid that small animal could carry in its bladder.

In the spring, when I wandered about the fields, hares were a common sight and I caught several leverets simply by walking up on them. The method I used was by approaching them at an angle without turning my head to look at them directly. The nearer you got to a crouching hare, the smaller it appeared as it pressed its body lower and lower on to the ground, and it was always handy to have a jacket ready to throw over the squatting animal. Years later I used the same stalking method to get within rifle range of adult hares. I took one of the captured leverets home – yet another pet – but the poor creature never settled and appeared highly strung. I took it back to the field the next day.

Another pet was a shop-bought grass snake which cost me three weeks' pocket money. My father refused to let the snake stay in the house and the reptile was left in the garden overnight in an old aquarium with a sheet of glass placed on top and a house brick on top of that for added security – but by morning the snake was gone. I hadn't had time to form a close bond with this new pet, but the financial loss was upsetting enough. The neighbours were not very enthusiastic about helping with the search, and some of them were unnecessarily alarmed.

The Killing Game

Killing a wild *thing* for the first time was a shock to the system, and the initial experience was one of shame and regret.

At the age of fourteen, I spent all my savings on an ancient but serviceable air rifle. The transaction had been done furtively, largely because my father despised guns after his wartime experiences. He had been an anti-aircraft gunner on merchant ships in the Atlantic and Mediterranean and had been sunk twice by U-boats, losing many of his friends.

One day my brother Peter brought home an unexploded German incendiary bomb which he left on the mantelpiece for the family to admire. Apparently the device had crashed through the roof of an outdoor toilet during the Blitz and had been kept as a souvenir by a lady my brother knew. When Dad got home he was furious and took the bomb to the river, where he dropped it from the bridge into a deep pool. At the time we all thought he was a spoilsport.

I concealed the newly acquired air rifle in my big brother's old canvas golf bag, which was never used; the few clubs in it were all rusty. I bought ammunition from the gun shop the following day, and ran all the way home to test the weapon. I sneaked up to my bedroom and sat by the open window with the loaded rifle, careful not to poke the barrel beyond the curtains in case one of the neighbours spotted me.

A few small birds flitted about the garden, none of them in range. Eventually there was the monotonous cheep of a house sparrow on the roof above. The unfortunate creature hopped into view to take a drink from the gutter and was a sitting target at a distance of only twelve feet. I closed one eye, took aim, and squeezed the trigger. 'Thwack': it was a direct hit. My hands were shaking as I shoved the rifle under the bed and ran downstairs and opened the front door. The poor bird was lying on the doormat, feet up, stone dead. I picked up the tiny body, which was warm and soft, and there was blood coming from its beak. No one had witnessed the crime, but I was ashamed of what I had done. I dug a hole in the garden and buried the body.

After several days the guilt began to subside, and the temptation to test my marksmanship became a stronger impulse. Birds were everywhere, in the garden, on the roof and in the trees. The next target was a starling sitting on a neighbour's chimney about fifty yards away. It seemed an impossible distance to hit something so small. I took aim, then decided not to shoot, but aimed again and this time did squeeze the trigger. The bird fell from its perch and rolled down the roof into the gutter, where a wing-tip was all that could be seen. It was unnecessary to dispose of the body.

I realized that shooting something for sport could never be justified and I knew it was wrong, but my hunting instinct was extremely strong, like a drug; I could think of nothing else. During the school holidays I would be out in the woods and fields looking for game. On one occasion I was out in the early morning on a golf course; it had been a dry summer and the pond there was only a few inches deep. I saw a golf ball just below the surface of the clear water, took aim – and learned a valuable lesson that I would never forget. The pellet ricocheted straight back, parting my hair and grazing my scalp, drawing blood. A little lower and I could have lost an eye.

Dragonflies became a tempting target as they flew slowly past, hunting midges and I hit one with a lucky shot, snapping it in half; another wasted life.

Rats

One evening I walked past our municipal rubbish tip in the failing light and there were rats running everywhere. I sat and watched for a while. They made very difficult moving targets. When they stopped it was only for seconds and they used every available bit of cover as they sprinted across small clearings.

I heard a shot from an air rifle and noticed someone else sitting in the shadows; I went over to investigate and found a youth not much older than myself. He had a very curious profile: his face was distinctly rat-like in that he had no chin, a prominent nose and a sloped-back forehead, and his hair was trimmed in a crew cut, which emphasized his odd appearance. But he was a good marksman, and there was a row of freshly killed rats lined up neatly at his feet. When it got too dark to see much, the rat-boy produced a torch, which he fixed to the barrel of his rifle. He was an excellent shot and rarely missed and I enjoyed watching a master sniper at work. The boy was shy and didn't say much; he got bullied at school, and told me that he was waiting to get plastic surgery to fix his nose.

In my younger days I once put my hand down a small hole in the riverbank, looking for sand martins' nests, and felt something soft in my hand: it was a rat's face, and I soon felt its teeth when it bit my finger and drew blood. After the initial shock, and narrowly avoiding a tumble in the river, I kicked out at the retreating rat and disabled it before picking it up by the tail and twirling it round in the air to avoid being bitten again. An elderly man cycling past on the bridge stopped and insisted on crushing the rat's head with his hobnail boot. The old chap told me the tail was worth a shilling, but I threw the rat in the river and sacrificed the bounty money.

I had no love for rats and took every opportunity to kill them. However, the novelty of shooting them soon diminished when I realized it was an expensive waste of pellets that could be better used for hunting edible species.

Initial Success in the Hunting Field

My first success in the hunting field was the shooting of a woodpigeon. The plump dove was roosting in the top of an elm tree in the early evening and I fired from directly underneath it, getting a crick in my neck from the acute angle. The pigeon dropped like a house brick, landing on my head. In its crop were twenty-four acorns. I plucked the bird on the way home and presented it to my mother. She made a bread stuffing and roasted it for me. There was something very satisfying about bringing home wild meat. I liked the flavour and was keen to get more.

I knew that early morning was the best time to be out hunting; animals and birds were more active and there was less chance of being seen by anyone else. I was able to dismantle my rifle in two parts so that it could be concealed under my coat, the stock and the barrel hanging on opposite sides of my chest from two coat-hanger hooks attached to a thick piece of string around the back of my neck. I had to carry a screwdriver for reassembly. My father was still unaware of this secret weapon.

A grey squirrel was the next experimental culinary treat. Apparently the Americans found them a great delicacy but the roast carcass was a great disappointment: the meat was tough, rubbery and very unappetizing, although the strong, thick skin made a nice addition to the cover of my rifle case. There were also bounty payments on grey squirrel tails, but I discovered that I could sell them to the fishing shop for making trout flies and so traded squirrel tails for air pellets at a favourable exchange rate.

One autumn day I stalked a pond where I had heard wild ducks calling, and managed to crawl through the long dry grass to a good vantage point to get a better view. Ducks have remarkably good eyesight and are very wary. There was a pair of mallards on the water, near the middle of the overgrown pond. There was a slight ripple on the surface. I aimed at the drake. The pellet hit it in the head and the bird flapped all over the pond before lying still in the middle with its head below the surface. I had to strip off and wade out to claim my prize, but there was enough meat on the duck to share with the others at home. I sold the wings to the fishing shop, the blue wing flashes being used for fly-tying; the soft downy breast feathers we kept to re-stuff an old pillow.

Trout Fishing

I bought an old trout rod I had seen advertised in the local newspaper; it was nine feet long. The only fish I had ever caught before were minnows in the burn, using a net, so I sought angling advice from a neighbour who was a keen trout fisherman.

Rab Douglas knew the best places to go and had a moped to get there. He told me to forget about fly fishing, and to start digging in the compost heap for worms; the best ones were the small reddish brandlings. The docken grub was also recommended as bait. These large, white, maggoty grubs were found inside the thick root of the dock weed, but it was hard work digging the plants up with a garden fork. They usually grew in fields where cattle grazed. Only about one in ten plants produced a grub, although occasionally two could be found hiding in the same hollowed-out stem. We kept the worms in sphagnum moss overnight to scour them and keep them firm and moist.

In the morning, Rab came round for me at 5am; it was still dark. The moped lurched up into the hills along rough tracks that were better suited to the Land Rovers that had made them. We stopped at a gate where a deep, narrow burn flowed down from the hills, and parked the bike. The surrounding vegetation was rough sheep grazing, rushes and deep heather. All was silent up there except for the occasional warbling call of a curlew.

Rab told me that if you saw a trout in a pool then you probably wouldn't catch it and that the real skill in hooking these wild fish lay in remaining unseen. He demonstrated his technique by crawling nearer to the bank, on all fours, after 'reading the water' upstream and seeing the likely places where fish would be lying.

Our tackle consisted of a small hook tied to eighteen inches of fine nylon line, which was attached to a heavier, green, sinking fly line on the reel. The reason for this was simple: the slightest breeze allows the baited hook to dance in the wind and makes it difficult to plop the worm into the water in a natural way, allowing it to sink deeper and flow with the current. If a feeding fish sees the bait dragging on the surface, it will take fright and dart under the bank to hide. I followed my companion's instructions and knelt in the heather just a little way from the bank. I flicked my line forwards and managed to drop the bait nicely into the shallows above a pool and watched the line drift downwards. There was a tug on the rod and I had caught my first wild brown trout.

It was a small fish, only about five inches long, but I was elated. It was one of the most beautiful things I had ever seen. The small hook came easily from its mouth and I admired the silvery flanks and bright red spots on its sides. Rab told me to release the fish downstream so as not to frighten the others. Upstream worming was the preferred method of catching hill trout. If they were facing into the current then you were approaching them from behind with less chance of being seen. Between us we caught another six undersized trout, none of them big enough to take home.

After hooking a fish it was necessary to take a step back and flick the rod over the shoulder away from the water. Sometimes fish were able to grip the worm without getting hooked and fell back into the water before they were landed. I was a little over-enthusiastic in landing my second fish and managed to flick it off the hook, into the heather some distance behind me and it took a five-minute search to find it.

Trout left slime on the hands and a very distinctive smell but I liked the pungent odour. Going home empty-handed was no disgrace: I had learned a new skill.

Trout fishing became an important part of my life, and I was able to get to many fishing places on my bicycle. There was something very satisfying about being alone in the hills, and carrying a fishing rod drew far less attention than carrying a gun. Any shepherds I met were usually friendly. I became familiar with many of the clear, narrow, meandering hill burns, and soon learned where all the holding pools were. If you ever caught a fish in one pool, then you would almost certainly catch another on a return visit. The biggest fish in the pool would normally get caught first, due to the pecking order when feeding, although very big fish were understandably too smart to get taken easily.

On one of my trips I noticed a slender pole that had been laid across the burn to act as a bridge for stoats and weasels. There was a sprung Fenn trap hanging by a chain underneath it. Gamekeepers often set them like this and caught other creatures by accident. They were non-selective if badly set, and this one had a moorhen trapped by the legs. It must have walked across the trap, then fallen and drowned. I left the trap as I found it. The following week I saw the trap again and this time it had a blackbird in it. I felt quite justified in removing the trap, which I hid in the bracken, to pick up on the way back. As far as I knew, no one had seen me removing or concealing it and I thought I could put the trap to better use myself.

I lost all sense of time and distance when climbing the hills following a swift-running burn. The fish were correspondingly smaller in size nearer to the source and I noticed that the colour of a fish often matched its immediate surroundings. For instance, if a resident trout was caught in a deep, slow-moving, shadowy pool, then it would be slightly darker in colour than the bright silvery fish from the swift-moving shallower water.

On one occasion I made an unexpected catch with my rod. I approached a pool that I knew well near a shepherd's cottage, close to the track. A stone wall, built to support the road, formed the near bank. The burn was about five feet below the road level.

I had fished this pool many times before and usually caught a trout. The method, as always, was to remain unseen by keeping well back from the edge and lowering the baited hook gently down into the upstream current, allowing it to sink mid-water and then drift down naturally into the pool. The line went tight, more like a snag than a nibble. The rod bent double and the line ran off the reel with a screech. I held up the rod, as I had been taught, and watched in amazement as a mallard duck tried to fly away with my tackle. The duck had been lightly hooked in one leg and was airborne, attempting to make its escape by flapping as fast as it could in the direction of the hill opposite. It was a surreal moment, without a witness. Who was going to believe what had happened?

I managed to wind the unfortunate bird in safely and discovered that she had been shielding six small ducklings under the mossy bank below. The little ones splashed upstream, diving underwater like little fish, and were hidden from view in seconds, well camouflaged in their brown and yellow coats. It took less than a minute to release their captive mother, who flew downstream before circling back overhead and landing upstream where her brood had concealed themselves.

On a previous occasion, near the same place, I had flicked a worm under the opposite bank and watched it drift downstream in the slow current. There was a tiny splash near the bait. It wasn't a fish, but a weasel that had dived into the water from the far bank to investigate a possible meal. The skinny wee animal doggy-paddled towards me, but when it saw me it did a U-turn, hauling itself out on to a rock, then into the long grass where it disappeared.

One of my friends went fishing with me. It was a twenty-mile round trip to my favourite trout stream in the Pentland Hills. It was a bright, sunny spring morning and a nice day for a cycle ride, although not ideal for fishing. My friend Gareth was not a country boy but he was game for anything, and we caught a few small trout and enjoyed the walk up into the hills.

On the way I stopped to admire a solitary bunch of wild yellow primroses that came up every year under the same rowan tree on a steep bank, and which had miraculously survived the grazing and trampling of the blackface sheep in the area. This was the only place I ever saw those flowers on the hill. I walked on ahead, and my companion came after me calling for me to wait. Then he came alongside, proudly displaying the looted prize in his grubby hands: he had dug the primroses out of the riverbank to take home for his mother. I was furious, and never took Gareth fishing with me again.

I explored every possible fishing place for miles around, and having a bike gave me a wide range. Someone told me about a place that had good-sized trout, wild brown and rainbow. It was in a narrow stretch of water between a reservoir dam and a wide river, and I had been advised that I would need waders and the ability to climb over fallen trees and slimy rocks. The place turned out to be extremely productive, although the down side was that for every fish hooked, only half were landed. This was because of the trees and low overhanging branches, which restricted the movement of the rod. The small hooks regularly got snagged on the branches and I lost several lengths of nylon. The banks were carpeted in wild garlic and the smell was overpowering, but a few leaves added to a cheese sandwich made a tasty lunch.

On the way up to the dam, a pair of roe deer jumped across the burn upstream, and dozens of woodpigeons came clattering out of the fir trees where they were nesting. The place was teeming with wildlife. When I got to a grassy clearing, I almost trod on a rabbit in the long grass. The bunny ran uphill as fast as its legs would carry it to a warren on the sandy bank above. Just as the rabbit was about to plunge into the hole, a black cat appeared and caught it by its flanks with both paws. The momentum of the rabbit took the cat down into the burrow with it.

I dropped my rod and ran up the hill to the entrance hole where the pair had disappeared, and lay on the earth listening to what was going on deep underground. There was a muffled thumping and bumping and something was getting a damned good kicking. After about ten minutes the cat reappeared tail first. It was covered in sand and had a torn ear and a closed eye. It hadn't been pleased to see me when it surfaced and limped off into the bracken.

I have never been very fond of cats. As a small child I witnessed an incident on my way to school, which left me with a strong dislike of the feline species. There was a chaffinch feeding on a grass verge under an oak tree and the finch was caught by a cat, which stalked it from behind the tree. I watched as the bird was crippled and then played with, for the cat's amusement. I picked up a rock and chased the cat down a garden path, where I took aim as it stopped to look back; but before I could launch the missile, the front door opened and an elderly woman stood watching me. It was her cat.

She was surprisingly sympathetic and told me that the cat was always bringing birds into the house. She was quite apologetic and pleased to hear that I was so interested in birds. She told me to wait while she went inside for a few minutes and came back out again with a book on birds' nests with beautiful colour illustrations, which she gave to me to read. Unfortunately for the bird population, the book gave me a new interest in identifying and collecting wild birds' eggs.

Beginner's Luck

I took my big brother Peter to try his hand at trout fishing and managed to borrow a spare rod so that we wouldn't need to share mine. I also took a landing net, although I had never used one before. We went to the wild burn between the river and the reservoir and I felt proud that I could teach my older brother something I knew more about than he did. We caught a few smallish trout that were just about big enough to eat, and Peter was enjoying himself catching anything at all.

When we reached the uppermost pool, which was below the high dam, I baited Peter's hook with a fresh worm. The pool was only about twelve feet across, but was deep and dark and there was a fallen tree lying half-submerged, diagonally, making snagging very likely. I thought I would let the novice have the last shot at the fishing. I showed my brother how to make a gentle cast above the log and let the bait sink smoothly beneath it. Straightaway there was a great splash and thrashing on the surface of the water and I was flabbergasted when I saw the size of the fish, a big rainbow trout. I bawled at my brother to keep his rod up while I got the landing net under the fish. The trout weighed three and a half pounds, and was the biggest fish I had ever seen there. A half-pound trout was considered a good specimen from this burn. The small hook had hardly penetrated the fish's mouth and without the landing net it would have been 'the big one that got away'.

Brotherly Love

Peter and I always had a turbulent relationship as children. There was an age difference of three years between us, and sometimes Peter didn't know his own strength. My father once brought home a pair of boxing gloves a colleague at work had given to him, and we brothers had sparring matches with each other using one glove each. But I got fed up with being used as a punchbag by my brother, who soon forgot his promise not to hurt me.

One of the most dangerous contests between us was with German cavalry sabres. The swords had been acquired by a relative as souvenirs from World War I. The engraved blades were curved and had decorative basket hilts with sharkskin handles. One morning we lunged at each other all over the garden, trampling the flowers as we went. I was wounded in the hand when my brother's sword tip penetrated the pierced design in the steel guard of my sword. The blade tip sliced into my index finger above the second joint and slid along the bone and there was a lot of bloodshed. My old battle scar still remains visible today. My mother was blissfully unaware of these shenanigans and inflicted wounds were usually explained as 'I just tripped over in the garden and landed on something sharp.'

There was also a Samurai sword in the house. It was a relatively short one, from World War II and standard issue for a Japanese army officer. It, too, was a souvenir, brought back by a POW from a Japanese prison camp. The scabbard was plain brown leather with a long handle that had a cut-out design with indented diamond shapes woven in white silk. I liked to play with this sword, which was best used with both hands and would wander around the garden slicing the heads off flowers; but one afternoon I took the sword up to my bedroom to test its cutting ability on something more substantial. I placed a chunk of wood on the edge of my bed, then I gripped the handle, adopted the stance, and brought the sword down with all my might. The wood was sliced in two, but so were the sheets, blankets and mattress. There was even a nick out of the metal strip that held the springs – but the sword blade was undamaged.

The Opposite Sex

When I developed an interest in the opposite sex, my fishing expeditions became less frequent. One of my fantasies was to meet a gorgeous girl of my own age who was equally interested in hunting and fishing and wasn't too squeamish when it came to bumping something off for the pot.

I seriously misjudged the sensitivity of a girl I had become very fond of. We had been out together a few times and usually ended up snogging in a grassy field somewhere. On one of our dates I had taken along an air pistol, which I thought she would find amusing, shooting at inanimate objects. As we walked along the riverbank we looked up at the swallows and house martins that were feeding in the sky above us. The birds had a very predictable flight path and flew above our heads, low and straight. I took out the pistol, loaded it, and waited for a swallow that was flying towards me. I pointed the gun, aiming about six feet in front of the flying bird and pulled the trigger. Thwack! I couldn't believe it. The bird came down on to the path about thirty feet away, stone dead.

My girlfriend was most certainly not impressed, she was mortified. The untimely demise of this innocent creature through casual gunplay brought an abrupt end to our promising relationship. Barbara was convinced that I made a regular practice of knocking swallows out of the sky with my deadly weapon.

Holiday Jobs

During the summer holidays I had several jobs. One of them was working in a market garden, which was hard work but reasonably well paid. The highlights of the day were the mealtimes; the portions of food were huge, and nothing was ever left over. Work began at 8am, with a break for sandwiches at 11am, and then dinner at 1pm, always thick slices of meat, new potatoes and two green vegetables. In the afternoon there was a sandwich break at 3.30pm and the day's work ended at 6pm.

Some of the chores were backbreaking, such as hoeing between the long rows of cabbages and lettuces or, even worse, weeding by hand between the hundred-yard rows of rhubarb plants. Occasionally I would see a fieldmouse or a toad, which would break the monotony of the work. The farmer's son always carried a twelve-bore shotgun in the tractor. Every morning he would see the same rabbit in the lettuce patch and take a pot shot as it ran for cover, but he was never able to hit it and probably did more damage to his crops than the rabbit did.

2
Flying the Nest

College Days

After leaving school I went to Art College to study graphic design. My brother Peter had already been there for three years, doing the same. For me, the next four years were bliss. I left home at the age of seventeen and got a place in a flat, sharing with two girls, Liz and Sue, who were fellow students, doing fashion design. The flat was in a rambling Victorian house, which had been sub-divided into three apartments; there were street pigeons on the roof, mice in the kitchen and rats in the basement.

I was never a tidy person, but the girls were even worse. Dishes were never washed and were left piled in the sink until someone needed a plate or cup; only then would someone bother to wash up. We were like three children enjoying our first taste of freedom, and we didn't let the rules of basic hygiene inconvenience us.

Domestic Warfare

That was until the mice appeared. The kitchen had bare floorboards with big gaps along the skirting boards and walking into the kitchen in bare feet and switching the light on was a good way of coming into close contact with wildlife. I bought a couple of mousetraps and set them each evening, baited with cheese. At first they were successful and caught several small mice, but the surviving rodents showed remarkable intelligence in avoiding the death traps. The killing machines became a 'no go' area, and mice were still running around the kitchen.

I had my reputation to consider and a gun would have to be used as a last resort. The problem was how to shoot these creatures without damaging the house? I had already converted my air pistol for killing houseflies and wasps. This was done by chewing up a small piece of paper – a bus ticket was ideal – then rolling the pulp into a torpedo shape and ramming it down the barrel. It was safer to do this before the gun was cocked to avoid shooting yourself in the hand. I would then shoot the bugs as they rested on the ceiling. Throughout the house were little blobs of dry paper pellets attached to the ceiling, some of them with flies underneath.

I devised a sniping plan for killing the rodent problem, positioning articles of clothing behind the surfaces where mice usually appeared to catch any ricochets, because this time I was using lead pellets. I made myself comfortable sitting in the doorway facing the gas cooker, and didn't have long to wait. A tiny mouse appeared and sat upright on the breadboard. I raised the pistol very slowly and took aim at the mouse, which was looking in my direction. I fired, and wasn't sure whether I had hit it or not, but the bloody grey smudge on the wall behind confirmed a direct hit. The remains were minimal, slim pickings: an ear, a tail and a couple of detached feet.

Further attempts were less successful and pellet holes multiplied in the kitchen walls. One ricochet cracked the kitchen window.

At night the rats appeared in the garden and could be seen by the light from the street lamp. I practised shooting downwards, through the first floor window, and soon had the range accurately calculated. The rat shooting was more successful. They sometimes squeaked when they were hit and the local cat dragged them off into the neighbour's cellar.

Urban Warfare

One Saturday morning, I was in my bedroom getting ready to go out when there was a loud crash at the window and a small round hole appeared in one of the panes. My room was at the back of our house and overlooked a row of identical terraced houses from the gable end, so whatever had been fired must have been from this street – the hole in my window was exactly in line with these. I went outside and walked up the narrow lane at the back of the houses. The yards all had brick walls around them, about head height and the view was limited. As I was heading back down the hill, I saw two hands above the wall, drawing back a catapult in the direction of our house.

'Hey! Don't you f—ing dare!' I bawled.

The wooden door in the wall was bolted on the inside and I couldn't get into the yard. But my blood was up and I was ready to punch the culprit's head when I got him. I ran back down the lane and round to the front of the house, identifying it by the colour of the drainpipes, which were the only red ones in the terrace. A respectable-looking woman answered the door and I told her what had happened.

'My son has been working on his bike all morning.'

As far as she was concerned, her boy had done nothing wrong. I stormed back to the house and checked my bedroom. Eureka! Lying on the carpet under a dent in the wall was the chrome nut from a bicycle spindle, which matched the hole in the window perfectly.

When I went back to the sniper's house, his mother answered the door again and I held out the incriminating evidence in the palm of my hand. The boy was called to the door and admitted what he had done. His face was as red as a beetroot and he stared at the floor. His mother accepted responsibility for his actions and went to get her purse; she handed me a ten bob [shilling] note, saying, 'That should be more than enough for the repair.'

'I'm sorry,' said the boy, grudgingly. I bet he got a real bollocking when I left.

I went straight round to the local hardware shop and bought a pane of glass and a tub of putty. I borrowed a long, heavy ladder from the neighbour and set it up against the back of the house. I was not the most organized person when it came to doing DIY jobs, and I scaled the ladder wearing only a pair of flip-flops on my bare feet. The foot of the ladder hadn't been secured and the floor in the yard was smooth cement covered in slimy moss; it was an accident waiting to happen, and it did.

While I was at the top of the ladder, digging out the last of the shards of jagged glass from the window frame, the ladder began to slide down the wall. I held on to one of the rungs with both hands, but the balance of the ladder shifted and it flipped over, leaving me hanging from the underside with my bare feet thrashing about for a foothold. The ladder continued to slide downwards, momentarily slowing down as it bounced off the window ledge below. I lost my grip and went into freefall, landing upright on the broken glass below. My flatmates were away for the weekend, so it was useless seeking help.

I had broken glass in both feet and they were bloody and filthy. I got back into the house on my hands and knees and was able to wash my feet in the bath and pick out some of the larger pieces. Fortunately, there was a bus stop at our front door and the local hospital was on the route. My feet were X-rayed and the doctor told me that I was lucky because it was old window glass and had lead in it, which showed up nicely on the film. I didn't feel lucky.

Living Dangerously

Our flat was a virtual death trap. In the bathroom there was faulty electrical wiring inside the plaster wall against the bath; this was an external wall which became damp after heavy rain, so there must have been a leakage problem on the roof. We flatmates received the occasional electric shock when we took a bath, but these only occurred when a certain combination of limb positions occurred. Thus, to get a shock, you had to have one hand on the tap, one hand on the damp wall and one foot in the bath. It was necessary to instruct guests on how to take a bath safely. Eventually the landlord sent an electrician round to check the complaint. He stuck his safety screwdriver into the damp plaster wall and the handle lit up.

Late one night the girls were awakened by noises on the roof above their rooms. Liz had a trapdoor in her ceiling, which opened directly on to the roof. I got the air rifle and whispered to the girls to open the trap slowly because there was someone moving about above. When the trapdoor was opened, I poked the gun barrel through the gap, and there was the sound of a body sliding downwards over the slates. There were voices below and whoever was there managed to make their escape down the drainpipe. In the morning light an inspection revealed damage where the thieves had stripped the lead from one of the gutters. It seemed a high risk venture for such small profit.

During my stay at the flat I bought a pair of fencing foils. I couldn't afford any safety gear like protective facemasks or padded vests, so my only concession to safety was leaving the small rubber stoppers on the tips. After an introductory skirmish with a fellow student, I experienced severe bruising to my ribs. Later I learned that the first thing you are supposed to do with a new foil is to bend it: this basic procedure allows the blade to give and reduces the risk of serious injury or death. Fencing duels became a regular fixture in our flat.

One of the rooms at the top of the house was well suited for these contests. It was a long, narrow room with bare floorboards and a low ceiling: the perfect swordsman's gallery. The room had no furniture in it and only a single naked light bulb dangling from the middle of the ceiling.

My chief opponent was a friend who had an equally cavalier attitude to mine where his own safety was concerned. We were quite well matched in fencing skills and soon got bored with the daily duels. To make things a little more interesting, we began to fence stripped to the waist and took the rubber tips off the foils. We agreed that the winner would be the first person to draw blood and these matches became rather more dangerous. We both received a variety of slight wounds. The ribs were the main target area, but I managed to get hit in the ear lobe and the neck. My friend got hit under his right eye. We didn't wear gloves and both of us developed scarred pinkies on our right hands.

On one memorable late night session, we had a long contest that was more like a chess game. We both knew each other's moves and were becoming more defensive in style, anticipating each other's attacks; my partner's eyebrow would often twitch before he lunged. We made a simultaneous strike and both hilts rammed together, forcing the blades upwards. The light bulb smashed and we were left in total darkness, with broken glass on our heads and shoulders. Sometimes you just know when a game is over.

Working on the Docks

In the sixties most students got paid jobs during the summer holidays, except for the wealthy ones who sponged off their parents and it was largely a matter of luck whether you found something cushy or not. One guy I knew had a highly paid job in an abattoir as a 'grade 3 killer', whatever that entailed; it sounded more like he should have been doing serious time in prison.

I had a friend at college who was studying medicine because both his parents were doctors. We were planning on working together during the holiday, but events overtook us. The Six Day War broke out in June, and he went to Israel to become a paratrooper; his name was Dan Cohen, and he was a Jewish boy committed to the survival of Israel. At that time the world thought that Israel's Arab neighbours would wipe out the Jewish State.

When Dan came back from Israel he was a different person. A sniper had killed his best friend as the two of them had sheltered in a doorway, and his friend's brains had been spattered all over him. He told me that when his company had attacked Arab villages, some women and children had been killed by Israeli grenades tossed through open windows. He was sickened by what he saw over there and his conscience bothered him. Back at college he switched from medicine to business studies, but he couldn't settle down as a student again and went to work in the City. I never saw him again.

That summer I got a holiday job through the Manpower Commission, working as a docker on the Manchester Ship Canal. The wages were very poor for the work that we did and the reason for this was because we worked in a small warehouse and not on the main dock, where the labour force was well organized and better paid. The job was a form of slave labour and most of the regular guys were struggling to make a living; some of them would have been better off on the dole. The work we did was almost the same as the men on the main river docks, except they had bigger ships. We unloaded barges from the canal on to lorries and vice versa.

The materials we handled were varied: there was cement, corn, chocolate, whisky, cotton imported from India and carpets exported to America. One of the bulkier loads was the great spools of newsprint that came in from the Swedish paper mills. The massive spools had to be levered off the truck by hand, using a specially shaped, long-shafted wooden wedge called a bodger. Materials needed to be handled in a certain way and we had to learn the skills quickly. The experienced crew showed us the ropes and then laughed when we screwed up and struggled with the jobs that they made look easy. It was a place where an unwary person could be very easily injured. The total workforce numbered thirteen and they were a mixed bunch of guys, most of whom didn't rate students very highly. I was one of three students working there for the summer.

Workmates

The foreman was universally disliked, and was not considered 'one of the lads'. He was a boss's man. He had been a tank commander in the Korean War, but had been captured by the enemy and tortured until he had nearly died. He hated all Orientals – and in Manchester the Chinese community formed a significant section of the population.

One of my favourite guys was a Glaswegian called Alec. He was as hard as nails, but was really kind-hearted and he looked after me. He showed me a scar down his back almost the full length of his spine. Alec had grown up in the Gorbals area and had been involved in many gang fights as a teenager. In one of those fights a rival gang member had chased him down the street with a sword and slashed him from behind and the tip of the blade had sliced through his full-length leather coat and his shirt; Alec seemed more concerned about the damage to his coat than to his body. He left Glasgow and headed south soon after being released from hospital.

His brother Jimmy worked on the railways, shovelling coal to feed the boiler of a steam engine and one of the perks of the job was an unlimited supply of whisky from an unlikely source. Jimmy's engine shunted past a whisky bond every day where his pal worked. The pal had access to the casks and would fill an empty rubber hot water bottle with the maturing spirit when he was unobserved. Each morning, when the train passed, his pal hurled the bottle over a high security fence on to the coal stack behind the engine. These events occurred before the days of security cameras.

Sam, from West Africa, was another guy I liked. He came to work each day wearing a suit and then pulled on a baggy old pair of trousers, tying them up with string. Sam was a philosopher, never in a hurry to do anything. He was also lazy and knew every hiding place on the premises. He would disappear on the upper floors and could usually be located by his snoring, fast asleep on a cotton bale, with his clipboard on his chest and a pencil in his hand. Sam could wake up writing and tell us that he was stock-taking.

The dock warehouse had been built alongside the canal for easy access to the barges, four floors high and a very attractive example of Victorian architecture. On bright days, sunbeams would shine through the grubby windows and illuminate the dusty, dark interior, turning the worn timber floors and hessian bales into gold. This was Sam's domain. He had graduated from labourer to warehouse checker, which was less strenuous for a man approaching retirement.

Sam was a religious man, and attended church every Sunday with his large family. He was also very superstitious, and told me scary tales about Africa and his childhood. He was convinced of the power of witchdoctors, who were respected and feared in his society, and when Sam looked me in the eye and told me things that had happened in his village I got a chill down my spine. He would make the tea for our morning break (exactly fifteen minutes), while one of the lads ran to the nearby café for bacon rolls. The air in the hut was thick with the fug of cigarette smoke and everyone played cards or dominoes for small amounts of money.

Dave was another chap I liked. He was in his thirties and had three young children. Before his present job he had worked in the city morgue where the wages had been a great deal more than he was getting on the docks. It had taken him a while to get used to assisting the pathologist cutting up bodies on the slab, but he packed in the job when he saw children the same age as his own being dissected for a coroner's report.

Working for Peanuts

The first week was the hardest and, not being used to tough physical labour, I was wrecked when I got home at night.

Next to the old warehouse was a relatively new barn of a building where lorries drove in for unloading, and there were two forklift trucks parked in the far corner. I really fancied driving a forklift, and one of the guys gave me a little demonstration of the basic controls, which were quite simple.

During the morning tea break I sneaked into the building for a test drive. The only vehicle that I had ever driven before was a bumper car at the fairground and that should have been an omen. I clambered into the seat, turned on the ignition and put the vehicle into forward motion, successfully steering around the sacks of grain, which were stacked on pallets, about fifteen feet high. I continued driving around the maze of sacks until I reached the edge of the canal where there was a sheer drop into the filthy water below and dead pigeons floating on the oily surface. Instead of putting the truck into reverse, I hit the wrong lever and went forwards. The only thing that stopped me somersaulting into the canal was the fully lowered position of the forks which jammed against a shallow lip of concrete on the quayside. I should have quit while I was winning, but I still had eight lives left.

Studying the very simple control lever, which any idiot could have figured out – forward, neutral and reverse – I set off with a bit more confidence, even though I was still trembling from my close call with the grim reaper. I drove the vehicle back to where I'd found it parked, and reversed it neatly into the gap.

The problem was that I was going too fast. SMACK! Right into a tower of peanut sacks. I looked up to see the uppermost sacks coming down on top of me. Fortunately for me, this machine was the one with the safety guard over the seat. Four sacks came down, two of them bursting on impact and showering me with peanuts. They streamed down my neck and into my shirt and underpants. I did a quick strip: even my boots were full of them. When I glanced back over my shoulder, the place was a real mess. I was hoping that, when it was discovered, it would look like the sacks had just tumbled down all by themselves.

It wasn't until the afternoon tea break that the foreman came over to the hut looking for the culprit.

'Okay! Who knocked the f—ing peanuts over?'

There was a long pause; nobody spoke. I raised my hand – it was like being back in school again.

'Right! Get a f—ing brush and a f—ing shovel and sweep every f—ing peanut back into those f—ing sacks.' I couldn't believe that I hadn't been fired on the spot. The other guys couldn't believe that I had owned up to my crime.

'Yer daft b—er, yer shudda sed f— all!' said one of the lads after the foreman had left.

I started to feel more like one of the lads after the second week, and the piss-taking on us students began to ease off a bit. Lunchtimes were spent playing cricket in the yard. If you broke a window it counted as a six, but you had to pay for the damage. Two of the office workers came out to join us. This was the only time that the men in suits mixed with the men in overalls.

I was beginning to feel very physically fit, and had more energy at the end of the day. Most of us helped ourselves to peanuts, and took some home to salt and roast in a dry frying pan. You really could say we were working for peanuts. Such were the perks of the inshore longshoreman.

Health and Safety

Health and safety at this place was a big joke. One morning we had to load a lorry full of asbestos in damaged sacks from pallets on the floor. There was fine dust everywhere, and it was known as a major health risk even in those days. We were given useless facemasks without filters which had been worn by other workers before us, and it was impossible to breathe when we were doing such heavy work.

Another safety issue in the old warehouse concerned the loading bays on the upper floors. Cotton bales were swung out from the building on slings and low-ered on pulleys, usually a two-man job, and the only safety equipment supplied was a thick pair of gloves to reduce rope burn. Each bay had iron rings set into the wall where there used to be safety harnesses at some time in the distant past.

One worker had already fallen from the bay, landing on top of a lorry and seriously injuring himself. The workforce all knew about this incident but never complained about the lack of basic safety equipment. When I asked the lads about this dangerous practice, they said that you just got used to it. When it rained the bays became wet and the floorboards slippery, and if you let the rope slip then you would take a dive on to the cobbles in the yard far below.

In the first week I was the victim of an initiation ceremony referred to as 'buried alive'. This was a seriously frightening experience, and anyone who suffered from claustrophobia would have met an early death for real. The warehouse always had a lot of rolled carpets stacked on the floor to be packed into containers for shipping to America. Just before tea break I was grabbed by two of the guys, while others tied my hands and feet together. Two long rolls of heavy carpet were laid parallel and close together on the concrete floor in the big warehouse. I was jammed between them while other rolled carpets were laid crossways on the top, forming a confined space like a coffin. As the carpets settled down, I could feel the pressure on my chest and head. At this stage I was beginning to panic, fearing that I would suffocate. I was left there for the whole fifteen-minute tea break, which felt more like hours.

During my premature burial I had visions of wreaking revenge on all those involved. However, I was glad when I heard my torturers returning from their tea break in high spirits. I did ponder for a while on the idea of accidentally knocking one particular individual from one of the loading bays on the top floor of the warehouse.

The next day another little surprise was arranged for us three students. We were bundled separately into one of the empty metal containers and locked in. This metal cube was then lifted by an overhead crane and suspended just a couple of feet above the ground. The crane driver then swung the container to and fro, so that you had to sit on the floor to avoid banging your head on the sides. Outside, two of the guys beat the container with iron bars, and it was like being inside a church bell tower with the Hunchback of Notre Dame, The Bells! The Bells! After about five minutes the container was dropped with a clang, leaving the victim hard of hearing and slightly bruised about the knees and elbows.

Obscene messages had been chalked up inside these transatlantic containers, such as 'Yankee Wankers' and 'Up Yours! You Limey Motherf—ers'. We maintained the tradition and added our own rude insults, like naughty schoolboys.

Working in the City Jungle

One of the 'highlights' of the job was the unloading of a barge, and we got extra money for opening up the hold. First we hauled a big tarpaulin back from a large rectangular raised cover centred on the steel deck, and then lifted the wooden boards that were slatted one against the other, side by side: two men stood opposite each other on either side of the hold and lifted half the boards to the bow and half to the stern, exposing a dark chasm below. Then it was all hands on deck until the last of the cargo was lifted by crane from the hold. An empty hold always produced several rats and it was company policy to kill them all; there was so much foodstuff around the docks that contamination was a serious problem. We had to tuck our trousers into our socks and put gloves on before going after them with pickaxe handles. Inside the smooth-sided steel hold they were prisoners and couldn't escape, and the hunt was like some primeval sacrificial ceremony and not for the squeamish or faint-hearted. Poor ratty had few friends in that neck of the industrial waterways.

The foreman brought his little terrier with him one day, but it was young and not much use; it chased a large rat around the hold, but backed off when the rat turned on him. The little terrier ran away whimpering and the boss was mortified. The pup was called Tiger.

Hundreds of grubby street pigeons roosted in the rafters of the big warehouse and these were also fair game. One day the foreman put me in there with an air rifle to clear the place. Once I got the range it was like shooting at a fairground, and they kept coming and coming even though their companions were falling in full view and thudding on to the sacks of peanuts below. We collected ninety-three birds in total, and they were thrown into the canal, providing a feast for the rats, one pest eating another. Two days later the same number of pigeons would be seen again roosting in the rafters.

Other things were sometimes thrown into the water. I watched one of the younger lads in the old warehouse hurl a sack of cement from the top floor just because he liked to hear the loud smack it made as it hit the water far below. What a waste of resources.

Bobbins of wool were aimed at unwary heads as we rookie workers walked between the cotton bales on the upper floors of the warehouse. It was like being ambushed by the Viet Cong. We were working in a city jungle.

I discovered that pilfering was widespread in the docks and was considered to be a perk of the job, enabling the underpaid rebellious workforce to make some extra cash. One consignment of bales from India contained large bath towels. A bale was broken at one corner and a few of the tightly packed towels could be hauled out, leaving the pack apparently still full. Chocolate biscuits were also removed from large cardboard boxes, leaving little evidence of tampering. But when whisky was unloaded it was under the watchful eyes of the Customs and Excise men, and not a single bottle ever went missing.

Of the two other students, one was a really nice guy, Ralph, a Londoner reading English at Manchester University. He was the quiet, thoughtful type, and had swapped his daily newspaper, *The Guardian*, for the more acceptable *Daily Mirror*, the favoured tabloid in the hut.

The other student was a Mancunian, a person most of the workforce found patronizing and cowardly. Two incidents spring to mind. The first was when it was my turn to get teased by the lads, when they were carrying me towards the canal for a mock throw-in. I was being held by my arms and legs and couldn't move. The sly student, Daniel, came alongside me and punched me in the balls; this was his idea of being one of the crew. He would normally run a mile to avoid being the victim of a stunt himself and was not known for being a good sport. Alec, the Glaswegian, realized I had been hurt and told the others to let me go. I could hardly walk and was doubled up with the pain. At that moment I saw an iron bar propped against the wall, and grabbed it and hurled it at Daniel's head as he ran between a lorry and the warehouse wall. It missed him by a few inches, fortunately, but I can well understand how it is possible to kill some-one in the heat of the moment. I'm sure that Daniel's mother thought he was a lovely boy.

The second incident occurred when we got the call to provide extra manpower at another part of the docks, where they were supplying maize to Kellogg's factory for the production of cornflakes. During the lunch break we were sitting in the site hut with an elderly caretaker, who brewed the tea; he was the only person there who didn't curse and swear. As we lounged about, waiting for a job to be allocated by the boss, we looked out of the hut window and saw a very attractive, well dressed young woman approaching.

Daniel piped up, 'Cor! I'd like to shag the arse off that!' and even worse things.

The girl came into the hut. 'Hi, Dad!' she said to the caretaker and handed him a packet of sandwiches. Daniel on this occasion was shamefaced and in need of a hole to crawl into.

I left the job after about six weeks and went travelling again. Several months later I met the nice student, Ralph from London and it seemed that I had had a close shave. I had left the job one week earlier than the others and gone to Amsterdam. The Customs and Excise men had raided the houses of everyone still working there and searched every inch of every room. Most of the guys had been convicted of theft and fined, then sacked. It seems that almost everyone except Sam and the foreman had at least a couple of Indian bath towels and a large amount of peanuts squirrelled away for the winter.

My criminal record would be put on hold for the time being.

3
Into Adulthood

My first full-time employment after college was as a conductor on the Edinburgh corporation buses; we were more commonly known as clippies. This new job provided an unlikely opportunity for country pursuits. The terminus on our route was at the edge of town where there were farm fields bordering a golf course and plenty of hedgerows for game cover. Carrying a gun on the bus was out of the question, and there was probably something in the regulations covering such matters – but carrying a couple of Fenn traps was a different matter, as they could be concealed discretely in my duffle bag with my sandwiches. When I was on that bus route, I set a couple of traps in the morning on the first shift and would check them at the end of the day on the last run. I got one cock pheasant at the first attempt. My driver kept a lookout for me.

Semi-wild ducks were another favourite food supply for me. There was a river that ran through the city, and its meandering course took it through some very secluded overgrown banks that were not overlooked from the road or the houses. I carried out my initial reconnaissance of the river from the top deck of the bus while I was working and there were always large numbers of mallard ducks on the water.

In the evenings and at weekends I did some detailed exploration of the river-banks. Early morning was the best time for duck hunting with so few people about and I became proficient at hitting moving targets as they paddled along, similar to target shooting at the fairground. Shooting over water was an easy way of calculating the range, but retrieving dead mallard ducks as they drifted swiftly downstream required a high level of physical fitness and some climbing skills. A change of clothing would also have been useful on occasions.

On the Buses

I worked for the transport department for seven months with various drivers and was amazed by the cross-section of society, men and women from all backgrounds and nations. The uniform made everyone look the same and it was like being back at school. I hated mine and avoided wearing the cap. There was something very militaristic about the uniform, especially the long winter greatcoat; I felt like a refugee from Tsarist Russia. Even the crossed leather straps on the chest, holding the ticket machine and cash bag, looked soldierly.

I made several friends at the depot and there was a certain comradeship between the workers. One of my friends was a Geordie boy from down south; his name was Victor and he was the same age as me, but married and with a new-born baby. He had been in the merchant navy since leaving school, but his wife hadn't been too keen on his long absences from home. I asked him why he had left Newcastle, and he told me that he was escaping a vendetta.

Just before he sailed on a voyage, two thugs in the city had beaten him up and robbed him and his last night had been spent in the hospital getting patched up in the A&E department. He sailed with a broken nose and two broken ribs. He was back home in Newcastle two months later with plenty of money to spend and bought a brand new Norton motorbike with his wages. On his second day of leave he took his wife to the local supermarket and left the bike in the car park. When they came out of the store, he could hardly believe his eyes: there was a guy fiddling with his new motorcycle, trying to unlock it.

Vic recognized the thief as one of his pre-voyage assailants and he described to me with great pleasure what happened next: 'I spotted this c—t trying to nick my f—ing bike. I would never forget that face and he was still wearing the same f—ing leather jacket with the studs on the back which made a star shape. He had his back to me when I sneaked up on him. I dipped into the shopping bag and took out a can of Heinz beans. I calmly walked up behind him and let him have it – I smacked him right across the back of his head with it and he went out cold. There were no witnesses. I kept the can as a souvenir; we never opened it. There was a nice big dent in the side.' Victor was still laughing...

My favourite driver was a tall, gangly black guy called Clarence. He was an American from Alabama and had been a sailor with the US Navy, stationed in Holy Loch on the Clyde. He had married a local girl and they had six kids. Clarence had a wicked sense of humour and was well known around the town. We sometimes went to the pub together on the way home from work. He made friends easily, and people liked that slow southern drawl of his; it was a big novelty to Scottish ears.

When our bus stopped at traffic lights one day in the city centre, someone he knew tossed a reefer to him through the driver's window; he smoked it at the terminus. It didn't seem to affect his driving ability, which wasn't great anyway. He once drove away from the bus stop in George Street, leaving me on the pavement with a young mother I had been helping off the bus with her baby in a pram. It was usual for the driver to wait for the conductor to ring twice before the bus moved on. It was ten minutes before Clarence realized he had left me behind and came back to pick me up.

On another occasion he watched me in his rear view mirror, counting my money at the end of the night. I had rows of coins lined up on one of the seats waiting to be bagged, to save time back at the depot. The bus was empty of passengers and Clarence decided it would be fun to play a practical joke on me: he made an emergency stop and all the coins on the seat flew forwards to the front of the bus. They were all over the floor and under the seats – but he did have the decency to help me retrieve them.

Soon afterwards Clarence went back to the States, leaving his wife and family behind. He had often told me that he was homesick and missed the food and climate of the Deep South.

I left the job soon afterwards. For me, the novelty of conducting buses had worn thin. I had applied for the job initially after seeing a very cool-looking clip-pie rolling a fag one-handed while he crooked the other arm round the upright bar on the open-ended bus, while the vehicle turned a corner on two wheels. There were no doors on buses in those days. I was impressed by his grace and dexterity. Collecting fares on a moving bus required sea legs just like on a boat at sea.

One time our bus had been going down a steep hill on a windy day and there was a cyclist following close behind us only inches away from the open platform. My driver braked to avoid rear-ending a taxi in front and the cyclist made an unexpected visit to the lower deck of the bus. Rather callously, I pointed to my ticket machine and asked him how far he was going. We had some laughs.

Hunting

For hunting purposes my main mode of transport was a bicycle. My trusty steed was an old Raleigh with an all-steel frame and it had Sturmey Archer three-speed gears. It was heavy and robust. I got fit cycling and covered great distances on this machine.

The first thing I did when I bought the bike was to paint it dark green to match my hunting clothes. I always wore a camouflage jacket and green trousers and when my hair began to turn prematurely grey I wore a tweed bunnet. Having suitable clothes was a great advantage when it came to concealment: it was the difference between being spotted and caught, and getting away.

I had quite a few narrow escapes over the years and ruined a fine pair of dyed green jodhpurs during one of those mad dashes. I was hunting for rabbits in an urban area that was patrolled by the police, although I think they were more concerned with burglars than poachers. When you are hunting without permission on other people's land you develop a habit of constantly looking over your shoulder. You also avoid crossing open spaces where there is no cover.

It was a summer's morning at about 5am and I was stalking a rabbit on the driveway of a stately home near the city outskirts. I saw a police car approaching from behind. I had already worked out my escape route through nearby woodlands and was quite confident that I could get away easily. When I reached a barbed-wire fence I dived along the ground to go under it – but the seat of my jodhpurs caught on the wire in two places and ripped out like a trapdoor. I was up and running, but my arse was hanging out and I wasn't wearing underpants. I was lucky to have the bike to get back home on, thereby retaining some sort of modesty. After that incident I always carried a couple of safety pins in the lining of my jacket.

It was possible to take a bike almost anywhere that you could walk; it was also easily concealed and could outmanoeuvre a gamekeeper using a Landrover in dense woodland. My rifle, in its green canvas case, was fixed along the crossbar with two leather straps. I had to make a quick exit from woodlands several times by manhandling the bike over a drystone dyke to escape.

On one memorable occasion I cycled down a steep hill on a golf course fairway out of control, with no possibility of braking or slowing down because the grass was soaked with the morning dew. At the bottom of the hill on a right-hand bend I narrowly missed two golfers who were putting on the green and passed between them. They looked rather bemused and one of them shouted after me, 'Is this point-to-point or cross-country?'

It was that kind of cool, witty retort that made you proud to be British.

Fair Game

I had a love/hate relationship with golfers. The courses were great places to hunt rabbits, hares and partridges in the early morning and the greenkeepers weren't too bothered about what happened to the rabbits, which were destructive vermin, always digging up the greens. One beautiful sunny morning I was heading home along the edge of a golf course with two brace of rabbits over my shoulders. My rifle was in its case and I was feeling pleasantly content listening to the skylarks singing overhead in a clear blue sky.

I waited a few minutes for a group of four golfers to tee off, so that I wouldn't spoil their concentration. As we approached each other on the path, the first three sportsmen passed the time of day cheerfully. The fourth one must have been having a bad game. He ignored my 'Good morning' and thundered past with a glower on his fat red face, huffing and puffing in his attempt to catch up with the others. He was wearing a baseball cap with an assortment of small metallic badges all over it. If I had had to guess this man's profession, I would have labelled him as a pork butcher.

'*Excuse me, but are you a member of this golf club?*'

I turned round to confront my inquisitor. 'Yes, as a matter of fact I am,' I lied.

'Oh! Sorry, it's just that we get some strange people wandering about here.'

'Please don't apologize. I frequently challenge trespassers on the course myself.'

Enjoying his embarrassment was a lovely feeling, and I was still laughing ten minutes later.

Trapping

Over the years I had collected a number of Fenn traps. All of these traps had been removed from places where gamekeepers had left them for non-legal purposes. Their design was intended for the killing of ground pests such as squirrels, stoats and weasels, but sometimes I found a trap that had been set on the top of a post with a dead tawny owl or sparrowhawk hanging from it. The keeper was breaking the law, so I didn't consider the removal of these traps to be stealing.

I discovered by trial and error that these traps could be used for other prey, and in particular were excellent for catching pheasants. Dried maize or pigeon corn could be glued on to the trigger plate, and the traps set in places frequented by game birds.

My favourite trapping sites were beneath yew trees. The reason for this was that pheasants like to dust themselves daily to deal with parasites in their feathers. Tell-tale feathers in the dust bowls beneath the trees gave a good indication of usage and the earth there was usually dry, even in wet weather. Another advantage with yew trees was that they provided good cover, right down to the ground. A casual observer passing by would be unlikely to spot anything suspicious.

There was a real skill in setting these traps and the important thing was to catch the prey that you were after. When I first started pheasant trapping, I fixed a wooden peg to the chain on the trap, but hammering the peg into the ground was noisy and could attract unwanted attention and there was always the possibility of a predator such as a fox uprooting the peg from the sandy soil in an attempt to remove the catch from the trap. Each winter season I used the same trap sites under the same trees.

When I was still using the wooden pegs I carried a large hammer with me, but it seemed stupid to lug this heavy hammer on every trip, so at the end of one season I hung it in the fork of one of the yew trees, where it was well concealed. The following season I went to reclaim my hidden tool and discovered that the tree had fully embraced it – I simply couldn't budge the damn thing and so left it where it was. Whenever I was in the area I would take a look at the disappearing claw hammer until there was absolutely no trace. I imagined the possible reaction in the distant future when a forester came to cut down the old tree; there would be some colourful language.

I developed a better clip-on method for fixing the trap, which made it into an immoveable object: an eyed screw could be attached to the base of the tree and a dog clip to the end of the chain. This system enabled the trapper to work quickly and quietly. Next, a shallow indent was made in the soft earth. The trap could be pre-set with the safety catch on the trigger mechanism, to prevent broken fingers. The Fenn trap is an efficient and humane killer, but it is also powerful enough to do serious damage to an unwary or careless hand. In the flat, pre-set position the trap can be safely worked into the hollow so that the baited plate is flush with the ground. I used an old spoon to sprinkle sand and earth over the trap, leaving only the bait visible.

The next step was to make a tunnel of twigs above the trap to prevent any creature accidentally walking across it. A few well placed pieces of maize on the ground is a good way of leading a bird into the contraption. When a pheasant stretches its neck forwards and pecks at the glued bait, the trap springs up and snaps its neck. In all the years I have used this method, every bird has been instantly killed. On rare occasions I would find a dead grey squirrel in the trap, and sometimes a passing stoat or weasel would eat the neck of a dead pheasant before I had uplifted it.

I usually set the traps in the early morning and collected them at sundown. Pheasants were often wary of these sites for a few days after one of their number had been caught.

Mr Tod

Twice I have caught pheasants that have been removed by foxes, with only the heads left in the traps. I got my own back on one particular fox that I knew by sight which had unusual white markings on its tail. This fox used to hunt the same ground as I did; we even ambushed our prey using the same route.

Early one morning I was out with my rifle on the golf course and saw the white-tailed fox heading in my direction, carrying a large rabbit. I was well concealed and waited until Mr Tod was only about ten yards away. I deliberately fired a shot over his head to give him a fright, and the trick worked – he dropped the rabbit and ran back the way he came. He had eaten the rabbit's head, but the body was undamaged and still warm. I felt no sense of guilt, and considered two pheasants for a rabbit fair game, in his favour.

I have always had a grudging respect for the crafty fox because we were brothers in the field, playing the same game and over the years I have met hundreds of foxes going about their natural business. Only once in my life have I ever killed a fox and that was a mercy killing – but more about that later. If they didn't bother me, I didn't bother them.

I knew a shepherd called Callum, who had a fox on his land. It was an upland sheep farm with a salmon river below and forestry above. His fox never bothered the lambs in the springtime and he often watched it trot through the sheep field with the newborn lambs, ignoring them completely. His neighbour J. W., however, who lived on the opposite bank of the River Tweed, had constant problems with foxes that frequently killed his lambs. Jim always shot foxes on sight, using a lamp at night, with the help of a gamekeeper friend. One year he managed to kill a dog fox and four young cubs, but he was unable to get the vixen and she killed nine lambs during the next two days, in broad daylight.

Callum was of the opinion that if his fox didn't bother him, then he would leave it alone. A new fox coming on to land to replace its predecessor might have more destructive feeding habits. Better the devil you know.

Back to Work

After leaving the buses my next job was as an artist with a sign-making firm: my artistic career had finally been launched. The interview went well, and I was able to convince the boss that 'I could handle a set of French curves'.

The company made big signs for shop fronts and pubs and one of my first duties was to draw scaled-up letters on to sheets of perspex. A light projector was used to enlarge the image on to a wall in the darkroom. When my part of the work was completed, the sheets of perspex were passed on to the machine shop to be cut out on a bandsaw. The finished letters had female locators glued to the back of them, and the corresponding male parts were screwed into place on the shop front using a template for accuracy. If the job had been done properly, the perspex letters popped on to the corresponding locators easily, using very little pressure.

One of the machine operators was called John, a refugee from the Ukraine who detested all things Russian. He had been on the losing side during the war and was lucky to escape with his life. John gave me a souvenir, a star from a Russian soldier's uniform; he wouldn't give me any details as to how he came by it, so I could only guess.

John showed me an interesting weapon that he had adapted from the material we used to fix the signs. It was a giant peashooter/blowpipe, with the hitting power of an air rifle. The female locators we used were cut into ¾in lengths, from a long piece of rigid, clear perspex tubing with a similar bore to a peashooter. The ideal length of weapon, which had been tried and tested by my colleague, was about three feet long. It was a wise precaution to smooth the ends with a fine piece of sandpaper, to protect the lips from lacerations.

Almost any object of the right calibre could be propelled along this barrel with devastating effect and the accuracy was truly impressive. It was possible to snuff out a candle from twenty paces, and we practised our marksmanship on the dartboard. The best ammunition was the male locator, which was tailor-made to fit the tube and formed a perfect air lock.

Most of the guys working beside me had their own personal 'shooter' and all of us suffered from snipers when we least expected it, the backside being the preferred target area. Occasionally an angry victim would go berserk and throw a stool at their attacker. I have to admit that I became an enthusiastic player in the game myself and dodged a few heavy objects that came my way. Those were the days before some genius invented paintball and made money out of potential psychopaths who wanted to kill each other.

I was employed for less than a year with this company. I was officially made redundant because of the downturn in orders, but the truth, as I found out later, was different: my job had been given to the boss's nephew, who was employed at a cheaper rate. I kept in touch with some of my old workmates and our friendship lasted many years.

Unemployment: Blessing in Disguise

My newfound freedom turned out to be a blessing in disguise. By this time I was married with a baby son. I signed on the dole for a couple of months and was content to enjoy my time away from the rat race. I went to the local library and read my way through just about every book they had on hunting, shooting and fishing. There were some great books on poaching, but I soon discovered that the theory didn't always match the practice. I read about sure-fire ways to catch all kinds of game using clever contraptions, or 'engines' as the Victorians liked to refer to them. I also constructed several primitive traps of the type used by our Stone Age ancestors. The problem with using ancient methods in modern times is that of being able to avoid landowners and gamekeepers; setting a trap in the best place for success could also make it obvious to a passerby.

I put a great deal of time and effort into experimenting with various methods of trapping game; I even soaked raisins in gin and scattered them where pheasants liked to feed. Many poaching books describe how drunken pheasants fell out of their roosts and were gathered up in a sack by poachers waiting beneath the trees. I watched as a bunch of pheasants fed all around my bait without eating a single raisin. At least I tried.

Hunting for the Pot

I soon discovered that the deadliest of all traps was the snare and that brass wire was the best material for making them. They were efficient, very light and easy to carry. For many years I used them, without pegs; I carried about fifty of them in an old sporran under my jacket. The eyelets were obtained from recycling old shoes by cutting around the reinforced lace holes. I always carried a stiff piece of leather for pulling the wire through to take any kinks out and fixed most of my snares along wire fences where rabbits made runs. There was always a risk in being seen setting snares and I usually set mine at night while it was still dark. Early morning was the best time to check them and I sometimes caught pheasants in these runs.

One morning at first light I saw three pheasants in a stubble field. I walked along the hedgerow and watched them move slowly towards a five-bar gate at the top of the hill. The two hen pheasants flew over the gate and the cock bird ran under it. The next morning I went back to the same place, half an hour earlier while it was still dark. This time I set a snare under the gate and walked back round to the bottom of the hill; as the sun came up I saw the three pheasants in the same place as the day before. I walked into the field and followed the hedge-row again, keeping my fingers crossed. And the gamble paid off: the birds did exactly the same thing and the cock pheasant ran straight into the snare under the gate.

A Royal Feast

There is a great advantage in knowing a piece of land really well, because often animals and birds are very predictable in their habits.

I did get an unexpected surprise one frosty winter's morning. I used to creep along behind a stone wall that bordered a stubble field, to get within rifle range of feeding pheasants. When I popped my head above the wall, I saw a couple of pheasants and a peacock. They were all feeding with their heads down, tails in the air. The peacock was about sixty yards away, which was about the maximum range for an accurate shot with an air rifle; at that distance there was an element of luck involved and birds had to be hit in the head or the neck to knock them over. I took a shot and missed. The two pheasants flew away from me but the peacock came towards me and flew over my head into the top of a pine tree, more than a hundred yards away. I waited for about ten minutes, squatting against the wall. We were watching each other. I began to creep towards it, moving very slowly, until I was within range. The head and neck were partly obscured by the upper branches of the tree, but I took very careful aim through a narrow gap.

The pellet hit the bird smack in the head and down it came, crashing through the lower branches.

I had to get out of there fast. It was a still, cold day and sounds travelled far in those conditions. My game bag was too small and I had trouble carrying the damn thing. The tail had to be wrapped around the bird and the long legs tied close to the body and I cycled home with my jacket over the top of the bag.

My wife was taken aback when she saw this multi-coloured offering. There was no recipe in the cookbook specifically for peacock. The meat tasted just like pheasant and I kept the primary feathers for fletching arrows – but more about that later.

Holding the Baby

I had an Irish friend called Martin around this time who was also unemployed. We used to go to a lot of places together and get into a bit of mischief. Our wives were also friends. One particular morning the women had gone shopping together and left us holding the baby. We took the infant for a stroll round the park in his pram. It was a miserable rainy day and there were not many people about. The ducks on the pond were relatively tame and hungry.

A mallard drake with a broken leg came limping up the bank looking for a handout; the poor creature looked in a bad way and I wondered if it had been attacked by a dog. I took a quick look around: there was no one watching. I bent down and grabbed hold of it. It was either a trip to the vet's or Saturday dinner, but we were skint and it didn't take us long to make our minds up. I shoved the bird under my jacket while Martin grabbed the pram and we made a rapid retreat from the pond to find a place where we were not overlooked. As soon as we reached the trees I took the duck from my jacket and wrung its neck. I shoved it under the pram cover and we left the scene of the crime, hurrying back to Martin's flat on the High Street before our wives got back. We didn't think they would have approved of a hunting trip involving a minor.

We carried the pram up the tenement stair to the second floor and felt safe once we were inside the flat. But the duck had bled all over the smart cream knitted blanket in the baby's pram and we had to get a move on in order to clean things up before the women got home. We almost made it. We put the duck in the kitchen and threw the bloody blanket into the bath to give it a quick wash. We heard the key in the door while we were in the living room attending to the baby. Unfortunately my wife went straight into the bathroom to use the toilet. There was a shriek and she came charging straight through to the living room, ashen-faced, expecting that something terrible had happened to the infant. But the baby was dozing peacefully, safe and sound on the sofa. I plucked the duck in the kitchen while the oven was heating up.

A Goose

Next time Martin and I went to the Queen's Park, it was six in the morning and the place was deserted. This time I took my catapult with me and left the baby at home. Martin had his dog with him. We were hunting for food again. Times were hard, as they say. It was a lovely sunny morning and we walked over the hill looking for rabbits for the dog to chase. When we reached the big loch, there was a greylag goose paddling just within range of the sloping bank. I missed with the first two pebbles, but hit it in the neck with the third one. Its head went under and it thrashed about on the surface, drifting further away from the shore. Eventually it lay still, leaving a ring of ripples on the calm surface of the loch.

'Fetch!' we told the dog. He didn't understand what we were talking about, and just looked puzzled. The retrieve was my responsibility, as it was my kill. I stripped off and waded in through the muddy shallows and when the water reached my chest, I started swimming out towards the bird. But as I reached it, it came to life again: it had only been stunned. I grabbed one wing and started swimming for the shore, while the goose paddled furiously in the other direction. I was struggling, but had no intention of letting go. It was too late to give up now. It had been a hard-won meal, enough to feed two families. The dog was running up and down on the shore, and Martin was having a good laugh at my expense.

We got home safe and sound without running into the park rangers. Martin's wife roasted the goose with potatoes that same night and the gorgeous aroma coming from the kitchen filled the whole flat. We waited patiently for the timer on the oven to indicate our royal feast. I had the honour of carving the bird. It looked delicious, all golden brown and glistening, with a crispy skin.

Unfortunately that hard-won meal turned out to be one of the worst that I had ever tasted. The geriatric goose was as tough as an old boot, the meat dry and stringy. The dog got a significant portion of it, though the carcass did make good soup.

A Bolt from the Blue

Martin and I made a few hunting trips together. One notable excursion was an early morning visit to a golf course near the zoo, where there were usually plenty of rabbits and a few brown hares. The course ran alongside a large woodland area on one side, and the grounds of a private castle on the other. The castle grounds included a large paddock with horses and cattle and it was a good place for rabbit warrens. The castle boundary had a great thicket of brambles growing along the fence line and was a great place for flushing rabbits.

On this occasion I took a crossbow with me so that Martin could use my air rifle. The crossbow had been a spur-of-the-moment purchase several years earlier and I had often regretted buying it. The bow was an extremely accurate weapon when used for target shooting – it was possible to hit a cigarette packet with a bolt at fifty yards. The main problem with the weapon was retrieving the bolts when they hit the ground: they vanished, even in an area with short grass such as a golf course. They flew at a great velocity and because they were so short in length, they tended to disappear into the ground; even if you saw where they had landed, they could be extremely difficult to locate. I lost many bolts that way and was often reluctant to take a shot on rough ground. One option was to carry a spade and dig them out.

As we walked alongside the bramble patch, we saw a rabbit hopping deeper into cover, very close by. Martin got in a quick shot with the rifle and missed. At the sound of the shot, a big long-legged hare broke cover, running out of the thicket and up the fairway, towards the wood on the hill. I brought the crossbow up to my shoulder and fired, aiming instinctively well above the fleeing animal, a good distance in front of it. I saw the hare somersault forwards and then lie still in the grass, belly up, white fur showing.

Martin and I looked at each other in amazement, then ran up the hill to claim our prize. There was a lot of blood. The bolt had penetrated the back of the hare's head and had come out through its mouth between its teeth; it was exactly half way through the head. It was a macabre scene, but death had been instantaneous. As I stood with the crossbow in my hand and the dead hare at my feet, I could see the turrets of the castle above the trees, giving the incident a timeless quality.

A full-grown hare provided a lot of meat for a family. I usually filleted all the meat off and put it through the mincing machine twice. I mixed in onion, ginger, salt and garlic, and then made hareburgers; I always thought it tasted more like beef that way. The women in my family were never very keen on hare meat, but the boys liked it.

To me, the hare was a magical sort of animal. I had observed them for many years and I liked to watch them in the spring when there were three or more of them chasing and boxing each other; there was a gracefulness about them that never failed to impress. When they ran away at your approach, they often circled and watched you from a distance. I learned a valuable lesson of escape from these wonderful animals.

When I was a young man, hares were relatively common in many places. I have to admit that people like myself were partially responsible for their demise in urban areas, but loss of habitat was probably the main cause of their disappearance. Over the years I took several hares in the vicinity of the old castle.

A Brush with the Law

One morning I shot a hare in the castle grounds. Only the head had been showing above the long grass, and its twitching ears had given its resting place away. A shot to the head almost always killed these animals cleanly. This particular hare was a large specimen and a heavy weight to carry and the combined weight of the game and the rifle made for slow progress across the golf course to where I had hidden my bicycle.

As I reached the greenkeeper's shed, next to a tumbledown dyke, I saw the top of a police car craftily concealed close to the wall. They must have been watching me heading towards them over the open ground. I didn't hang about: I ran like hell, back towards the castle. Fortunately I had a slight advantage because they decided to pursue me in their vehicle, rather than on foot, and they lost valuable time finding a gap in the wall they could drive through. I ran towards the top of a low hill, running to the right, but as soon as I was out of their sight, I turned to the left and ran in the other direction. I had watched hares doing this when dogs were chasing them and it was a smart move. I hid the hare in a hole in a dyke and kept on running.

When I got to a good vantage point I stopped and watched the police car. They had to choose their route carefully to avoid driving over any of the greens and leaving tyre marks. When they realized they didn't have a hope in hell of catching me, they turned back. I made a wide circle and came up behind them near a disused quarry. I watched them for about half an hour and sneaked up close behind them so I could hear their conversation. I went back for the hare later, after hiding the rifle.

A Life Saved?

On the same golf course the following year I met someone else hunting in the early morning light. I had already shot three rabbits and stashed them in a hollow tree nearby. I wrongly assumed that this young man was poaching, like me, but it turned out that his father was the owner of this celebrated and exclusive golf course. His weapon was rather more serious than mine, a live, bolt-action, .22 rifle with a range of about a mile, a potentially dangerous weapon when used in an urban environment. The chap turned out to be quite friendly and we chatted about hunting. His rifle had telescopic sights which he was still getting used to.

As we spoke, he spotted a pheasant about a hundred yards away against the skyline. He took aim and had his finger on the trigger, ready to squeeze.

What he hadn't seen with his narrow telescopic view was a man's head coming into line behind the pheasant. It was a greenkeeper on the slope below, walking from right to left, straight into the firing line.

'*Don't shoot!*' I cried.

He didn't, and avoided what could have become a front-page news story, nationwide. He was slightly shaken by the experience and offered me a shot of his weapon.

We exchanged rifles and walked over to the far side of the course where it was much safer to shoot; at least there were no ground staff about up there. We walked along a dyke and spotted a hare feeding on the other side about eighty yards away. I liked to be a little nearer than that, being used to an air rifle, with a more limited range. I was shown how to take the safety catch off and have the gun ready. I ducked behind the dyke and sneaked a little closer to the hare, which was still feeding and hadn't seen me. I peeped over the dyke and instinctively lined up the cross-hairs on the scope at the animal's head and fired. There was a loud crack from the gun. The hare remained in the same position and hadn't moved, so I was trying to figure out how to reload the weapon for another shot. I pulled the bolt back and ejected the shell case.

'You killed it,' said my companion, but I wasn't convinced.

I was used to seeing a shot animal thrashing about when I hit it with a pellet from my gun. It was explained to me that a high velocity round penetrated the target so fast that it didn't have the slow punch of an air pellet. We walked over to the dead hare and examined it. The small bullet had entered the ribcage just behind the right shoulder; the exit hole on the opposite side was extremely large and the whole of the left front leg and shoulder had disintegrated into mush. I offered my companion the better half of the hare and he was happy with the division. I never told him about the rabbits I had stashed earlier.

As we were leaving the course, the greenkeeper came over to check us out. He recognized the boss's son and was polite and friendly towards us. Whenever I had seen the greenkeeper in the past, I had always avoided him. The keeper was blissfully unaware just how close he had been to disaster only an hour earlier.

Rabbits

Rabbits were the main haul in my game bag and I could make a few shillings selling them to butchers and fishmongers. My wife had asked our local butcher if he wanted to buy any fresh rabbits from me and he told her that he only bought trapped ones that weren't damaged.

'Oh, that's okay, he uses an air rifle and he shoots them in the head,' she told him. Understandably the butcher was cynical and said, 'If you tell him to bring some in, I'll have a look at them.'

I was at the shop at 8am the following morning with six fresh rabbits, all of them hit in the head. The butcher had an interest in shooting and was impressed by the condition of the rabbits; he said he was surprised by my marksmanship. He used a shotgun himself. He bought as many rabbits as I could supply throughout that season. Occasionally there would be a black one amongst them, and when that happened, it was hurriedly shoved out of sight under the counter in case any of his customers thought it was a cat.

I began to get a regular supply of rabbits and had to take them to different butchers to sell them all. For me the arrangement was ideal because I never had to skin or joint them so it was less work for me and I was paid by the weight. I always gutted them immediately on the hill and left the entrails for the foxes and crows. One butcher was happy to trade meat instead of a cash transaction and was very generous with the exchange. My own family was sick of eating rabbit, stewed, curried, roast or fried. I kept the livers and made delicious paté with them, but it suited me to come home from an early morning hunting expedition with a gamebag full of sausages, chops and steak. Of course selling game was illegal and I only ever sold rabbits. Our bathroom in the flat usually had game hanging over the sink, dripping blood; our friends never batted an eyelid when they used the bathroom.

The rifle I used was a .22, BSA Airsporter Mark I, with an under lever to cock the spring. The great advantage with this particular model was the very fine open sight. I never used telescopic sights: they make a gun heavier to carry and clumsier to handle and you can't make snap shots with them. Most important of all, calculating the range with an open sight is very easy to do. The trajectory of an air rifle is very simple to calculate, the best place to test various distances being on a pond. Once you figure out the range of the target, you aim either high or low to hit the mark. The majority of rabbits were shot within thirty to forty yards and if you are shooting downhill, then you have to aim slightly under the target.

Occasionally I would hit something I wouldn't have thought possible and it was always worth trying a snap shot at a moving target. Wild ducks will often fly up vertically from a small pond when there are trees around. I shot several by firing above them as they came up and they were usually hit in the neck. A single .22 pellet could hit quite hard.

Duck

One cold, hard winter's day, I cycled for miles along a river to some low-lying farmland where there was a marsh, which was good cover for wild ducks. I was there at first light and there was a gale blowing and I was wishing I'd stayed in bed. A pair of mallard came up before I had the chance to get anywhere near the water's edge and flew away from me downwind. I watched as they circled and came back round. As they flew above me, about seventy feet high, I aimed at least three feet in front of the nearest one and pulled the trigger – and down it came.

To say I was gobsmacked would be an understatement. The height and momentum of its flight carried the drake about fifty yards on and it landed between the ridges of a ploughed field which were frozen hard. I ran as fast as my legs would carry me. I picked the warm body up and examined it, to see where it had been hit. There were no visible wounds and no sign of blood. I had to wait until I got home to conduct an autopsy. When I plucked the bird in the kitchen, the only sign of injury was a slight bruising on the left side of the breast. I could only imagine that the pellet had struck a glancing blow in that place and caused a heart attack, because the duck appeared to have been dead before it hit the ground.

There was another incident involving a duck, with a surprising and unexpected outcome, on a cold, frosty winter's day. I was up in the hills in a fir wood plantation walking quietly through the trees, when I spotted a solitary duck sitting on a small pond at the bottom of a slope. There was a slight ripple on the surface of the water and the bird was bobbing gently on the waves. I crawled nearer to the target on my stomach and elbows, braving the cold ground to get within range and hid behind a tree for cover where I was able to get into a good shooting position. I guessed at the range, took aim, squeezed the trigger – and thwack! I hit the duck in the head. But it remained upright, and lolled from side to side – and the sound of the strike was not what I had expected. In fact the duck turned out to be a rubber decoy, anchored to the bottom of the pond. I did feel a bit stupid, but was pleased with the accuracy of the shot and wondered if anyone else had done the same thing.

I suppose my marksmanship must have improved with the constant practice, day after day and I took it pretty much for granted that I would hit what I aimed at. If I wanted to test the sights, I used spent 12-bore shotgun cartridges as targets placed at various distances, because they were about the same thickness as a pheasant's neck.

A Million-to-One Shot

I used to visit a golf course on the edge of a beech wood where the rabbits grazed close to a wall on a little mound. I always arrived there just before dawn in the grey light and if I peeped over the dyke very carefully, I usually got a shot. One morning I saw a large rabbit silhouetted against the sky about forty yards away. I took a shot, thinking I had missed when the creature didn't appear to react.

It hopped forwards about six yards and stopped again, still facing in the same direction. I managed to get a second shot and this time it keeled over.

It wasn't until I got home and skinned the rabbit that I discovered something unusual: there was a single hole in the left side of its ribcage, but when I took out the liver I found two new pellets inside it welded together. If I hadn't seen this with my own eyes, I probably wouldn't have believed it possible. I showed my wife the pellets and explained what had happened. She didn't seem very impressed, which was disappointing, since I wasn't looking for praise, just recognition of a million to one shot.

Partridge

During the autumn months, I hunted over a farm that usually had a covey of partridges on the stubble fields next to a golf course, so early one morning I cycled over to take a look, sneaking along a drystone dyke to where there was a five bar gate in the wall overlooking the sloping field below. As I peeped through the gate I spotted a brace of partridges less than fifty yards away – but they also saw me. The pair flew away downhill, fast and close to the ground, but I managed to get a snap shot just before they dipped over a rise. Several breast feathers parted from one of the birds and drifted on the breeze, so I knew that one of them had been hit. I vaulted the gate and ran down the hill as fast as my legs would carry me to the spot where I found the feathers – but no bird. I searched further down the hill to a hedgerow on the boundary but without success, and assumed that the pellet had only struck the fleeing bird a glancing blow with no serious harm done.

The following season almost a year to the day, there was a remarkable coincidence. I looked into the same field round the same gate and saw two partridges sitting in almost exactly the same place; the only difference this time was that the field had been ploughed and the fine soil rolled flat. I took a carefully aimed shot and hit one of the birds in the head. The unfortunate victim began to somersault backwards. This is not unusual with a head shot; I've seen it many times before. What did surprise me was the other bird's reaction, because the second partridge began to peck at the spinning bird and made no attempt to fly away. I always instinctively reloaded my rifle immediately after taking a shot, but my hands were shaking and the adrenalin was pumping with the excitement as I rested the barrel on the gate and fired again. The second bird died instantly, hit in the neck. I thought it must have been fairly uncommon, shooting a brace of partridge within seconds, using an air rifle.

A bigger shock came when I got home. One of the birds had what appeared to be a short brown stick protruding from the lower part of its breast; when I pulled the object out, it left an indentation in the skin about ½in deep and ⅛in wide. There was no blood or obvious wound, although I could feel a small cyst in the muscle. I took a sharp knife and made a small incision in the little hard lump under the skin. Inside the grizzle was one of my .22 airgun pellets. The angle of the pellet matched the angle of the shot that I had made the previous year. The pellets I used were very distinctive and easily recognized. What I had thought was a stick protruding from the unfortunate creature must have been what I can only describe as fossilized feathers that had been formed by the pellet that had pushed them in; otherwise the bird appeared healthy and in good condition. I often found shotgun pellets in pheasants that I had snared.

I always felt guilty about killing partridges. Compared to a pheasant there is not a great deal of meat on them and they are beautiful creatures that are becoming scarce in many places due to the loss of so much of their habitat. I love the soft, natural tweedy colours of their plumage and the chestnut horseshoe on the breast. Their dumpy, well rounded shape is also quite endearing. I learned to call the birds to the edge of a field when the coveys were scattered, feeding amongst the green crops in the late summer. I would make a squeaky ratchetting sound by blowing my lips into the top of a closed fist through the folded index finger. The covey signalling sound was easy to make and the birds answered back as they came slowly nearer to investigate. It was an easy opportunity for a hard-hearted hunter to shoot one, but I never did.

I also blew a 'trapped rabbit squeal' with a blade of grass between my thumbs to get a fox to come running when I spotted one in the open. Gamekeepers shot foxes using this method. Crows also respond to the 'rabbit in distress' call, as do weasels and stoats.

4
A Double Life

I saw a job advertised in the *Evening News* which sounded ideal. The position was for a graphic artist in an advertising agency in a large retail store on Edinburgh's High Street and the wages were a lot better than my previous job. I was successful in the interview and started work the following week; however, I had mixed feelings about losing my newfound freedom and those glorious early morning rambles. I was in the habit of sleeping during the middle of the day when I came back from my early morning hunting trips.

My New Job

The studio where I worked had six people in the team and was set up like a school classroom on the top floor of a handsome Victorian building, facing south. There were large windows with balconies outside overlooking the High Street. I liked it there, and soon got to know the others. George, the oldest member of the group, was very keen on film making, using a Super 8 cine camera, and he was also interested in still photography, so we had something in common. George was an old soldier and had seen action in the North Africa campaign, carrying a miniature camera with him throughout the conflict. This act was risky and illegal because of the risk of the information being of use to the enemy if it were captured. George bore a striking resemblance to Benito Mussolini and shaved his head every morning.

Home Movies

I had been forewarned by the others in the studio about the epic home movies that George showed in his house whenever he came back from his continental holidays. He anxiously awaited the 'rushes' from the film processors. Eventually I got my official invitation to his house with the rest of the studio team to see the current release: this turned out to be a meandering epic lasting three and a half hours with no end in sight and was truly tedious. We were seated, crowded into a tiny overheated sitting room with a coal fire blazing in the hearth, and George's wife made a stack of delicious sandwiches and fresh cakes for us that we were given during the intermission.

Reel after reel was loaded on to the projector and the second half of the movie seemed endless. It was the deafening soundtrack that kept us awake, 'Classic Theme Tunes' from Hollywood Westerns. The bulk of George's home movie featured Cannes and Monte Carlo in the South of France, so the cowboy theme seemed most inappropriate. Much of the film's footage was repetitious shots of the road ahead of George's car on that winding coast road. The camera was fixed on to the dashboard with a home-made bracket.

We all made polite remarks and thanked George for a lovely night as we trooped out through the front door into the welcome cool of the night. His wife was a dab hand at baking and we had in all honesty thoroughly enjoyed that.

The Blowpipe

Media advertising for the store was seasonal and we had high and low periods of work activity. Most of our work was done for newspaper ads or slides for television. It was usually quiet for a couple of months following Christmas and in January and February we could bring in our own projects – unofficially, of course. I thought it was about time to introduce my new colleagues to the wonders of the blowpipe they had heard so much about. Most of them were sceptical and demanded a practical demonstration – and I was happy to oblige.

I bought a pound of dried peas; they weren't the ideal ammunition, but they did the job. The office junior was the most enthusiastic member of the team. They all wanted to know what the maximum range of the weapon was. We were on the fifth floor of a building overlooking the busy High Street, which was an excellent position from which to test the range and trajectory. Down below there was a gap site on the opposite side of the road, with high wooden hoardings where a man was reading the *Evening News*, fully opened. He was standing on the pavement leaning against the boards, facing in our direction and his body was visible only from the waist down.

I leaned over the balcony and lined up the blowpipe. The first attempt was straight, but way short of the mark; the dried pea landed in the middle of the road and bounced a couple of times before landing in the gutter. The second shot was spot on, hitting the centre of the newspaper and leaving a dent. In the studio we instinctively dived for cover, but needn't have bothered because the victim had absolutely no idea what had hit his newspaper and soon began reading again. I managed to hit the chap's paper twice again before he moved away, looking all around him but never looking up. This impressive sniping incident soon became folklore in the office.

When things were quiet in the studio we wandered round the store chatting to the girls in the various departments. A favourite game of ours was to walk through the bedding department where the newly invented waterbeds were displayed, and if there was nobody looking we would take a running dive on to one of those beds and experience the thrill of a soft landing followed by a heavy swell.

However, all good things came to an end when we discovered that our advertising department was being transferred to Glasgow and none of us wanted to re-locate. I was one of the lucky ones who managed to get a new position in one of the best advertisement agencies in town, just before the move to Glasgow took place.

New Job

The new job was a great improvement in both salary and conditions. The agency was a much bigger operation than the previous one and I was working with some interesting and talented people on a wide variety of clients. Word soon got round about my unusual urban lifestyle when I started selling rabbits at work and I was nick-named Bob the Poacher. My new colleagues seemed to be amused by my double life; not quite Jekyll and Hyde, but outwardly respectable with a hint of criminality.

Many city people regarded poaching as a bit of a joke, not really a criminal activity unless violence was used or gangs were involved; poachers still had something of the 'Robin Hood' reputation. There continues to be a historical resentment by many people towards present-day landowners who have thousands of acres of the best countryside, from which peasants like myself are excluded. Many well-to-do country landowners are aware of good public relations when it comes to promoting a tolerant attitude towards the 'local man' who catches something for the pot for his family – but when it comes to pounds, shillings and pence and the business of gamekeeping, all poachers are likely to feel the full rigour of the law.

Two years later, I was in the Sheriff Court myself, charged with a poaching offence in the Scottish Borders – but more about that later.

One fateful day I took my blowpipe into the studio and demonstrated its impressive power for the last time. Everybody wanted a shot and we took turns to hit the paper cups positioned strategically around the room. This time our ammunition was made from soft balls of putty rubber, normally used for rubbing out pencil marks on art board. There was a very tall chap in the studio called Colin who smoked king-sized cigarettes and I couldn't resist the temptation to target him. He was standing about ten feet away from my desk in the middle of the floor and while lighting a cigarette with a match, presented the perfect target profile. I took a snap shot and snapped his fag exactly in half. Colin was furious, the only person in the room that didn't see the funny side of it.

Later that day I made a big mistake: I shot Colin again, this time in the arse as he was leaning over his desk. I knew I had gone too far. He was a volatile personality with a quick temper and he grabbed the first object that came to hand from his desk, a hefty giant roll of double-sided adhesive tape. It came my way with an impressive velocity and struck me on the right side of jaw. I felt as though I had just met Mohammad Ali and had no one to blame but myself. I can't remember what happened to the blowpipe, but I lost interest in it soon after this incident.

Jack the Ferret

Young Frank, the office junior at the agency, told me that one of his old school pals was 'mad keen' on hunting and thought that we ought to meet each other. There was a big age difference between us; I was older than Jack by ten years. A meeting was arranged at the local pub a few days later.

Meeting 'Jack the Ferret' was a significant milestone in my life. Jack was a young man with an old head on his shoulders, a heating and plumbing engineer by trade. He had the dark eyes of a gypsy and a serious countenance and he struck me as someone who didn't suffer fools gladly. His surname related him to Romany stock from the Scottish Borders.

Our first meeting was a little uncertain because we were assessing each other, and I sensed that Jack regarded me with some caution. He was a working man who could handle himself and I was an ex-student with an arty-farty job who didn't get his hands dirty; we were also wary about discussing our unofficial hunting activities. However, after a couple of pints we both felt a bit more relaxed with each other. Jack's passion was ferreting and this meeting was to open a wonderful new world for me because I knew absolutely nothing about these intriguing little stoat-like creatures. By a strange coincidence, Jack and I had been hunting in one of the same areas for rabbits, although we had never bumped into one another; it was behind the City Zoo.

Although our backgrounds were very different, we had much in common and became friends. We were both outdoor fanatics and loved the natural world. I admired Jack's attention to detail; anything that he made was absolutely sound and reliable. He was good with his hands and a natural problem solver.

My Introduction to Ferrets

Our first combined hunting trip was on ground that we were both familiar with. We met before dawn under a distinctive tree on a hill that we both knew;

Jack went by foot and I rode my bike. This was the first time I had handled a ferret. There were two sandy-coloured jills in a home-made carrying box that Jack had made; it was lined with straw and looked very cosy. I picked the creatures up under supervision and found them friendly and inquisitive; they smelled of honey musk.

For a novice, hunting with ferrets was truly magical, watching those little animals doing their job instinctively. We set purse nets on all the holes in a small warren. Jack checked them all meticulously, as a badly set net allowed a bolting rabbit to escape. I was a willing apprentice and searched for any possible bolt holes around the perimeter. The net laying was done in complete silence and any communication between us was done with hand signals. We tiptoed quietly from hole to hole.

Eventually one of the ferrets was slipped under a net at the nearest hole, where it quickly disappeared below ground and it was less than a minute before there was a furry explosion into the nets. Half a dozen baby rabbits managed to get through the large mesh in the nets, where Jack scooped them up and put them in his pocket for their own safety. When the ferret resurfaced again, hot on the trail of the escapees, he picked it up and put it back in the carrying box, then returned the tiny rabbits back down the hole. 'We'll get them next year, when they've grown a bit,' he said. It seemed a sensible approach to me.

Later that morning we saw some rapid action, as big rabbits bolted at high speed into the nets. Under Jack's instruction I rushed about laying a fresh net over any hole where a rabbit had been bagged. Occasionally a fleeing rabbit got back-netted, as it shot out from one hole brushing the net aside and into another hole with an unseen well placed net over the entrance. This silent method of hunting rabbits with ferrets was productive and discreet; there was something very satisfying about hunting with natural predators without the use of guns and the ferreting expeditions became a regular feature.

Cold Comfort

Jack was given permission to ferret on a small farm in the Pentland Hills, but we had to rely on his mum to drive us out there and collect us at the end of the day. It was a major expedition carrying ferrets, heaps of nets and food supplies enough to last us for two days. The farm was unattractive, bare and exposed. It was late winter and there was a cold blast from the north-easterly wind with very little shelter, only a few spindly beech trees along the fence lines. The farmer told us that we could start ferreting anywhere we wanted and wouldn't be in the way, so we found a small warren in a far corner of a field at the furthest point from the farmhouse. There were about a dozen holes in the banking amongst the tree roots.

It took us quite a while to fix about a dozen nets over the holes because the ground was frozen hard and we couldn't use the wooden anchor pegs. As we were preparing to put one of the ferrets down a hole, we saw the farmer approaching in his tractor, towing a muck spreader behind him, fully operational. Jack and I looked at each other. 'Surely to God he's not coming over here?' I said. He must have been able see us because there was hardly any cover. We watched in disbelief as he rumbled towards us sending shit flying in all directions. We dodged behind the skinny trees, from where we could hear the slapping of slurry all around us but were just out of the firing line – but the unattended ferret box received a coating of shit. The farmer was either mentally retarded or taking the piss and gave us a friendly wave as he slurried by.

The expedition continued as it started, a shitty day and hard work all round; it took a whole day to catch just three rabbits, one being brought down by my home-made throwing stick as it slipped under the net. The stick was made from a heavy, seasoned yew branch and was originally designed as a priest for killing fish with. It had roughly the same proportion, as a police truncheon, with a slight curve, tapering towards the handle. A straight stick would not fly true when thrown. I got to be a dab hand with this primitive weapon at close quarters and was usually prepared whenever a pheasant rocketed out of the grass under my feet.

We stopped at the farmhouse to thank the farmer for allowing us to ferret on his land and offered him one of his own rabbits. He politely declined our generous offer. We never did go back to Cold Comfort Farm.

Archery

I was still enjoying my job at the advertising agency, working amongst a nice bunch of people and at that time I had a new hobby: making long bows. My basic knowledge came from library books and the skills I developed were learned the hard way, by trial and error.

Finding a suitable bow stave was not easy, my preferred timber being yew wood, which I harvested in some very strange places. The recommended seasoning for green yew wood was four years, which was frustrating and impractical for me because I was keen to start right away. I discovered that it was possible to find dead branches on yew trees and that these could be worked into bows and so I became a hunter of trees, always on the lookout for any yew tree that could provide me with a bow stave. I cycled great distances and examined any suitable trees that I came across for suitable branches: I searched country estates, local parks, private gardens and hospital grounds. The yew is a relatively common tree in this country, but to find one with a stave of the right dimensions and without side branches is a very lucky find, a rarity.

When I did spot a likely looking branch, I climbed the tree for a closer inspection and depending on the tree's location, whether it was private or public, would make a return journey on a dark windy night to claim my prize. When removing a limb I was always careful to rope it to the tree for support; this prevented the stave from falling and splitting. Eventually I built up a stock of suitable green wood, which I stored in the attic for future use. Some of those yew logs were heavy and cumbersome when I strapped them on to my bike to transport them home. Often I would have to push the bike many miles, having a seat only when I could freewheel downhill. Emergency braking was another useful skill on those expeditions.

Archery

Like most boys, my introduction to archery was at an early age. As children we made our own weedy bows out of privet branches or split sections of bamboo poles from the garden. The arrows we used were cut mainly from hazel bushes if they were straight and of the right dimensions and the flights were cut and shaped from Kellogg's cornflakes boxes or old playing cards. The bowstring was the weakest link and was usually retrieved from parcel bindings after carefully unpicking the knots. The wear on the string could be slowed down a little by rubbing candlewax into it; at that time I hadn't discovered beeswax.

I can remember buying three beautiful but rather expensive arrows from a sports shop, after saving my spending money for about two months. My friends and I fired them in relay from one end of the street to the other, into a grass verge, avoiding the tall trees by aiming high. There was an accident one day when a local girl called Eileen was hit in the head by an arrow, as she came out of her garden gate. She was taken to hospital in an ambulance on a stretcher with the arrow sticking out of her head just behind the ear. Fortunately she made a full recovery. One of her brothers was responsible for the deed and afterwards archery practice was frowned upon so we had to go further afield.

Making Bows

My adult bow-making skills progressed with experience and the tools needed were simple. A sharp axe was useful for whittling down the bulk of the wood and roughing out the basic shape. Yew has an ideal close, even grain in the heartwood, which is easy to work, having good elasticity and great strength. The art in making a successful longbow is to retain the heart and sapwood together so that it forms a natural laminate. The heartwood is a beautiful dark reddish or gold colour and the sapwood is off white, like ivory. When an archer draws a yew bow, the sapwood faces away from him.

I used the angled edge of a broken file to smooth out the adze-like scars left by the axe on the surface of the stave. Shaping the limbs and getting them to bend evenly was the most difficult part of the operation and it was necessary to fit a string to the bow before it was anywhere near finished. Knocks had to be filed at the tips to take the loops on the string.

The bowstring was made from multiple strands of linen thread and there was a knack in getting the string to match the length of the bow. For this task I knocked two nails into the doorframe, one at the top and one at the bottom. One end of single thread was anchored to the top nail from the bobbin, looped around the bottom nail and then back up again. The process was repeated until the combined thickness of the string matched the knock in the arrow.

Before the thread was removed from the nails, I rubbed beeswax into its entire length and hooked a lead fishing weight to the bottom loop, which kept an even tension on the string. The weight was then spun to bring the threads together as one, while the beeswax was worked into the string with a piece of thick leather. This twisting motion shortened the finished string by about six inches from the original span pegged on the doorframe. The end loops were then served with a double strand of waxed thread to reduce chaffing and wear from the knocks and the centre of the string where the arrow was knocked was dressed in the same way. Dental floss was a good serving material for this job.

Making Arrows

One of my favourite archery chores was the making of arrows, which I normally did in the evening when the children were in bed so that I could set myself up at the kitchen table undisturbed. I bought plain cedar-wood arrow shafts, which had the most delicious fragrance, from the sports shop. The correct length of an arrow to suit an archer was measured by placing one end against the middle of the chest while holding the shaft at right angles between outstretched hands. The point of the arrow should be level with the middle fingertips.

The first stage in the manufacture of arrows was to cut a knock at one end of the shaft square across the grain so that the string wouldn't split the arrow. A needle file was ideal for this job.

I made flights for my arrows from goose or swan feathers and wasn't interested in any of the new-fangled soft plastic flights available. The wild or greylag goose has provided archers with an excellent natural material for centuries and I was able to collect swans' feathers from city ponds during the moulting season.

A standard arrow has three flights in a triangle formation. The top one is the cock feather and should always be uppermost and at right angles to the knock when placed on the bow. The two feathers below, which rest against the bow, are the hen flights and there is a good reason for this configuration when launching an arrow from a bow: the two hen feathers give a smooth passage because they slide across the bow evenly spaced; if the cock feather were downward, then the released arrow would jump. I always used the white swan's feather for the top flight because it was a sure indication that the arrow was the right way up.

Only the stiff primary wing feathers were used for the fletching. I split the quills lengthways with a scalpel on the breadboard: you need confidence and a steady hand for this simple action. Bostik was the best adhesive for sticking quill to wood, as it is waterproof and lasts for many years. A dressmaker's pin at each end of the feather held it into position until the glue dried; the feathers could be trimmed to the required shape the following day. Because of the natural curve of a feather, each arrow had to be fletched only with right-winged feathers, or vice versa.

Accuracy was everything with bow hunting. I waterproofed my arrows with varnish to give them a longer life.

A floo-floo was another type of arrow, with a fletching that was entirely different from a standard arrow. A single feather was split down the middle and then one half was glued on to the shaft in a spiral form. The effect of this shape was to slow the arrow down by making it spin and it was for shooting at flying birds. If a standard arrow was fired skywards, it could disappear from view and land almost anywhere; a floo-floo would stall after reaching about a hundred feet and could be easily retrieved. It was a safer hunting method and less likely to cause injury.

I painted coloured rings on the arrows, purely for decoration and could just imagine a gamekeeper finding one of my lost arrows near his pheasant pens and uttering those immortal words 'Comanches, this far north?'!

Testing the Equipment

Trying out a newly completed bow could be an unnerving experience and I broke several. When a yew bow breaks, it fragments like a hand grenade and the sharp splinters fly in all directions. One of my most embarrassing moments was when I took a newly finished bow to the local park to try it out, standing beside a tall elm tree to make myself as inconspicuous as possible. Late summer evenings were ideal for these trials because the park was usually deserted. On this occasion, however, a young couple stopped to watch, as I fitted an arrow to the bow and struck the classical archer's pose, one of grace and balance.

But as I drew the bow fully back, there was an almighty crack. The arrow landed at my feet and the bow broke into three parts. One of those parts, the tip of the bow, still attached to the string, catapulted round the back of my head and cut into my right earlobe. There was blood dripping down my shoulder, but what was more painful was the sheer embarrassment of having been seen. I tried to look cool and unaffected, but was in agony.

Those little setbacks were a part of the bowyer's craft and a bow that didn't break became a much valued weapon.

I needlessly broke a favourite bow of mine about a year later when I went out hunting rabbits, one cold and frosty morning. I took that bow from a centrally heated kitchen into the local park and had shot only a few arrows when it suddenly snapped in half. An examination of the break showed no obvious weak spots in the bow. Later, however, an experienced archer told me that it was common practice to leave a wooden bow outdoors overnight to acclimatize it before use in the winter. It was a lesson learned the hard way.

I became addicted to practising with the longbow and it was very satisfying using a weapon that I had made myself. I also made a leather bracer for the left forearm and a tab to protect the finger tips on the right hand from being rubbed raw by the bowstring. My son's old school satchel provided suitable stiff leather for the job.

I made a set of target arrows with the peacock wing feathers that I had saved, but finding a place to practise archery without being a member of a club was difficult, so I made regular evening visits to the local park, alongside my favourite spot beside the elm tree, where it was possible to shoot arrows without being observed. My first mobile target was a large cardboard egg box placed at a distance of eighty yards. The box became too easy to hit, so I started using balloons tied to a garden cane and was amazed at the accuracy of the bow, occasionally splitting the cane with an arrow. I placed the target in an open area where I could see anyone approaching, waiting until they had passed safely, unaware of the archer in the shadows. One evening, an unobservant policeman passed close by without comment.

Seeing Stars

One beautiful, calm midsummer evening while standing beside the elm tree with my bow, I watched a big, heavy guy walking towards me. He was wearing greasy overalls and carrying a carburettor under his arm. His hands were filthy, covered in oil and his greasy black hair was slicked back, Elvis style.

'If that thing touches me I'll rip yer f—ing heid aff.' He had a rough, broad Glaswegian accent.

I looked around in case I had to make a run for it. He must have seen my face turn white and started laughing, then asked me about the bow and the home-made boomerangs lying at my feet. The big guy's natural voice was an educated Scottish one, with just a hint of the west coast. He had a weird sense of humour and I was very relieved not to have been pummelled. I demonstrated throwing the boomerangs for him and invited him to have a shot himself, but he declined the offer saying that he didn't want to get oil all over them.

'You're a bloody walking ethnic museum,' he told me and we parted on friendly terms.

At work the following day I told one of my colleagues about my close brush with danger and he started laughing. 'That would have been Robin Macmillan. He does voice-overs for us, for the radio ads. His hobby is fixing up old American cars. He's brilliant at accents.'

The next time I met this 'scary guy' he was wearing a white suit, at our office party. His stage name was Robbie Coltrane.

Hunting with the Bow

The novelty of target shooting soon wore off once I had become a reasonably competent shot with the constant practice. With the help of a few willing daredevil friends, I shot arrows at flying kites in the park and at cardboard boxes dragged along the ground with string; tin cans tossed into the air provided another inter-esting challenge. For safety reasons, I had fitted some arrows with rubber blunts, rather than target piles which were sharp and pointed.

In Britain, hunting with the bow is illegal and I suspect that the majority of people would be against it.

Some Observations on Hunting

All hunting has an element of cruelty involved and in the natural world I often witnessed incidents that could be described as cruel, occurring without the involvement of human kind. I watched cats playing with their victims, apparently for their own amusement and sometimes intervened. Once I watched a well known tabby cat at our local duck pond stalk and kill a mallard duck after disabling and playing with it for about ten minutes. Cat owners are usually very defensive about their pet's depredations on the local wildlife: 'She's just doing what comes naturally,' is a familiar retort. They regard dog owners rather less philosophically, so perhaps a dog chasing a cat is unnatural.

On more than one occasion I've watched weasels and stoats eating a rabbit alive while it screamed in terror, with the muscles on the back of the neck eaten first, right down to the vertebrae. Logically I know that I shouldn't interfere with these natural acts, however mercy killing an unfortunate victim always seemed the right thing to do at the time and occasionally I took a small part of the meat myself.

I've always had a respect for predators and particularly raptors, though my own enthusiasm is unlikely to be shared by many gamekeepers.

I never really thought of myself as a poacher, because I was a self-taught hunter with my own code of practice. Giving game a sporting chance was a nonsense to me. Why risk wounding a bird or an animal that you were trying to kill, by letting it put distance between you? Many times I have shot crouching pheasants from a distance of only a few feet and it's surprising just how well camouflaged those creatures are when they are sitting still; often it's just their bright eye that gives them away.

I wanted to test myself with the bow as a hunter, because using the rifle seemed too easy. When I was stalking the countryside in the early morning at dawn hunting for game, I felt a strange link with the past. People like me had been doing this for thousands of years; I was continuing an ancient tradition and the local hares were probably running along the same ancient paths as their own ancestors crossing the hill. Modern-day humans have become so far removed from their food source that many of them would probably starve to death if they were suddenly left to their own devices.

Experiences in the Hunting Field as an Archer

The golf course provided a perfect testing ground for a novice bow hunter because rabbits often grazed at the perimeters near to the woodland edge. Theoretically the bow had a much greater killing range than my air rifle, since it was easily 150 yards. I developed the useful knack of being able to carry six arrows against the bow handle while I had one knocked on the string ready to shoot. This method enabled quick reloading while you kept one eye on the quarry.

My first attempt to shoot a sitting rabbit was farcical. The range was about eighty yards and I fired a total of ten arrows. The rabbit looked round after each shot and continued grazing, unconcerned. It was almost penned in by the circle of arrows; some of them were very close. I then ran out of 'ammo', as they say, and the rabbit scampered off when I wandered over to retrieve them.

My self-confidence was undermined, but I didn't lose heart. On the way home I walked silently through a wood and got to within fifty yards of a hare that was sunning itself in the corner of a field. It hadn't seen me, so I took careful aim and calculated the perfect trajectory. Unfortunately the sound of the arrow slapping against the bow alerted the creature and it jumped to one side, causing the arrow to miss its mark by inches. When I got home I fitted a piece of rabbit fur above the bow handle to silence the arrow for future hunting trips.

It was a long time before I had success in the hunting field as an archer. My first kill was almost a carbon copy of the jumping hare, in reverse. I shot an arrow at a rabbit sitting seventy yards away, but the rabbit heard the incoming arrow and jumped sideways and the arrow hit it. If it had remained still, the arrow would have missed it. It was a fluke, but I still went home with the prize.

I started using rubber blunts on my hunting arrows for small game, because the shock impact had sufficient killing power and the arrows didn't snake into the grass and disappear. It took about an hour to make an arrow from scratch, so it was worth hunting for a lost one for about the same length of time.

One of the strangest bow shots that I ever made was next to my allotment on a sloping field where I sometimes practised my archery. At the top of the field I could see a carrion crow pecking at an object in the long grass at a distance of ninety yards. I aimed well above the target, allowing for the range, but the arrow fell short by about ten feet, although it was dead in line. The crow paused, then continued pecking in the grass so I shot a second arrow, making an allowance for the shortfall of the first one. The second arrow dropped on to the target from a great height and the crow fell backwards flapping its wings and then lay still. I climbed over the dyke and started up the hill, but before I reached the first arrow, the crow had recovered and had flown away. I discovered that my second arrow had impaled a large potato hidden in the grass and the shaft had pivoted with sufficient force to strike the bird a glancing blow, which stunned it for a few minutes. The potato had several peck marks on it.

This field became the ideal archery range for me because it sloped down towards the park below and the duck pond. In the early evening, groups of mallard flew from the pond to the nearby woods to feed on the river there. The ducks flew over the field at a height of a hundred feet to clear the trees on the boundary and on a quiet night you could hear them approaching by the whistling of their wings. Their flight path was predictable and their timing like clockwork. I stood in the field with my bow and waited for them to appear at dusk. It was a great opportunity for me to test the floo-floos, using the ones with white feathers when the light was dim because they were easier to find afterwards in the grass.

The ducks came over in waves, side by side, sometimes in pairs and sometimes in larger groups. The evening flights lasted for only a few minutes and I waited until the birds approached within range, directly overhead, before shooting arrows well in front of them. I wish I could say that I had brought down a few of those fast-flying birds, but I never did hit one. My arrows often missed them by inches.

Hunting with a Catapult

I took quite a few wild mallard ducks from a flooded quarry on the local golf course using a catapult. The most accurate ammunition for the catapult were the musket balls that I made by pouring melted lead into a mould set up in my garden. I was always on the lookout for discarded lead pipes in city skips and once retrieved yards of the stuff which had been dumped in the Union Canal.

Using a bow and a catapult required a similar technique. I carried a catapult whenever we walked in the countryside and often killed pheasants and wood-pigeons in relatively public places. On one occasion when we were pushing the pram along the curved driveway to a stately home, I spotted a woodpigeon perched directly overhead, on the branch of a tall cedar tree. I looked behind to check all was clear and let fly with a pebble, scoring a direct hit. There was an explosion of feathers above and the bird dropped, landing beside us next to the pram, where it was shoved hastily into our picnic bag. When we looked round a large group of people had turned the corner behind us and were looking upwards at the mysterious cloud of feathers drifting down on the breeze.

5
Self-Sufficiency

Gathering Winter Fuel

I was keen on self-sufficiency and by the time we had our second child this lifestyle extended to heating the house. We had an open fireplace in the living room and it was possible to gather enough timber from the nearby park to keep the fire burning all winter. The park was on the south side of the city and was a very public place with commuters swarming to work at peak times. After every windy night I made the rounds early the following morning collecting as much fallen wood as I could carry, using my bicycle for the donkeywork.

During a prolonged cold spell I became a little more ambitious in collecting firewood and developed a more efficient method of obtaining logs. The majority of the mature trees in the park were elm, lime and ash and most of them had some sizeable dead branches about twenty feet above the ground. I used an old washing line with a lead weight tied to one end, which I swung up over the tip of the dead branch. It was possible to lock the rope on to the branch and grip it by twirling the loose end of the rope around the hanging lead weight. The next step was a little trickier. When a strong tug on the line brought a hefty log crashing down to the ground, quick reflexes were necessary to avoid being brained. I amassed a good supply of logs for our fire this way.

As the winter progressed, most of the easy reachable timber in the park was gone. I knew almost every tree in the vicinity and had my eye on an elm tree with a large amount of dead wood on it next to the footpath. The limbs were far too big to snap off with a rope, so I waited for a dark and rainy night with few people about, then hauled myself up into the tree with a heavy climbing rope and a logging saw. Elm is extremely hard wood and takes some serious cutting. I perched precariously on a bough and started sawing through a dead branch, stopping when I spotted anyone approaching along the footpath. Not one passerby looked up; I was invisible in the dark.

I had sawn almost right through the branch when I looked down and realized that I was being watched from below. There was an angry man's face looking up.

'What the hell do you think you're doing?' He asked.

'Er, I'm doing some dry wood pruning,' was the best excuse I could come up with on the spur of the moment.

'I'm going to phone the police,' he said, and strode off towards his house. I recognized the man by sight: he lived opposite the park, in one of the nice little Georgian houses and had the reputation of being a very aggressive and unpredictable person.

I managed to saw through the log and climb down from the tree in about five minutes. I balanced the timber on the bike and managed to wheel it up the road before the local constabulary arrived on the scene.

A Man Without Support

About two weeks later, I was in the park early in the morning, gathering up kindling for the fire. There had been a powerful gale in the night and there was plenty of combustible twiggy material strewn about the grass and one of the giant ash trees beside the main road had lost a sizeable green bough.

I was about to leave the park with my bundle of dead twigs, when two policemen approached me.

'We have received a complaint from a local resident regarding someone fitting your description, in connection with criminal damage.'

'When was this?' I asked.

'This morning, about an hour ago,' he answered.

'Well, I was still in my bed at that time,' I told him.

'Do you have anyone that could vouch for you?' he asked. I replied 'Yes, my wife.'

The policeman asked me where I lived and I told him my flat was just around the corner. We walked round together and the policeman insisted on knocking at the door. My wife was having a late snooze, seeing that this was the weekend and took a while to answer the door. She was wearing her goony and was still half asleep.

'Can you confirm that your husband was still in the house about an hour ago?' asked the policeman.

'I don't know what time he went out. I was fast asleep.' She yawned.

I was a man without an alibi, let down by my own family. The cops told me that the complainant had seen me sawing up the green ash log earlier that morning. He had told them about my previous crime two weeks before and I didn't deny that one, but I did protest my innocence on the ash bough rap. They gave me the benefit of the doubt and advised me to stick to collecting fallen timber in the future.

About a fortnight later, I identified my doppelganger in the park. We both had beards, but there any similarity ended and we bore no resemblance to each other. It was he who had been sawing up the green log on that fateful morning. In retrospect it was quite funny. I was glad that the police witness hadn't been involved in a similar capacity in a murder case.

Taking on an Apprentice

I made another good friend at the agency with one of the copywriters who had a twelve-year-old stepson called Scott. The boy had a passionate interest in nature and was a natural born hunter and surprisingly knowledgeable for his age. Scott was a good kid and very eager to learn, so we gave him some sound advice: 'Get yourself a hat to cover that blonde hair of yours.' At that time, Jack the Ferret and I were both dark-haired and naturally camouflaged in the great outdoors.

I made a longbow for Scott and he became a skilled archer.

Young Scott made a few mistakes and learned the hard way; one of his most painful experiences was learning how to use my air rifle. I discovered a place where a small colony of guinea fowl was roosting. Poultry breeders often used these birds as guards because they gave an alarm call when they detected predators; that included humans. I had shot one of these birds the previous week and the meat had been delicious.

I took Scott on an early morning hunting trip and set him up to shoot his first guinea fowl. It was still dark as we located the roost and there were three plump birds high above in the branches, unaware of our presence below. We tiptoed into position, avoiding snapping any twigs on the ground. Scott attempted to cock the rifle with the under lever, which had a very strong spring. He accidentally pulled the trigger and the lever whipped up, crushing his left hand. The poor boy was in agony.

The birds hadn't moved, but were now aware of our presence below. Scott was rocking to and fro with both hands jammed into his armpits and his teeth tightly clenched. He said he wanted to try again, so I instructed him in the safest way to handle the gun, which had become a reflex action for me. I watched in absolute disbelief as he did exactly the same thing again. Words failed me. This time he was on his knees with his forehead pressed against the ground, groaning. He had broken his pinkie, which was an odd shape and swelling fast.

I picked up the rifle, cocked it, loaded it and shot one of those guinea fowl out of the tree with a neck shot. I reloaded and brought a second bird down. The third bird didn't hang about, so I missed out on a hat trick, but at least it hadn't been a wasted journey. To give that boy credit, he soldiered on and made the best of the rest of the day.

At a later date, young Scott's enthusiasm for hunting led him into another spot of bother. I showed him how to set a Fenn trap to catch a pheasant and gave him one of my own traps as a present. I was sure he would be successful in using it. He lived with his family in an old mill in the Scottish Border country. The cottage was on the edge of a shooting estate, which was protected by two gamekeepers.

What I hadn't anticipated was the boy's keen enthusiasm overriding his common sense. He was so desperate to catch a pheasant that he ignored the unexpected snowfall that came down that night. In the early morning he set out through the snowy fields and woods and set his trap where the pheasants were usually fed. It didn't take long for one of the keepers to figure out where this poacher lived, since the nice crisp footprints led to his back door.

Young Scott was lucky, but one of his friends who bore a slight resemblance to him was not. The friend had been making a call from the public telephone box in the village later that afternoon and the under keeper from the estate, who was in his late teens, had seen him. But it was a case of mistaken identity. The young custodian of the pheasants had hauled the innocent friend out the phone box and punched him in the face. 'That's for raisin' ma f—ing pheasants,' was the justification.

No charges were brought for the assault, or for the poaching offence. The estate landowner made a discreet visit to Scott's cottage; he was one of the gentry from the old school and knew Scott's father. He wasn't very happy about the boy's clumsy efforts at poaching his pheasants, but he knew that the young keeper had acted badly in attempting to mete out his own rough justice. Both parties made a gentleman's agreement, which suited both of them. The police were not involved and criminal records were avoided. The innocent party, who was the real victim in the drama, turned the other cheek to help his friend.

The Three Amigos

Jack the Ferret, Scott and I became firm friends. We were an unlikely combination of people from different backgrounds, but it was our passion for hunting that bonded the friendship: we had an assortment of skills that were mutually beneficial.

Jack was one of the most reliable and organized people that I had ever met. He was a rough diamond. He had left school at the first available opportunity and started an apprenticeship as a heating and plumbing engineer. His father had the same trade. Jack was no intellectual but he was extremely intelligent, with a natural problem-solving ability; he knew how things worked and could take things apart and, more importantly, unlike me, he could put them back together again.

Scott had an open and enthusiastic personality and you couldn't help but like the boy. He was very knowledgeable about falconry and had connections with people who practised the noble art. He was also friendly with one of the local farmers on the estate who didn't see eye to eye with the gamekeeper and who gave us permission to ferret on his upland sheep farm.

Eddie the farmer was very helpful in giving us free range to hunt over his land and saved us valuable time by advising us where all the best rabbit warrens were. Unfortunately Jack was unable to make our first trip due to work commitments, so we had to borrow a ferret from a friend of Scott's called Dougie. I met the young friend as I walked along the road from the bus stop heading for Scott's house; we had never met before, but I guessed who he was when I noticed what could only have been a live ferret bulging in his coat pocket. We arrive at Scott's house together and were formally introduced.

It was a freezing January day, wet and windy, so we kept off the exposed hill and headed towards the woods. It felt good wandering about the land, being legally in pursuit of game. An old chap in tweeds came hobbling along the track bawling at us,

'Hey! Where do you think you're going?'

Scott tried to explain what we were doing there, but it was a waste of time because the old boy wouldn't listen and didn't bother to identify himself. We walked away but he followed us.

'Where's the gun?' he demanded.

We had heard a distant shot about a minute earlier; it must have been miles away, but the old boy was convinced that we were concealing a firearm. We attempted to explain to him that we were ferreting, using nets, with the full permission of the farmer, but he became more abusive and eventually we had to barge past and ask him to speak to Eddie. We continued into the wood and watched Mr Grumpy standing on the path with his hands on his hips, still glowering at us. I suspected that he was heading for a **well-deserved heart attack**; we never did find out who he was.

In the woods we had to clear brushwood away from the holes on a steep-sided warren. It was a mature spruce plantation, which was overgrown and littered with dead branches. We did the preparation as quietly as possible and caught eight rabbits; two of them back-netted as they bolted from one hole then into another.

Dougie received a painful bite to his finger as he scooped up his ferret without due care and attention; he had tried to snatch it away from a struggling rabbit in one of the nets.

It was a successful hunt. We started back to the house as the sun went down, sharing our furry load. We were glad to get back to the house next to a warm fire and tea and toast. Scott had a large family, and his long-suffering mother made us very welcome.

Our next visit to Eddie's farm was the following February. Jack now had a car so we didn't have to get a bus at the crack of dawn. It was a freezing day with a heavy frost and blue skies above. This time we had plenty of ferrets with us. Scott was delighted at having the convenience of a vehicle to get us up into the hills, but his questionable advice on just how far we could take a family saloon along a frozen moorland farm track was suspect and we got bogged down almost immediately in deep ruts left by a go-anywhere tractor. Jack reversed the heavily laden car back down into a stubble field that was still frozen hard and we parked it beside a dyke on firm ground.

The air was sweet and sharp as we made our way across the heather to the top of the hill where we could see a row of old grouse butts. The ground was rock hard. There were sheets of ice where the sun had melted the snow the day before and the snowmelt had frozen again in the night, making a smooth, polished slide for the unwary. Green moss was encased in the thick, clear, ice and looked beautiful in the bright sunlight. We tried a couple of small warrens but there was nothing in either of them; the ferrets showed little interest at the holes and seemed happier when they were returned to their warm and cosy carrying boxes.

We followed a faint farm track to what was left of a derelict grey stone cottage on a remote part of the hill. The timbers had perished long ago and the gable end, with its well-built fireplace, stood like a monument to its previous occupant. The only sign of human habitation were the little clumps of snowdrops along the north-facing wall. An old woman had last lived in the cottage in splendid isolation; it must have been a lonely life for her. She had been burned alive in her bed before anyone could reach her, the fire it was thought started by a candle. We had our breakfast amongst the ruins and rested for a while.

It was a frustrating day and when we did eventually find warrens that were occupied, the rabbits refused to bolt; five that were in there had to be dug out. Jack did the lion's share of the digging with his army and navy multi-purpose folding shovel and by late afternoon we had ten rabbits. As the sky darkened and the wind freshened, it was time to head back to the car. Jack stopped for a cigarette, and in a rare moment of forgetfulness left all his nets hanging on a fence, only realizing his mistake when we got back to the car two miles down the hill. I went back up the hill to retrieve them – it seemed only fair since Jack had carried all the rabbits down the hill, single-handed.

When we got back to Scott's house, his mum was feeding her hungry brood of children around the big kitchen table and struggling to keep the peace. There was a delicious aroma of home-made lasagne filling the room. Jack and I glanced at each other. We had been invited to stay for tea, but we didn't want to impose because things looked a little chaotic.

I whispered to Scott, 'I think your mum's had enough, we'll just get off.'

Scott replied: 'No, she hasn't, I can always tell. She's not had enough yet!' I was to remind young Scott of this innocent remark many years later when he had a family of his own and he looked a bit sheepish.

Our Very Own Ferret

We left the flat where we had lived happily for ten years because we needed more space for our two children. Our neighbours had been very kind to us and we knew we would miss them, but the new house had a lot more room for a growing family and a decent-sized, sheltered garden. The garden at the flat had been a communal one, and keeping livestock there had been out of the question.

We soon acquired our first ferret: a polecat jill, with the most beautiful markings. Its face was panda-like, with big black patches around the eyes and there was a thin black line along the middle of its pale cream belly; Scott's stepfather Mike said, 'That's where God sewed 'em up when he made 'em.'

This young animal was christened Bramble, after a family vote on the name, and we couldn't have chosen a better one for a creature with such sharp, scratchy claws. My daughter spent more time than any of us raising this endearing little hunter and knitted it a miniature red woollen scarf, which it seemed happy to run around the house wearing. However, its cute household appearance didn't quite fit the killing machine role that I had envisioned for it myself. Nevertheless, a ferret that is handled a lot is a much easier to work in the field, being less likely to bite; they also make great pets for children, who learn how to handle animals safely.

The new ferret was installed in a wire cage in the garden; its sleeping quarters were in a square wooden box stuffed with soft hay. Extra bedding was put into the cage every second day and the occupant would pull this into the nest box; the hay reduced in bulk as the ferret turned round and round inside the box to make itself a comfy nest. Bramble was brought into the house to play in the kitchen and sometimes managed to get down into the basement through a secret passage behind the fridge. Two resident house mice in the kitchen soon disappeared.

Bramble

As soon as Bramble was fully grown, we began to take her on hunting expeditions. Ferrets didn't need very much training when it came to popping down rabbit holes. Whenever we fed Bramble we rang a little falcon bell that young Scott had given me as a present and which had belonged to a goshawk. Bramble always associated that high-pitched tinkling sound with meal times and came running when she heard it and this proved very useful when she was underground for a long time or out of our sight in the long grass.

We carried the ferret in an old fishing creel stuffed with straw. Most of our journeys were made by bus, but as an apparently respectable couple with two small children, we were an unlikely looking gang of poachers and our few nets were easily concealed under my jacket. On one of our first hunting trips we went to the seaside; it was a long walk from the bus stop over flat sandy fields towards the beach and on our way we saw a fat rabbit disappear into a three-hole warren. This was an ideal opportunity for our apprentice ferret to test her mettle.

We looked around to check for danger, but the area seemed deserted and safe from gamekeepers, so we placed a net over each hole and my daughter lifted Bramble from her cosy nest and placed her under a net for a sniff at the fresh rabbit scent. Bramble shook herself and slipped quietly underground. No sooner had we done the deed than a Landrover came hurtling towards us from the distant tree line, leaving a trail of dust behind it. We were lying prone on the ground, listening for tell-tale sounds of movement below. We scooped the nets up and I managed to shove them inside my jacket before the Landrover pulled up alongside us. We were on our knees with no incriminating evidence in view and the family pet was unseen below wandering about in the underworld.

'Have you got a ferret down there?' asked a ruddy-faced man in a tweed jacket, leaning out of the window, not bothering to get out of the vehicle.

'Yes we have, it's the children's pet. We're heading for the beach and it's gone walkabout,' I told him.

'Look, it doesn't bother me, but my gamekeeper might get a bit upset. You would be much safer on the shore,' he told us.

Bramble popped her head out of one of the holes and checked out the Landrover. The driver smiled and drove off giving us a friendly wave and we scooped her up and high-tailed it for the beach. We caught two rabbits later in the dunes along the coast.

Bramble became a constant companion on our weekend trips into the country-side and we rarely came home without a couple of rabbits in the bag. Fresh meat and plenty of exercise was essential to keep a ferret in good health. We even took her with us on our holidays during the Christmas break. My wife's parents lived in the Border country and seemed happy to have the children and their hunting pet to stay with them. However, I think they may have had reservations about my unofficial hunting activities in the fields around their house. I usually went for walks alone in the early morning and set a few snares. I caught several pheasants and hid them in the garden until I could sneak them unnoticed into the bottom of their freezer.

Bramble is Lost

In January, following the Christmas holiday, we lost Bramble. One of the children, who shall remain unnamed, was careless in putting her away one evening. The wire cage in the garden needed a brick placed on the roof to keep the trapdoor secure, because a ferret is a very strong animal and can squeeze through the tiniest spaces. It had snowed in the night, turning the garden into a Christmas card scene, and before we had breakfast I went out to bring Bramble into the house for a saucer of milk, which she liked.

The cage was empty. The brick, which should have been placed on the roof, had been left on the ground. My heart sank. I thought of my own childhood again, and experienced the same awful sensation of loss. The whole family was upset and it was even worse for the poor soul who had been responsible for the escape.

All our neighbours were informed about the missing pet. We were worried about Bramble being able to survive such icy conditions in the wild, but she was a keen little hunter, so she stood a reasonable chance of fending for herself. We lived alongside a railway line and the embankment provided a good environment for wildlife – there were mice, voles, shrews and all sorts of birds and there was even a burn flowing alongside the track with fish in it.

A few days later we heard a second-hand report of a giant 'weasel' that had been seen in a local garden, nibbling at bread that had been put out for the birds – but by the time we followed it up, the trail had gone cold. We continued to put food into the open cage in case Bramble found her way back home but we never did see her again.

An Adopted Ferret

Some months later, Eric, one of our elderly neighbours, acquired a female ferret as a pet – he had no intention of hunting with it. The polecat jill was called Viccy, and Eric played mad games with it and turned it into a hyperactive lunatic; you had to watch your fingers when you handled that furry little bundle of joy. But Eric was a kind-hearted soul and he was well aware of the grief we had suffered as a result of losing our much-loved pet. One day he asked me if I would like to have Viccy.

My initial reaction was a little cautious. I could just picture this mentally unbalanced animal gripping one of the children's noses with its needle-sharp teeth. Sometimes ferrets do bite people and refuse to let go – there were numerous old wives' tales on how to deal with such a painful experience. One of them was to hold a lighted cigarette under the animal's rectum, though as a non-smoker this was a non-starter for me; besides, if someone shoved a lighted cigarette up my backside, I think I would bite even harder. The family discussed the offer of a new pet and it didn't take long for them to make a decision: the children wanted any ferret, even a mad one.

Eric was more than happy to hand over his crazy pet for adoption and knew that Viccy would have a more interesting life with a family of hunter gatherers. He also gave us a large, secure, well made wire cage with a nest box made from thick cork and there was plenty of room in this cage for Viccy to run about and exercise.

The adoption of this over-excited little creature turned out to be a great success and in fact she calmed down with the appropriate kind of stimulus. We were not as manic as her previous owner in the games we played and Viccy turned out to be a first class hunter, accounting for hundreds of the rabbits that were recorded in the game book. The falcon bell we had used to train Bramble had been damaged and had lost its beautiful clear tinkle so, with its magic gone, we used a bicycle bell to train Viccy at feeding times.

The Rough Wooing

After the first rabbit-hunting season we decided to breed Viccy with a hob ferret owned by Scott's brother Simon; we knew several people who were keen to have one of her young ones. Furthermore my friend Jack was a great believer in populating the world with more ferrets and said he would help me to feed them.

We introduced Simon's great lusty hob to Viccy when she came into season, but the first meeting did not go well. Viccy was a liberated female who could handle herself with a big male three times her weight and initially it looked as if the powerful male was going to end up as an entry in the game book as one of Viccy's kills. It was my young daughter who had a great idea for making the love match successful:

'What about if we make Viccy run up and down the stairs for half an hour and then put her in the cage with that big randy hob?' she asked.

Out of the mouths of babes and sucklings, as they say. The plan worked a treat as Viccy was slipped into the cage with Romeo: this time he was not to be denied and grabbed his partner by the scruff of the neck and got down to business, providing the children with a graphic natural history lesson in the continuation of the species.

Viccy gave birth to eight kittens: five jills and three hobs. My daughter had been warned that newborn ferrets ought to be left alone until their mother allowed them to make a public appearance and we emphasized the dangers of interfering with a wild animal and her young. We knew that Viccy had given birth when we saw her new slim-line figure as we took her out of the cage to feed her. The young ones were sleeping out of sight in the nest box. After feeding, we put Viccy back in the cage and went indoors.

When I looked into the garden about ten minutes later, I saw my young daughter lying in front of the cage with one hand inside the nestbox and in a panic, I started wondering where our first aid box was. But by some miracle Viccy didn't seem to be bothered by the intruder who was removing her new brood from the warmth and safety of the nest. Her young ones were naked and blind and resembled chipolata sausages.

Finding enough food for the growing ferret family became a daily chore, but it was a point of honour for me to provide it without resorting to buying canned dog meat. A family Scott was acquainted with in the Borders had asked him if he knew of anyone who could remove rabbits from their garden and this was a good opportunity for me to get some fresh meat for the hungry brood. I got the bus out there the following morning and took Viccy with me; Scott met me in the village.

The house with the rabbit problem was a detached Georgian villa in a couple of acres of well tended garden on a steep hillside. We looked around the grounds and noted all the likely looking places for resident rabbits. There were three holes in the lawn at the furthest point from the house, next to a thick beech hedge. We took Viccy out of the creel, slipped her into one of the netted holes, then backed away from the warren and waited. There was silence for several minutes. We were bracing ourselves for a bolting rabbit.

The ferret's head suddenly appeared above the ground carrying something in her mouth. I wasn't prepared for this particular eventuality as Viccy trotted over to us with her prize: it was a baby stoat, unharmed and quite safe. Its coat was chocolate brown and one of its eyes still hadn't opened; it was probably no more than a few days old. Vicci was carrying the little creature by the scruff of its neck – she moved her own kittens around the cage in the same way and I was relieved to see that her maternal instinct was overriding any sign of aggression towards a potential competitor.

She returned to the warren three times and brought up another baby stoat each time, placed them at our feet; she then seemed to wait as if wanting to see what we wanted to do with them. Scott and I examined the little creatures: they were beautiful with their little blunt faces and tiny short round ears; only one of them had two eyes open. We put them all back down the hole safe and sound.

We left the garden through a gate in the hedge and went into the fields beyond, where we caught plenty of rabbits. It was only on the way back home, several hours later, that we came up with a plan to adopt one of the kittens for Viccy and went back to the stoat's nest. Viccy was still lactating and would have been able to suckle the newcomer with her own young. We put her down the same hole – but perhaps we had been a little over-optimistic in our plans, because of course the nest was empty: the stoat mother had returned and carried her brood to a safer nest elsewhere.

6
Living Off the Land

I had experimented with various forms of primitive hunting weapon and was a regular visitor to the Australian exhibits in the museum. The bow and arrow had been a universal weapon since prehistoric times and Australia was one of the few places on earth where human hunters had thrived without them and used, amongst other things, the boomerang.

Hunting with Boomerangs

I began to make boomerangs to amuse myself, first as toys, then as hunting weapons. It was very satisfying to get a home-made boomerang to come back to its launching point with consistent accuracy, but I got hit on just about every part of my body by boomerangs of every shape and size. One of the giant ones that I made would only fly in a gale-force wind; it looked like a cartwheel when I managed to get the thing airborne. Getting hit by this one would probably have resulted in a trip to the undertakers.

An important part in the manufacture of a boomerang is the ratio of width to its thickness and length; the under side is flat and the leading edge on the top side has to be bevelled more steeply than the edge that follows. It is the same shape as an aircraft wing, which is what produces the lift and flight. The knack in throwing these objects isn't strength, but a flick of the wrist. My children learned the dangers of returning boomerangs at a very early age – when I shouted '*Duck!*' they didn't need to be told twice, it was a reflex action.

At the time I was experimenting with these weapons, it was unusual to see a person throwing boomerangs in a public park. They attracted a lot of attention from passers-by and many people stopped and chatted; I spent as much time letting other people have shots as I had shots myself. One poor child threw one so well at his first attempt that it came back and knocked his glasses off! I had to explain to his mother that his injury was self-inflicted – at least his specs hadn't been broken.

My early boomeranging days became obsessed with the hunt for suitable timber. Sheets of plywood were often found with discarded broken furniture in the street and empty tea chests also provided plywood with the right thickness and strength.

With experience I could usually tell just by looking at a boomerang whether it would fly or not. I tried several 'genuine' articles from Australia that were totally useless; I think they had been cheaply and clumsily manufactured for the tourist trade with a view to decorating the mantelpiece back home.

As a weapon, there was nothing primitive about a returning boomerang: it was an extremely sophisticated piece of equipment. The real skill in using one was being familiar with its flight pattern, but the wind was a major factor in the way it flew and could make it unpredictable. A long-distance retrieve could be very irritating. An acute right-angled boomerang was easier for the novice to throw, but it broke easily if it hit the ground edge first; a pattern that was only slightly curved could absorb more shock when it landed hard on its edge. A damaged boomerang was not worth keeping for use and repairs were never very satisfactory.

Pigeons

I was forced into hunting with the boomerang when I had to find more food for the ferret and her hungry brood. In the month of July the elm trees in the local park were shedding seeds by the millions and this seasonal fare was much appreciated by the street pigeons in the area. Sometimes there were flocks of more than a hundred strong feeding below the big trees. I knew that the aboriginal people in Australia often hunted flocks of birds at waterholes where they congregated in large numbers, so it seemed a logical place for me to start hunting with my boomerangs.

I rose early one morning while most of the citizens were still in their beds – I really didn't want anyone to witness my anthropological experiment in the city park. I knew just how far the boomerang would travel in a straight line before it curved back and carried three of an identical size and shape. It was possible to throw all three simultaneously or in rapid succession.

I crossed the wide expanse of grass towards a large flock of pigeons busy feeding near the tree line and they showed no interest in me as I approached them. I threw a single boomerang towards the middle of the flock parallel to the ground and the birds exploded into the air as it passed high above them in a curving flight. The pigeon flock circled back towards me, well within range and I threw a second boomerang well ahead of their flight path with perfect timing. One bird was hit a glancing blow and came straight down; it was dead in the air. The flock circled again and then returned to the tree line, where they continued to feed. I was surprised by their lack of concern regarding the new danger in their lives and went straight home to feed the ferrets with this new source of food. They made short work of the pigeon between them.

I made regular daily visits to the park on my bike and pursued the pigeon flocks with great success. I tucked three boomerangs into the belt at the back of my trousers for easy access and became adept at throwing these weapons as I cycled towards the flocks as fast as I could pedal. Sometimes I would bring down two birds with one throw. I even practised uplifting the fallen pigeons Cossack-style without dismounting or slowing down and rarely went home with an empty bag.

All good things come to an end: I became overconfident operating in a public place with my guerrilla tactics and sometimes a member of the public would look on in disbelief, wondering if their eyes had deceived them. I knew it was only a matter of time before the local police were out looking for a bearded Caucasian on a bike who was decimating the local wildlife with aboriginal weaponry. This was a shame, because the ferrets had thrived on their pigeon diet.

Rook Hunting

Another valuable food source for me was an old rookery a few miles distant from the house. Squab meat had been a traditional delicacy since ancient times and young rooks and pigeons had been gathered as seasonal fare for many hundreds of years; the dove-cots alongside the great houses and castles made the gathering easier. Many city people regarded rooks in the same way as crows, as carrion eaters and unclean — but this is not the case, as rooks prefer to glean the fields for grubs and other non-carrion food items, although they are known to feed on sheep afterbirth at lambing time.

I always visited the rookery towards the end of May because this was the most productive time for getting plump young birds for the pot. Most of the nests were in the tops of tall sycamore trees and by this time the fledglings were out of the nests and perching in the branches alongside. There were about two hundred birds in the colony and I shot about twenty of them each season. Using an air rifle to shoot birds in the high trees directly above my head always gave me a stiff neck; marksmanship was difficult at this acute angle and sometimes it took me several shaky shots to bring down one bird. When a bird was hit, it dropped like a stone, usually at my feet. The musty smell of guano under the nest trees could be overpowering on a warm day.

Killing young birds in the spring made me feel a little uneasy, because the practice seemed to go against nature — but I was just another predator, like the fox that caught the fledglings on the ground. Our ancestors had no such qualms and the quality and taste of the meat was a great salve to a guilty conscience. I filleted the breast meat from the carcasses, which I usually left for the local fox, but when I had ferrets to feed I would take everything home for them.

Squab meat is very tender, it has a mild flavour and is ideal for making traditional pies using boiled eggs and mushrooms. It is also tasty when sliced thinly and grilled with a little garlic salt. One year I smoked a batch of rook fillets to make my own pemmican, but the experiment was not a complete success because the meat turned out dry, hard and massively over-salted. However, it did remain in a state of preservation for several months. There were occasions when we invited friends round for rook pie and everybody who tasted the meat enjoyed it, only discovering what they had eaten afterwards – and no one threw up in the bathroom.

Living in the Hills

Every year I spent a few days alone in the hills living off the land, staying in a makeshift campsite with a rough sleeping shelter that was well hidden in a dense fir plantation. Access to my den was by crawling along the ground on all fours under a maze of jaggy low branches and it wasn't the kind of place anyone would stumble across by accident. If I needed to make a fire to cook, then I used another site some distance away because I didn't want to advertise my presence with smoke signals. The area had a loch, a burn and acres of wild moorland above the tree line and there was even a pheasant pen less than a mile away in a birch plantation with good ground cover.

I carried some basic foodstuffs such as bread, bacon and chocolate. The only hunting tools that I took with me were about twenty rabbit snares, a couple of nets and a nine-foot trout rod.

Catching wild food was relatively easy as there were plenty of rabbits in the area, with well-worn runs under the sheep fences indicating their movements. I set most of my wires away from the fences, in the open. Gamekeepers and shepherds were observant people who were likely to spot anything suspicious along a fence line and I had no intention of being ambushed myself as I went to collect them.

Setting a trap line was best done as soon as possible. I considered myself a fit and healthy person, but my energy levels seemed to diminish with each passing day on the hill, as I covered a lot of ground to check the snares several times a day. Sometimes I would find a crow feasting on one of my fresh-caught rabbits; the eyes were always the first to go.

For a quick meal, I liked to roast the livers and kidneys of rabbits skewered on a wire coat hanger over hot embers because the heated wire cooked the meat on the inside and made the job much quicker. Small trout could be cooked in the same way.

One of the best fuels for a small fire on the open hill was the dead woody stems of the scrub heather that had been burned off the previous year. These gave off very little smoke and produced a fierce heat, but they burned very quickly so a good supply of twigs needed to be collected before cooking commenced. Dead branches snapped off the bonsai rowan trees were also useful in an emergency; these dwarfed shrubs were formed by the prevailing wind and poor soil conditions.

Fishing for my Supper

I felt less conspicuous in the landscape using my fishing rod, because an angler fishing a remote hill burn was less likely to attract unwanted attention from passing landowners in Land Rovers. Sometimes the narrow peaty streams cut deep into the soft banks creating surprisingly deep pools and a half-pound trout was considered a fine specimen from such a place.

One afternoon I passed a clear pool with three trout hanging in the current, one behind the other. It was the usual pecking order, with the big one up front. I observed them from a high bank without being seen myself. Their only cover was a large flat stone at the back of the pool on the bend. I managed to cast a worm into the middle of pool without success. The big fish glided across to the bait and inspected the wriggling worm, but was suspicious and made no attempt to take it. On my second cast, all three fish darted under the flat stone out of sight.

I lay in the heather and peeped down into the clear pool. The sun was on my back and I was happy to play the waiting game. I backed slowly away from the water's edge and took out my fly box. I had plenty of patterns to choose from, but only knew the names of about six of them. I tied on a brightly coloured wet fly and crawled back to the steep bank overlooking the pool. The three fish were back in the same formation, waiting for food to drift downstream. I let the soft breeze work the fly on the line and dapped it down gently on the surface of the pool. The big trout positioned itself, grabbed the fly from below, then it spat it out again in a split second. My heart sank.

The fish ignored the same fly when I presented it again for the second time and the three occupants of the pool were now suspicious. Each time I tied on a new fly, they showed interest and inspected it but none of them would bite. Novelty was needed to keep their attention if I was to stand any chance of catching one.

About half a mile downstream I had passed a long-dead sheep stewing in the hot sun, crawling with maggots and stinking. I was desperate to catch one of those fish, and there was only one solution if I didn't want to wait until the sun went down. I hiked back down the hill and located my smelly woolly bait bucket. The maggots were writhing all over the carcass and the stench was awful. I gathered a handful of the grubs in a plastic bag and carried them at arm's length. I had no way to clean them and was conscious of the health risk in handling them.

When I got back to the pool, the three fish were still there. I fixed the live bait to a fly called a 'bloody butcher'. The wriggling maggot was an impressive sight with its newly attached wings, and looked the business. I felt a lot more confident this time as I lowered the rod and dapped the 'fly' gently on the surface of the pool. The big trout came up like a torpedo and snatched it, hooking itself as it turned to dive. The rod bent double and I had it on the line. I stepped back, swung the fish up on to the bank and retrieved the fly, then waited for about ten minutes before I peeped into the pool below. The two remaining fish were feeding again, unconcerned by the disappearance of their larger companion, and I caught both within minutes, using the same fly with a fresh maggot attached.

It had taken me more than three hours to catch my fish supper and I was a happy man as I trudged wearily over the heather back to my cooking spot in the woods. The trout were delicious roasted over an open fire.

I slept like a log in my cosy shelter, exhaustion being an important factor for a good night's sleep. The soft sound of the wind in the fir trees above me was like the waves on the shore, and it was hard to stay awake. Once a tawny owl woke me from my slumbers in the middle of the night, hooting in the tree above me, and in the morning, I was wakened by a roe deer passing by. The roe has a bark like a dog, which might alarm a novice camper in the woods.

Observing Hawks

Much of my time in the wilds was spent on reconnaissance; I liked to find a good vantage spot and conceal myself to watch the local wildlife. If the wind was in my favour, I sometimes saw a roe deer pass close by, unaware of my presence. Five-barred gates in dykes served as useful crossing places for rabbits and hares to pass under. There were plenty of raptors in the area, and I saw buzzards, short-eared owls, tawny owls, sparrow hawks and merlin. On the moor above were golden plover and red grouse.

I watched a merlin pursuing a small pipit above the rough grazing where the sheep were feeding; the intended victim was twisting and turning and displaying impressive aerobatics to throw off its attacker. The small bird succeeded in eluding the falcon by crashing into a large tussock of rushes, and the merlin flipped over in an easy graceful movement, switching its pursuit to a passing woodpigeon overhead: it was poetry in motion. The pigeon accelerated towards a pine plantation and escaped into a tree by a hair's breadth. A sparrowhawk would have pressed on with the attack through the branches, but the merlin was more at home in the open country, where they also took swifts and martins on the wing.

The merlin is the avian equivalent of a guided missile: it locks on to its prey and follows its intended victim at every twist and turn, sometimes for long distances. When I was fishing a burn in the hills on a previous occasion, I watched a dipper rocketing towards me with a merlin on its tail. The dipper made an emergency dive into a small pool below with a big splash and the falcon passed over my head and disappeared downstream.

A shepherd once told me that he had been standing on the summit of a hill and was aware of a commotion above him in the sky. As he looked up, he saw a merlin high above, pursuing a small bird towards him. It was a skylark. The lark landed between the shepherd's feet and the merlin veered off to hunt elsewhere.

I had a close shave myself when I was ferreting in a pinewood and a blackbird flew towards me, clipping my ear as it passed over my shoulder, fleeing from a hen sparrowhawk close behind it. The hawk banked up when it saw me and rolled over like a spitfire through the tree canopy, continuing its pursuit of the blackbird, which had flown out of the trees and across an open field. Unfortunately I wasn't in a position to see the outcome of this exciting chase.

The Pheasant Pen

I made a visit to the pheasant pen early one morning with a view to varying my diet. There were several decent-sized birds strutting about the woods nearby.

I found a dog fox lying dead in a heavy wire snare, a magnificent large specimen in the peak of condition with a beautiful coat and a big bushy tail. The snare had been set beside a narrow deer track through the woods and the vegetation had been flattened all around the body. The poor beast looked as if it had had a painful and lingering death and I suspected that this fox snare hadn't been checked for several days. The gamekeeper therefore hadn't followed his legal duty by checking his trap lines twice daily and was clearly breaking the law.

I crept up close to the high chicken-wire fence around the pen. There was a fox-proof wire funnel on the ground, allowing free-ranging pheasants access to the safety of the pen to feed on the grain inside. I tied two rabbit nets across the divided funnel and backed away into the wood. I could see a few pheasants moving about the thick brushwood inside the pen and found a way in through a wire gate in the fence. I discovered that by moving slowly inside the pen, the birds were less likely to panic and fly over the top of the wire and it was possible to move them very slowly towards the exit funnel, keeping them on the ground, driving them around the inside perimeter.

I netted one pheasant and lifted both nets. My dinner was in the bag and the whole operation had taken less than ten minutes. I was careful not to leave any footprints in the soft ground and removed a few loose feathers.

A Lesson Learned

One evening I made a bad miscalculation after staying out on the hill later than usual, watching a woodcock circling over a pine plantation, intrigued by its flight and the croaking sound it made like a frog. The sun had gone down, the light was fading fast and there was no moon. I should have gone back to the den while there was still light to see by. It took me half an hour at a brisk walk to get to the fir wood where my sleeping place was. I had no torch with me and the wood was a pitch-black maze inside. I realized there was a real possibility of getting totally lost inside the wood attempting to find my sleeping bag and food cache in the darkness.

I didn't want to get hypothermia and freeze to death. I had suffered from the symptoms several years previously after being caught in a torrential downpour on the hill: my clothing had been soaked through to my skin, and I was on the point of collapse through cold and exhaustion. I had to stop myself falling asleep as I rested sitting with my back against a tree. I could feel the adrenalin pumping through my body and a warm tingling sensation from head to toe that was very pleasant; as deaths go, it would have been an easy one.

Luckily on this occasion I had a box of matches with me and was able to collect bundles of dry twigs by snapping off the dead lower branches from the fir trees. This material is highly combustible and makes excellent kindling. I lit a small fire just inside the wood for illumination and started to crawl on my hands and knees towards where I thought my bed was. I lit another fire, deeper in the wood and looked back to my first beacon, which had already burned down to a red glow. I was feeling a real sense of unease and was desperate to be able to retrace my steps in the event that I wasn't able to reach my den. I lit six small fires as I crawled through the wood. They flared up quickly and died down very rapidly.

Suddenly I saw my den close by and experienced a tremendous sense of relief. I had put myself in a very risky position by my own stupidity. I watched the fading red embers of the little fires to make sure they died out safely, and that night I slept the most delicious sleep imaginable. A five star hotel couldn't have been any more comfortable. Since that day, I always carry a small torch with me when sleeping out in the woods.

Returning to Civilization

After living in the woods for a week, I got used to being alone and enjoyed the experience. My vocal cords seemed to dry out and the first time I spoke to someone back in civilization, I croaked like a frog. My feet also became accustomed to the softer ground in the woods and hills and when I walked on to my first road, the hard surface seemed to come up to meet me. It was like stepping off a boat after a long sea journey.

7
Shotguns and Deer Hunting

Shotguns and Pigeon Shooting

Jack and I both bought shotguns. We were keen on the idea of being able to shoot flying birds, to increase our self-sufficiency. I had hunted woodpigeons for many years with the air rifle, stalking them in their roosts in the early morning, at the grey light of dawn and on a good day I could get half a dozen. The meat was excellent, the breasts delicious grilled with garlic salt, like the rook fillets. The carcasses made great stock for potato soup and the flavour was not unlike beef.

There were areas along the coast where it was legal to shoot between high and low tide: this was Crown land and peasants like us had an ancient right to hunt there. September was the best time for pigeon shooting. The cornfields had been harvested and hundreds of plump gathered to glean the fallen grain from the stubble. After feeding in the fields the birds flew over to the shingle beach to pick up the grit that aided their digestion.

As a shooter, it was best to be in position at first light. We wore camouflage clothing and made a rough hide on a flight line under an old beech tree. Pigeons are very wary birds and have sentries that position themselves in good vantage points for the benefit of the flock. Our tree was one of those places and it was possible to shoot a few birds as they landed in its top branches to take a peek at the gritty shoreline below – but after a few shots had been fired, the flocks became wary and moved away.

It was a waiting game. A few birds continued to fly on to the beach from the fields beyond. The top of the beech tree had been blasted by generations of shooters and the uppermost branches were mostly dead and leafless; they had been peppered with lead and the tree was probably worth more in scrap metal than it was for timber.

Jack and I were not brilliant shots with our newly acquired shotguns and we both needed practice. Flying birds seemed very difficult to hit. Most novices were unaware of the limited range of a shotgun and often took pot shots at birds well out of range; these optimistic snap shots were more likely to prick a bird and injure it. Forty yards was the recommended distance as an effective killing range.

The angle of aim was another complex problem to calculate. A bird flying away from the hunter in an upward direction had to be aimed at well above; likewise, a bird flying down towards the gun had to be aimed at in front and well below. There were so many different complications in sighting on a flying bird that you had to be a mathematical genius with lightning reflexes to have any consistent success and I was much impressed when I did see a fine shot.

We did get a few wild duck when we discovered good places to stand for the early morning flight, which depended on the state of the tide. Occasionally we bagged the odd pheasant that wandered on to the shore from the shooting estate, which bordered the coastline. Of course those game birds were out of bounds for us and protected by law, but I always found the temptation too much to bear and shot them on sight. We did have to be careful about concealing any pheasants, in case we met with the estate gamekeeper on the way home.

A Rampant Stag

Late one morning on the beach, Jack and I got more than we bargained for. We had shot a few pigeons from our hide under the beech tree and were heading back towards the car a few miles distant. The accessible shoreline that bordered the estate was very narrow when the tide was high and there was a deer park with a wall round it, quite close to the water's edge. There were shrubs and small sycamore trees along some parts of the wall. As we walked along a strip of fine sand just below the grassy banking under the wall, we saw the fresh footprints of a large red deer stag. We looked at each other and checked our weapons. What the hell was a big beast like that doing wandering along the shoreline?

A minute later we heard the sound of breaking branches and saw a magnificent stag break cover, with its antlers festooned with green leaves, stripped from the low-hanging trees that had barred its way. The animal was in a state of panic and turned away from us, bolting along the shoreline and disappearing round the next bend in the direction of the village.

'*Stay where you are*! There's a dangerous stag on the loose,' cried a voice from the far side of the wall. 'If you wait by the wall, we'll head it off and try to drive it back towards the gate before it reaches the road. Keep out of sight.'

The warning was a bit late and we were bemused by the incident. There were people rushing about in the deer park shouting to each other, and a couple of Land Rovers revving up in the field, but we couldn't see much of what was going on over the high wall.

We found a comfortable place to sit, side by side, with our backs against the wall between two shrubs and a clear view of the narrow beach along a short path about ten yards in length. The sea was lapping close against the shore and there was hardly a ripple on the water. Our guns were unloaded, leaning against the wall and the camouflage gear that we had on blended beautifully with our immediate surroundings.

We sat and talked quietly to each other for about half an hour before we considered a move. The excitement in the deer park had died down and it was a still, calm day without a breath of wind. Then we heard it, a snorting sound, heavy breathing, coming nearer and nearer along the beach. There was also the sound of hoof beats on shingle. Jack and I were expecting a nice view of the royal stag as it passed by in glorious profile, framed by the branches either side of the path, the perfect vignette. But instead of passing by, the stag made a left turn on to our path.

What followed next seemed to happen in slow motion. Jack and I stared in disbelief as this extremely large and dangerous animal ran directly towards us: it was fleeing in panic, unaware of our presence against the wall. It ran directly at me and then did an emergency stop, stomping its front hooves into the ground and driving its antlers down towards my face to within a few inches. My brain was telling me to protect my head and genitals, but my body had gone into shutdown mode and I was literally paralysed with fear and couldn't move a muscle.

The poor animal must have been reacting to sudden fear with aggression, which was logical and a defensive move.

My own experience was terrifying, made more so because I was sitting on the ground and looking up at a very large animal with a formidable set of killing weapons on its head. I have a clear memory of focusing my attention on the sharp white tips of the stag's antlers, only inches away from my face. The stag then wheeled round on the spot and galloped back along the beach. The last we saw of my would-be assassin was a big brown and white backside bounding back in the direction of the village.

'I thought you were gonna get a bit of a doin' then,' said my companion with very little emotion. I never did see Jack register shock at anything he ever saw. We discussed the possibility of him being able to load his shotgun while I was being gored to death. He thought he could have managed it.

On the soft ground before me was a splendid impression of two deep hoof prints. On the way back along the beach we followed the tracks of the fleeing animal for more than a mile. They eventually left the beach and disappeared into adjoining woodland where the fence was lower.

Twenty years later I had a conversation with an elderly employee on the estate, who recalled the incident of the escaped stag. In fact two stags had escaped and both of them had been shot after unsuccessful attempts to recapture them. They were considered to be a danger to the public running loose in the woods. They had been transported up from the south at great expense to introduce new blood to the resident herd in the deer park and it was a sad end for such magnificent animals.

A Hunter's Paradise

Scott contacted Jack and myself with an invitation to help him 'look after' his uncle's sheep farm in the Borders. His uncle was going away on holiday with his family so I took a week's holiday from work to take full advantage of unlimited hunting in a beautiful and wild part of the countryside.

Our duties on the farm were to check the flock twice a day and exercise the four working collies to keep them fit. After we had done this we were at liberty to wander freely over a wide area, which included open hills, forestry and a salmon river. I was in heaven.

Venison

There were hares, rabbits, pheasants and roe deer on the land. We had been instructed not to shoot any hen pheasants because they were the wild breeding stock for the following year. Technically the deer were out of bounds for us, being resident on the adjoining Forestry Commission land; you needed a licence to shoot them and hunting them without permission was trespassing and illegal. However, the marauding deer were inflicting serious damage on the newly planted hardwood trees, which had been planted on the farm by Scott's uncle who had a fondness for indigenous tree species. He was ahead of his time in the conservation movement and we had been given the nod that venison was on the menu.

Jack and I both had our shotguns and twenty-five buckshot cartridges between us. The killing range was no more than forty yards and in those days many roe deer were killed using twelve bores with heavy buckshot at fairly close range. Scott had a live .22 Winchester rifle, an ideal weapon for shooting deer at a longer range, but the small calibre of the bullet needed great accuracy for a clean kill. The recommended target area was the neck or heart. Any distance within a hundred yards was a reasonable range to shoot a deer with this rifle by a competent marksman.

We spent the first day and early evening watching the deer moving along the rides in the young fir plantations above the farm and inspected the soft ground near the fences and found their crossing places; there were fresh hoofprints and spoor everywhere. Deer numbers had increased rapidly with the planting of Sitka spruce on Forestry Commission land and the plantations provided the ideal breeding ground for our large mammals. There had been an explosion in the roe deer population and many farmers and shepherds took full advantage of this convenient source of fresh meat, although not always legally.

The deer were most active in the early morning and late evening. Jack, Scott and myself went out on the second morning into the forestry plantation where the trees were no more than six feet high. This age of woodland harboured the greatest number of deer, as there was still good grazing to be had amongst the young trees. From a hunter's point of view, the sightline along the rows of small trees was excellent, but the growing trees would eventually shut out the sunlight and leave the forest floor devoid of any vegetation.

We split up and took turns walking the rides between the trees. One person remained standing in a clearing, waiting for a roe to break cover away from the two beaters. When my turn came to stand and wait, a deer came bounding out in front of me down a steep hill at a distance of only thirty-five yards and I took a snap shot, aiming well in front of the running animal's head, as I would with a flying bird. *Bang*! The gunshot was deafening and the deer somersaulted downhill, with the forward momentum carrying it for a considerable distance.

My two friends came running at the sound of the shot. This was the first deer that I had ever killed and it was a big animal, although nowhere near the size of a red deer. Death had been instantaneous, with one wound to the upper neck and several in the head. The body was very warm to touch and blood was seeping into the green grass. The thick hairy coat was surprisingly rough and the deer's legs were long, slender and graceful. I felt pity for this animal and a sense of shame. It was a beautiful creature and I had just ended its life with a snap shot, a reflex action, with no time to think about it.

I was heartily congratulated by my friends, but experienced a mixture of emotions and still felt guilty; but by the time we got back down to the farm, the physical burden had outweighed the one on my conscience. A roe deer can be carried comfortably around the shoulders holding a front and back leg across the chest diagonally to keep the weight balanced, but even so, it was a heavy animal to bring down from the hill. We did the gralloching by the river to dispose of the evidence and the entrails and stomach were swept seawards by the swift current.

We hung the carcass in the barn and skinned it while it was still warm and easy to peel; the collies got the lower legs, the head and the lungs. The dogs were normally fed exclusively on dry mix, but the smell of blood brought them around us like a wolf pack.

We roasted a shoulder of venison in the oven for our evening meal, and the fresh meat was tender and delicious. My feelings of guilt had begun to diminish. I always found feasting with friends and family after a successful hunt to be a satisfying and happy experience. I liked to be a provider. I was never a very religious person, but I often felt a primitive urge to thank some superior being for my good fortune as a hunter.

The Fox Family

The days on the farm passed quickly. The air was clean and fresh and we could smell the wild thyme from the hill. Scott's uncle kept bees and had left us a large comb of dark, runny heather honey on a big, oval, willow pattern plate on the kitchen table. We dipped into this nectar with crusty bread. The only sounds we could hear around the farm were natural ones, sheep calling to each other from the hill and the wind in the trees by the house. Occasionally one of the collies would bark if a fox passed close by to the kennels.

There was a clear, swift-running burn that ran down from the hill, close to the barn and it was nice to sit and watch the sparkling little waterfalls in the autumn sunlight. In the early winter, salmon and sea trout sometimes swam up this narrow watercourse to spawn. I hadn't taken any fishing tackle with me, so we had to improvise in order to catch a few small trout in the pools along the burn. Jack provided an army camouflage-netting scarf and I went into the house to get a wire coat-hanger; we then threaded the wire through the green netting and tied off the loose end with baler twine. The finished article resembled a shortened version of a coarse fisherman's keep net. Fishing with a net required no tiptoeing along the bank or lightness of touch: we took turns wading upstream and splashing about in the pools to chase the wild brown trout under the banks where we could scoop them out with the net. Our total catch was modest, but we were happy at playing wild Indians, feeding ourselves with a varied diet.

I was the early riser amongst my younger friends and was well accustomed to being up before sunrise whenever I had a hunting opportunity. For me, the pursuit of game was like a drug: it wasn't a case of big numbers or filling a game book with long lists of furred and feathered victims. I did in fact keep records, because they were a very good way of making a note of where certain birds and animals would be during the different calendar months. Intelligence gathering and studying the ways of wild things was an essential part of being a successful hunter.

When I was a kid, I always wanted to be a Red Indian because they had better 'stuff' than white folks. The accumulated knowledge and hunting skills among tribal people was something to be amazed at, by us so-called civilized people. Many years later I had the good fortune to form a close friendship with a Native American, whom I met during a trip to the United States. It was a chance meeting on a city street in Albuquerque, New Mexico. Mr Redfox was a full-blooded Lakota/Sioux who had been born on a reservation in North Dakota. We were of a similar age and had similar interests, although his hunting experiences were related to larger prey than mine, such as elk, bear and wild turkeys. The buffalo had long gone from his birthplace, but some of the tribal lands and state parks had been restocked with wild bison herds that had narrowly avoided extinction during the 1800s. We had a mutual respect and admiration for birds of prey. Mr Redfox's first name was Lone Eagle and he had a twin brother called Crazy Thunder.

Back on the ranch, or sheep farm as we called it, we didn't get the opportunity to bag another deer, although we saw plenty – though they had usually seen us first and disappeared into the forestry. We had to take great care not to be seen with guns on the neighbouring land.

One morning I walked out with my shotgun and took one of the collie dogs with me for company. As I stepped into the field by the river, a big hare broke cover and started to run the length of a ploughed furrow. I had expected the dog to take after it instinctively, but man and dog stared at each other for a few seconds, equally puzzled. I then swung the gun up and fired above the running hare and killed it with a headshot, leaving no pellets in the body.

The farm collies were so well trained that they ignored their natural inclination to sprint after a bolting hare or rabbit. My own preference for a canine companion was something a little more racy, with its killer instinct still intact.

Stalking the Roe

For the following two years we were invited back to the farm and continued with the deer stalking. Jack was only able to stay with us at the weekends because of his work commitments. Scott and I spent most early mornings and evenings walking along the rides in the forestry searching for the elusive roe deer. We had seen a large buck in the area, several times. One evening we were walking quietly and silently along the tree line, measuring every step in slow motion. The sun was low in the sky and there were little pools of golden sunlight on the ground where the gaps crossed the rides.

Scott stopped ahead of me and nodded his head to the left. Just ten feet away from us was a beautiful red fox, fast asleep in the sun; it was curled up, with its bushy tail across its nose. I aimed my weapon at the slumbering animal for a couple of seconds and Scott moved his head from side to side – but I had no intention of shooting this dreaming creature, Mr Tod in the land of Nod and was content to study its magnificent form at close range. We had outwitted it by stealth and beaten it at its own game: the wind was in our favour and we stood for several minutes watching this wild animal, its life in our hands. As if by some sixth sense, the fox awoke, opened its eyes, did a double take, leapt to its feet and disappeared into the trees and safety.

I knew that Scott had shot a fox the week before and still regretted it. It had been done on impulse and he knew that I didn't approve. We had no luck that evening and went home empty-handed.

Because my stay on the farm was limited to only one week, I was more anxious than Scott to bag a deer and got lucky one evening when I went out on my own. I took my shotgun and a .22 rifle, which I borrowed from Scott; the rifle belonged to his uncle and had no telescopic sight. I was carrying the shotgun at the ready, in case of a snap shot at close range; the rifle was strapped to my back, ready to stalk an animal if I got the opportunity. I walked a couple of miles from the house, crossed several fences and made my way into the forestry. It was uphill all the way and there were boulders and rocks strewn all over the hillside. There were bare patches in the forest on the downward slope below the path, where the ground was too rocky for the trees to take root and it was in one of those clearings that I spotted a roe deer grazing.

I ducked down and kept dead still for several minutes, lying in the grass; when I peeped through the branches, it was still there. I unloaded the shotgun and laid it down on the ground beside me, then took the rifle off my back and pulled the bolt back as quietly as I could. I fumbled in my jacket pocket and managed to get one of the small .22 shells. My hands were shaking as I loaded the rifle, so I lay still for another five minutes, taking deep breaths to calm myself. I had never fired this weapon before, but the open sights were similar to my own air rifle.

The deer was about eighty yards away, at a very acute angle below. I managed to get myself into a good firing position without being seen. I aimed at the neck as the deer raised its head from grazing. The young trees obscured the body of the roe. I fired a shot and the animal disappeared out of sight. The shot echoed all around the hills and must have been heard from a great distance. I lay the rifle down and slid down the slope to search the spot where the deer had been.

At first I was convinced that I had missed the target. How could such a large animal be concealed right under my nose? Then I saw it: the roe had slid down the hill head first into a deep furrow between two rows of young trees; the grass was long and the deer well concealed. It was dead: the bullet had passed through the back portion of its skull, killing it instantly.

My initial excitement soon gave way to concern because it was going to be a hard task carrying my heavy burden and the two guns. Scott and I had agreed never to gralloch any beasts on forestry land, leaving evidence of our unofficial hunting activities. At least the way back to the farm was downhill most of the way, but the journey was cumbersome and I had to keep juggling the deer across my shoulders and balancing the two guns. I lost count of the number of times that I stumbled and fell, and was lucky not to break any bones. My knees were black and blue and my hands were grazed and sore. The hillside had many hidden rocks under the long grass and by the time I got back to the house it was dark. I could see a figure in the yard, by the light of the moon. Two of the collies came running to meet me.

'You lucky bastard,' Scott said, as I walked into the light.

'Luck has nothing to do with it, you lazy sod,' I answered.

We both agreed that luck only played a part in deer hunting and Scott would stand a much better chance of getting some venison once he got his backside off the sofa in the evening.

The next day, it was Scott's turn for success. We went for a stroll in the small field just behind the house where there were half a dozen pet sheep in the paddock that had been hand-reared as orphaned lambs. These unpredictable semi-wild woollies had to be watched, having very little fear of humans or dogs; a butt in the backside was a real possibility for the unwary. Scott took his Winchester rifle, in case we saw any pheasants near the house. They sometimes strolled down into the garden to peck at the vegetables.

I had good long sight and was usually the first person to spot a deer. Scott and Jack were both red/green colour blind and were often unable to see a deer that was standing in cover. Sometimes I had to lie beside them and guide their aim towards the target. As we walked along the boundary fence that ran parallel to the foot of the hill, we both saw a roe deer grazing on the steep slope alongside one of the forestry fences, at right angles to our own. We ducked down amongst the rushes in the corner of the field and Scott rested his rifle on the bottom rung of wire and looked through the scope. He fired and missed. The deer looked round but didn't seem to know where the shot had come from. Scott aimed and fired again, and this time the deer keeled over and rolled down the steep hill for a considerable distance.

We jumped the fence and scrambled up over the loose scree on the slope to get to the deer. The bullet had snapped the roe's neck at its narrowest point. The distance had been just under a hundred yards and I was impressed by the lad's coolness after missing the first time, then taking another well aimed shot in the space of five seconds.

A Final Visit

The following year was to be our final visit to the farm and the last opportunity for me to stalk another roe deer. Scott's uncle was selling up and trying a new financial venture on the Isle of Skye, so I was keen to make good use of our time as temporary custodians of the property, with the aim of filling the freezer with some wild venison.

Early one morning I slipped out of the house while Scott was still sleeping. I walked along the foot of the hill as the sun was coming up and watched a pair of carrion crows flapping towards the sheep pasture to feed in the dewy grass along the river bank. For some reason, the shepherds in this area referred to all crows as hoodies. I never understood why, because hooded crows were usually found only in the west and north of the country and were very rarely seen in this region. Occasionally a pair of ravens was seen, and easily identified by their guttural croaking and long, wedge-shaped tails. Those large corvids would usually return a greeting when it mimicked their croak, but kept a greater distance from humans than the carrion crows and jackdaws on the hill.

It wasn't long before I spotted two roe deer; unfortunately they had spotted me at the same time. The deer were high up on the side of the hill on a scree slope, several hundred yards away and well out of range for my .22 rifle with its open sights. The Sitka trees there were small, giving sparse cover for large animals and I watched the deer's progress from the track at the bottom of the hill, seated on a large boulder with my back against the dyke. They grazed on the scant vegetation between the small trees and finally disappeared over the summit of the hill. I knew that I had lost the element of surprise, but was prepared for a long hike up the hill to observe my quarry from a distance.

It took me almost an hour to scramble up to the top of the scree-covered hillside and get a view on to the next summit; the deer were visible several hundred yards away and still grazing. I was wearing full camouflage clothing and was well concealed behind a bushy, bonsai spruce tree, less than five feet tall. The rocky ground there produced stunted trees that were not going to grow any bigger, although from a hunter's point of view the land was ideal for deer stalking.

From my kneeling position behind the tree I observed the deer's movements by peeking through the branches without being seen – or so I thought. One of the deer, however, appeared to be looking in my direction each time it raised its head between spells of grazing. I knew I couldn't have been seen approaching the tree because I was on the blind side of the hill and the wind was also in my favour, but I felt sure that this deer was aware of my presence.

I kept stock still, anxious not to move a muscle, in an effort to remain unde-tected by my intended prey. The roe then turned from its side view and stood face on, staring in my direction and began to walk slowly towards me, stopping every so often and appearing to graze unconcernedly. My plan was to wait until the deer came within range and then to take a carefully aimed shot when I was confident of hitting the mark in either the heart or the neck.

The deer's slow approach seemed to take an eternity. I waited until it came within fifty yards and slid the rifle forwards very slowly, an inch at a time and got the butt to my shoulder. I was getting cramp in my arms from holding the rifle in position and the deer was still coming forwards. When I finally squeezed the trigger, the deer was less than twenty feet away looking directly at me. The bullet passed through its throat and exited through the back of its neck. I experienced a state of shock when it went down. It seemed too close for comfort and I felt as though I had just murdered someone in cold blood. Somehow I felt as if it were a breach of trust.

I laid the gun down and walked around the tree to look at the fallen animal, which was lying on its back absolutely still and not breathing. As I stood over it to examine the fatal wound, its hind leg jerked up and the sharp hoof caught me square in the testicles. My eyes watered and I knelt down to get my breath back while the deer twitched a couple of times before lying still.

Many years later I spoke to a deer stalker in the Highlands who had shot a red deer stag close up in very similar circumstances, although he had not been kicked in the balls afterwards.

8
A 'Criminal' Record

It was only a matter of time before I got caught red-handed while I was hunting 'unofficially' in the countryside. On the first occasion it was a combination of carelessness on my part and bad luck. I cycled to my usual haunt on a cold and windy March morning before the sun came up and hid my bike amongst the gorse bushes on the edge of the local golf course. The trees in the woods where I usually stalked roosting woodpigeons were empty and there were no rabbits in the adjoining pasture, so I wandered further afield in pursuit of game, crossing a road into a strip of woodland separating two ploughed fields. The land was typical partridge country, with small rolling hills and a burn running beside a farm track at the foot of the hill where there was a dense hawthorn hedge separating the track from the burn.

I looked across the open field ahead, spotting a cock pheasant down below, but it saw me and moved into cover. I never did like crossing open fields, but the coast looked clear with no farmhouse in sight. The pheasant was gone by the time I reached the muddy track so I crawled through a gap in the hedge and waded across the burn to sit down and eat a sandwich. I hadn't been there more than ten minutes when I saw a policeman's black-and-white chequered helmet pass slowly by along the top of the hedge. I sat tight: I was in a well concealed position and fully camouflaged. A few minutes past and I waited, sliding my rifle under the hedge to conceal it.

'Okay, come on out.'

I didn't move.

'I know where you are, come on out.'

I squeezed out of my hiding place and saw a young policeman standing close by, behind the hedge.

'Where's the gun?' he asked me.

'What gun?'

'Look, I saw you cross the field, where is it?'

I told him I would get it, but he told me to leave the gun where it was. Seconds later I heard two speeding vehicles driving towards us from the track above; they were police cars. There were three policemen in each vehicle and I was well and truly nicked.

'Where's the gun?' one of the new arrivals asked.

I told him where it was, and he went to retrieve it. There seemed to be a sigh of relief when the cop identified the weapon as an air rifle. I admitted that I was hunting for rabbits but hadn't managed to get any.

'Where's your wheels?' he asked me. He must have read my puzzled look. 'Where did you leave your car?'

'I don't drive, but I left my bike about two miles away.' With this revelation the cops started laughing.

'Well, I never thought I would catch a poacher in Edinburgh, and definitely not one on a pushbike!'

One of the policemen asked me where I lived and turned out to be a near neighbour of mine. He made a note of my name and address, and the serial number on the rifle. He told me they weren't too concerned about the incident, as the farmer was unaware of my presence there and there hadn't been a complaint. He suggested that asking for permission to shoot rabbits on the land might be a good idea.

When I asked him how they knew where to find me, it was my turn to share the joke. The young policeman who had caught me had driven his patrol car along the farm track so that he could have an unofficial 'skive', but his vehicle had become stuck on the bank of earth in the middle of the track that had been created by two very large tractor wheels on either side. He had been sitting marooned in his car, wondering how the hell he was going to explain his predicament and location to his colleagues, when he had the good fortune to observe a gunman behaving suspiciously nearby – and the low position of the bogged-down police car in the dip on the track was why I had not been able to see it when I crossed the field.

Caught Red-handed

A few years later I wasn't quite so fortunate and was caught red-handed in pursuit of game.

My friend Jack picked me up from the house in his Mini van, several hours before dawn, on a cold autumn day about a week before the official pheasant shooting season opened and we motored down to the Border country to an area I was familiar with, in order to bag a few early birds ahead of the paying estate guests. At this time of year, the pheasant population was blissfully unaware of what was in store for them with the coming of the shooters: a Blitzkrieg in the offing. Some of the quiet rural roads bordering the estates were handy places to snipe at pheasants from a vehicle with an air rifle, although the Mini van would have been more comfortable for a contortionist sniper. We had to be constantly on the lookout for landowners, farmers, gamekeepers and especially Land Rovers or jeeps.

When we saw a likely looking wood with pheasants on the ground, Jack would let me out and drive on, coming back about ten minutes later to pick me up. These hit-and-run tactics proved very productive and we bagged six birds without being observed. As more local traffic appeared on the little country roads, we thought it wise to move on and call it a day. The sensible thing to have done would have been to have gone home and not pushed our luck – but we didn't. As we passed close to the River Tweed, thousands of woodpigeons were circling over the forestry plantations along its banks and we thought it might be a good idea to bag a few once they had settled in the trees.

We parked the van in a quiet layby that was partially concealed from the road by the downward slope and a thick beech hedge running parallel to the road. It was the kind of place that courting couples would probably have found useful. I thought it might be a good idea not to leave the pheasants in the car, so we put the birds in a black plastic bag and stashed them in the hedge about twenty yards from the van. There was enough dry vegetation to cover the bag and it was well hidden.

From the layby, a narrow path went through the forest and down towards the riverbank. There were no houses nearby and no sign of human activity in the immediate vicinity. I managed to shoot a woodpigeon out of one of the tall trees alongside the path and slipped it into my bag. As we got down to the riverbank, dozens of wild mallard ducks took to the air when they saw us. They circled round and flew upstream, where they landed on the river again. Jack and I thought it might be worth stalking the ducks to get near enough to shoot one with the rifle. It would have rounded off the day's hunting very nicely.

There was a narrow, muddy path along the riverbank and plenty of cover on each side for concealment. By force of habit I walked beside the path on the grass, to avoid places that would leave footprints. We passed a fox snare, which Jack untied and shoved into his pocket. I didn't think that was a very good idea at the time. Those keen-eyed ducks were airborne again before we got anywhere near them, so we scrambled down the steep bank to take a look at the river. We watched the fast-flowing clear water for salmon heading upriver to spawn and occasionally saw one leaping.

We decided to head back to the van, which was less than a mile away. Jack scrambled up the bank ahead of me – and stopped suddenly in his tracks.

'Where the hell do you think you are going?' boomed a very angry voice.

I was still out of sight and couldn't see who was there. I assumed it might be a fisherman who was not too happy about the prospect of being accidentally shot by unidentified gunmen. I slipped my rifle in the case and clambered up the crumbling bank to join my pal. In retrospect I should have stayed where I was and hidden the gun while I still had the advantage of concealment.

Standing on the path above us was a Neanderthal-looking chap in a plus-fours, brandishing a primitive club in the form of a broken branch. He had curly red hair, a freckled face and was built like the proverbial 'brick shithouse'. His broad accent identified him as an Englishman from Yorkshire, probably in his early thirties.

'Right, hand over those guns,' he demanded. Jack and I looked at each other.

'Look, I don't want any trouble,' he told us.

'Who are you?' I asked him.

'I'm the under-gamekeeper on the estate and you two are poaching.'

It seemed pointless to deny these facts and as Jack and I were not thugs who would resort to physical violence to avoid capture, we were well and truly nicked by the duke's tweed-clad servant.

We duly handed over our weapons and walked behind him along the path. Jack was able to dump the fox snare without being seen. We were escorted into an open field where two estate foresters were sawing up a fallen beech tree in a meadow. The under-keeper sent one of the woodcutters to fetch the head keeper. While we sat waiting for his boss to show up, we had the most inane conversation with the under-keeper.

'Do you work in an office?' he asked me.

'Yes, I do,' I told him.

'Then how would you like me to walk into your office and scatter your papers all over the place? Because that's what poaching is.'

The comparison between my modest little workplace and a shooting and fishing estate on several thousand acres of the richest land in Scotland, owned by a member of the aristocracy, was not worthy of a reply. I felt sorry for the man and narrowly avoided giving him my political opinions, which would not have been helpful under the circumstances. Sometimes it's better to say nothing at all.

About ten minutes later, a small van appeared above the sloping meadow and parked on the grass. An elderly man wearing a tweed suit and a deerstalker hat got out and walked slowly down the hill towards us. He strolled over to the under-keeper, had a few words with him and then came over to us.

'Where did you leave your vehicle, gentlemen?' he enquired in a very polite tone. Jack and I had already agreed in advance to say that we had got the bus to the nearest town and had walked to the estate along the riverside. We were concerned about the possible confiscation of the van, which was owned jointly by Jack and his girlfriend Carolyne.

'When you walked from the town, how many bridges did you pass along the way?' he asked.

We knew the game was up. It was obvious we had not come the way we had told him. The old chap was a quite a decent sort, and had less to prove than his thuggish-looking under-keeper.

The local policeman arrived soon afterwards, parking his vehicle next to the keeper's van and walking down the field to the fallen tree where we were sitting. He gave Jack and me a very stern look, before taking a statement from the victorious young keeper who had apprehended us. He then came over to us and issued a caution before asking us if we had anything to say. We nodded our heads and said nothing. When he asked us if we agreed with the gamekeeper's account of what had happened, we said that we did.

We were then informed that we would be taken to the local police station and formally charged. The policeman took our rifles and put them in his car, while Jack and I were put into the back of the keeper's van with his wee dog. We got a friendly welcome from the little Border terrier, who licked us all over; the innocent little canine was unaware that he was fraternizing with the enemy. I was surprised by the civility of the head keeper as he drove us to the station, following the police car. It was all in a day's work for him and he had seen it all before, and I wondered how many other villains he had apprehended over the years. The younger keeper sat beside him and said nothing.

When we got to the unmanned village police station and the door was unlocked, we were ushered inside and told to sit down. The office was small and relatively comfortable; it was very much a one-man operation. It was only then that the policeman took my game bag and looked inside. He lifted the pigeon out by its wing tip and dropped it into a waste paper basket beside his desk. He then wiped his hands on a handkerchief before taking down a large law book from a shelf. The younger keeper smirked and made some remark about what great hunters we were.

'Trespass with a Firearm'

Once the policeman had browsed through the relevant section on poaching, we were formally charged with 'trespass with a firearm'. Apparently the poor woodpigeon was not considered to be game, and was therefore not relevant to the charge. If we had had a pheasant in the bag, then the charge would have been much more serious and we would have been prosecuted for being in possession of game without a licence and out of season, in addition to the firearm charge. The possession of the fox snare, which Jack had fortunately discarded, would have constituted theft and would have meant a further charge. The keeper knew that one of us had taken it, but had no proof.

The two keepers left the station and we were each given a mug of tea and a biscuit. The policeman turned out to be a very pleasant individual once we had got the official business out of the way and we discovered that the gamekeeper who had caught us was also a convicted criminal, having been charged in connection with the disappearance of the local pub's cat. He had been seen by witnesses carrying it from the premises one evening towards a footbridge over the river, and the pet moggy had never been seen again. One of the foresters, who had been cutting up the fallen tree, also had a criminal record for sheep stealing. It seemed like everybody in the countryside had been involved in some kind of mischief.

While we had been detained at the station, my wife had been visited by the Edinburgh city police, to confirm the address that I had given to the arresting officer. She had been told that her husband was helping police with their enquiries, in the Border District of Roxburgh. My wife had no idea where we had gone that day.

We were taken by the policeman back to the layby where Jack's van was parked. We were extremely concerned about the possibility of the bag of pheasants in the hedge having been discovered in our absence. The gamekeeper knew roughly where our vehicle had been parked and had had plenty of time to take a look before we got there.

'Is there anything in the van that I should know about?' asked the policeman.

'No,' I told him and looking him straight in the eye. I answered him honestly, and Jack gave the same response.

'I can search the vehicle,' he told us.

Jack offered him the van keys, but he didn't take them. He told us to drive safely and waved us off.

As we drove away from the scene of the crime, I discussed with Jack the possibility of nipping back to retrieve the birds an hour or so later. This was a stupid idea because the keepers might possibly have had the bag under surveillance and our fingerprints were all over it.

Recovering the Cache

Two days later, the thought of those six pheasants in that bag under the hedge was really getting to me. It was a waste of good food. The weather had been extremely cold and there had been a frost, which would have preserved the meat for several days longer. I mentioned the situation to an old friend of mine who was a schoolteacher with strong political views about the land-owning classes and their feudal relationship with the peasants. He was most definitely a willing chauffer for hire – at that time I was a non-driver – and one evening after work we made the fifty-mile journey south, under the cloak of darkness. I was still very much concerned about being caught in the act of retrieving the bag so close to the estate where Jack and I had been arrested. A passing dog might easily have sniffed out the hidden cache and betrayed the hiding place.

The drive down to the Borders was uneventful and we passed through the market town and along the narrow winding lane that led to the layby. As we made a right turn off the road into the layby, we saw a vehicle parked with its lights out, near to the hedge where the birds were hidden. Its engine was still running. At that moment I was in favour of aborting the rescue mission and driving straight back home again, empty-handed. My friend Maldwyn, however, was made of sterner stuff and was intent on a successful outcome. My fear was that the gamekeeper had been waiting for us to return so that he would have the satisfaction of catching us red-handed on a more serious charge.

But he who dares wins, as they say and so my friend drove towards the parked car with his headlights full up, illuminating and surprising a couple having sex on the folded-down seats. I was able to jump out of the car and retrieve the hidden bag in seconds. In the glare of our headlights the interrupted lovers would have seen nothing of us and would have been none the wiser about our sudden appearance at the scene.

We drove very fast along the lane with the bag on my lap and the windows wound down in case we had to jettison the evidence in a hurry on a blind bend. For a while we were followed closely for several miles by a vehicle that we were concerned about, eventually making a small detour just to be sure of a successful getaway and to convince ourselves that we were not being paranoid. It was a great feeling of relief to be in possession of our hard-won pheasants again. I was also aware that it would seem to soften the penalty of what was going to be a steep fine following our forthcoming court appearance.

The Judicial System

Several months later, following the summons, Jack and I made our appearance at the county courthouse in the beautiful Scottish Border country, wearing our best jackets and ties. We looked almost respectable, although were not feeling very comfortable in our unfamiliar restrictive collars and ties. We had to wait all morning and sit through numerous petty cases, most of the offenders being locals. Offences were mostly shoplifting, speeding, breach of the peace and domestic violence. I felt sorry for one woman, who had stolen a pair of sandals for one of her seven children. It was a first offence and she was a single mother and struggling to make ends meet; I thought her fine was severe. The presiding sheriff was known in the county as 'hanging judge P—', and was well known for his severity in dealing with lawbreakers. He also had friends amongst the local gentry with shooting and fishing interests, so I knew we would feel the full rigour of the law for our particular crime.

When our turn came to stand in the dock, we were informed that we were being charged with 'trespass with a firearm' and asked if we had anything to say. There was an embarrassing silence and I can remember mumbling something about not realizing that we were on private land, etcetera.

The fine was steep and our rifles were confiscated. We had been advised by the clerk of the court that it was possible to buy back our weapons after the case had been completed; an outside assessor from the local gun shop had valued our weapons to fix the price on each. I was fortunate in being able to get my beat-up old rifle back relatively cheaply because of its condition. I was extremely anxious to recover the old gun because of its remarkable accuracy and finely made open sights. Jack had to pay through the nose to recover his new rifle; the telescopic sights had greatly increased the value of his gun.

It was a relief to get the court case over and done with and there was much amusement at the agency where I worked. One of the partners there was a keen shot and paid handsomely for the privilege of shooting driven pheasants on a keepered estate in the county of West Lothian. As long as I was not operating on his hunting ground, he regarded my poaching activities as a bit of fun and gave me a ribbing for getting caught.

I must admit that I became more nervous about getting caught poaching, now that I had a criminal conviction. 'Trespass with a firearm' sounded very serious, more like someone walking into a supermarket with a sawn-off shotgun. The term 'firearm' included air guns, shotguns and all weapons using live ammunition. In the eyes of the law they all fitted the legal description and it was the propulsion of a missile along a barrel that defined a weapon as a firearm. I thought that maybe archery would have been a safer bet, although in the UK it was illegal to shoot any creature with an arrow.

What I found particularly annoying at the time of my own conviction, was what happened to an acquaintance of mine who had committed what I thought to be a far more serious crime. The difference in the geographical location of his offence may have been a factor in his financial penalty. He was charged with shooting eider ducks with a shotgun from a speedboat, on a sheltered sea loch on the west coast of Scotland. He was using a borrowed gun and had no shotgun certificate. He was shooting from a moving boat, which was illegal and he was shooting on a Sunday, which was also illegal in Scotland at the time. The nine ducks he had slaughtered were a protected species. The loch, which was adjoining the Clyde, was also used by sea anglers and weekend sailors and could have been described as a public area. The modest fine my swashbuckling pirate friend received for his multiple crimes paled into insignificance compared to the whacking great fine that I received for my single offence.

So much for the Scottish justice system.

9
Fishing and Ferrets

Sea Angling

In my early twenties I fished for mackerel from the old wooden pier at Newhaven on the Firth of Forth. There were usually a few optimistic anglers lined up on the rickety pier attempting to catch the fish when the shoals came into the Forth during the months of August and September. High tide was the best time for hooking one, although there were plenty of undersized coalies for desperate fisherman who only had cats to feed. I met some interesting characters on those fishing trips. One old chap described the fishing of his childhood when it was possible to catch mackerel by the hundred from Portobello beach and he assured me that it was possible to kill fish with a stick as they shoaled into the shallow water chasing the sand eels in a feeding frenzy. It seemed unlikely those golden days would be experienced again in my lifetime, however.

I received useful advice from this old-timer and he also told me about some of the best places to fish in the Forth area. The Figgate Burn on Portobello beach was a hotspot for catching flounder on the incoming tide in September and October, but the tide came in so fast, it was necessary to beat a hasty retreat from the approaching sea and not leave any of your belongings on the sand. Mackerel cut in strips seemed to be the most successful bait if there was no time to dig up lugworms or ragworms from the wet sand near the water's edge – though the hungry crabs often stripped the bait off the hooks long before the fish got anywhere near them. The mouth of the River Esk in Musselburgh was another useful place to catch flounder, although the competition there was fierce from other anglers crowded along its banks.

At Port Seton, to the east of Edinburgh, there was a coal-fired power station that pumped hot water into the Forth. The piped water outflow heated the sea water in a tiny harbour and attracted shoals of grey mullet, which fed there. The mullet could only be caught on very small hooks and were notoriously difficult to land. Even after hooking a fish you had to use a long drop net to secure the catch; there was a twenty-foot drop from the pier to the water and many of the fish that I saw caught, dropped off the line as they were being reeled in.

One young man amongst the anglers was more successful than the rest and he landed most of the fish that he had hooked, being skilled with the drop net. I watched in awe as he reeled in fish after fish in a confident and businesslike manner, while other anglers were effing and blinding as they watched their lightly hooked fish drop from their lines back into the water down below. This king of fishers was a native of Caithness in the far north, a crofter's son, with a very unsentimental attitude to putting food on the table or, in this case, in the freezer. James was a stocky chap with dark receding hair and spectacles; he was a man of few words and we were to become lifelong friends from that day onwards.

With my new connections I graduated to boat fishing on the high seas, as a member of an angling club. We were a mixed group of people both socially and age-wise, and our numbers were made up of several engineers, a shop assistant, an ex-gamekeeper, an ex-policeman, a chemist, a grocer and one unpleasant thuggish character who seemed more interested in firing cockles from his catapult at seagulls than fishing. Neither James nor I were people who enjoyed joining clubs, but it was a means to an end and we were able to benefit, sharing the expense of sea angling by hiring an inshore trawler for weekend trips.

The club's additional activities, such as fund raising to finance trips, seemed a bit cheeky to us. We didn't see why our fishing excursions should be funded by other people buying raffle tickets from club members and the monthly meetings in a local pub usually ended up as slanging matches by people who were on the committee. I tried to avoid the responsibility of being voted treasurer by claiming to have served time in prison for fraud. The ex-policeman didn't believe me, but said he would check anyway.

Our regular boat was the *Rachel Douglas* out of St Abbs on the Berwickshire coast. She had been built in the same year that I was born. Twelve anglers could fish reasonably comfortably by spacing themselves around the boat. I usually favoured the bow because it had always been a lucky place for me to catch fish and most of the anglers had a favourite place on the deck. The skipper Ian Wilson was a very likeable chap who came from a long line of fisher folk; he had baited the hooks with mussels on the long lines as a small boy on his father's vessel, a sail boat with no engine. In those days, rowing was the only way to move when there was no wind power. The shellfish bait was supplied by British Rail and came all the way from Norfolk. Ian was a well read, self-educated man with an interest in just about everything on the planet, but his favourite subject was the history of the Scottish Border country.

On some weekends we had a couple of English coal miners from Northumberland sharing our Sunday fishing trips when we were unable to get twelve men from the club to fill the boat. Their strong dialect was difficult for us to understand – for instance they referred to lugworms as 'loogs' and Tom as 'Toom'. While we used 1lb home-made lead weights to sink our hooks, they used large solid copper rivets that had been pilfered from their pit. Given the high price of scrap copper, it would have been worthwhile for a scuba diver to collect all the gear they lost on the rocky bottom where we usually fished.

Occasionally a couple of Glaswegians joined us for a day's fishing. There was a caravan park above the harbour where folk from the west came to stay during the summer holidays. Two of those holiday makers joined us early one summer's morning and were excited about the prospect of fishing in the open sea as opposed to the sheltered sea lochs they were familiar with on the west coast. Each of them had brought a carryout: six cans of Tennant's lager. As we sailed out of the harbour on the calm flood tide, one of them opened his first can and took a swig; he winked at me and said, 'This is the life, eh!' Then as we passed the breakwater into the open sea, we caught a fresh wind and a heavy swell and our friends from the west looked a little less confident. Two cans and two hours later they were heaving over the side and spent most of the remaining six hours lying on the deck, rolling with the motion of the waves under the boat. We were too far out from the coast to put them ashore and I suspected they would be fishing from the rocks for the remainder of their holiday.

The catches on these trips were sometimes very good and paid for the initial cash outlay several times over. Cod, haddock, saithe, ling and mackerel were the usual fish that came over the side, although we sometimes caught angler fish and the occasional octopus; Ian, our skipper, told us that he had once caught a large angler fish in the trawl with an undigested racing pigeon inside it. He retrieved the ring from its leg and managed to trace the owner to inform him of the bird's fate. The pigeon could have ditched into the sea from exhaustion or may have been whacked by one of the local peregrines that nested on the cliffs at St Abbs.

On the rare occasions that herring were caught, they were usually foul-hooked as a shoal passed under the boat. Those 'silver darlings' never seemed to feed on our bait by choice and were difficult to catch. One day a Sei whale surfaced close to the boat, when there was herring activity in the area. It was the sound of expelled air that first caught our attention, followed by a long, shiny black back and a big dorsal fin each time the animal breached. The whale's head and tail were never visible. Porpoises would sometimes suddenly appear beside the boat and ride the bow wave when we were heading out to the fishing grounds and those fleeting visits would be a very enjoyable experience for us anglers.

My friend James always caught fish, even when other anglers on the boat were not catching anything. He had a multitude of home-made lures of various patterns and shapes and if one wasn't catching fish, then he would try another – he was constantly experimenting; I even saw him wrapping the silver foil from his sandwiches around a bare hook and catching a sizeable cod. There was always a good-natured rivalry between the anglers on the boat and a cash prize for the heaviest fish. We all put a pound into the kitty when we got on board and the winner would take all at the end of the day.

During the winter months of January and February some of the club members fished over in the west on the Firth of Clyde, where nuclear submarines were the main threat to fishing activities as they steamed past on their way up river to their home base. The displacement wake from those gigantic craft churned up sand and mud on the river bottom and ruined the fishing for the rest of the day – and to add insult to injury, there was usually a bunch of naval officers in gold braid uniforms observing us through powerful binoculars from the sub's conning tower. We gave them the reversed victory V sign from our tiny dinghy.

Fish stocks on all parts of the Clyde were seriously depleted through over-fishing and disturbance from shipping and we were lucky to bring home two decent-sized fish each. One bonus for fishing winter cod was catching one that was heavy with roe. I found the eggs a great delicacy, although it wasn't the ideal way to propagate the declining species. Ironically we always stopped at a chippy in Helensburgh for a fish supper on the way home.

Independence on the High Seas

It wasn't long before my fishing pal James bought his own boat, in the shape of a basic fibreglass moulded hull; he fitted the decking and timber himself. The thwarts (seating planks) were made from recycled mahogany retrieved from a city skip. Edinburgh's New Town provided some fine cast-off building materials at that time because architectural salvage by builders was not commonplace in those days. Anything metallic on the boat was either solid brass or stainless steel, James's work being another useful source for 'recycled' objects for the new craft. The boat was painted blue and white and christened *Svanr*, which was the Norse word for 'swan'. It was a comfortable size for two people.

The trial run, with a big outboard motor, was a great success. The boat had a flat bottom and planed over the calm sea at a fair rate of knots. I wasn't mechanically minded and the technical specifications went right over my head, but James had an engineering background and was very knowledgeable on the subject of engines. As far as I was concerned it was a boat that would float and went fast. The convenience of owning a small boat and trailer meant that we could fish anywhere we wanted and whenever we wanted.

Dunbar harbour, with its convenient slipway, became our regular launching point on the east coast; even on the ebb tide it was possible to get the boat in and out of the harbour with a little knowhow. We had a system for handling the boat which made the job of getting it out of the water when the tide was low a lot easier for us. Some of the other boat anglers really struggled to get back up the slipway with their trailers and boats and there was sometimes a queue. James's winch and rubber wheel guides to line up the boat's keel on our trailer made hauling the *Svanr* out of the water much easier.

The magic time for catching fish was on the flood tide about two hours after sunrise and the majority of our day's catch was in the fish box by that time. Most of our best fishing marks had been discovered by trial and error and when we did find a productive hotspot, we took photographs of two points on the shore to fix the position for a return visit. Allowing for the tide and drift, we were successful in relocating those fish-rich rocky pinnacles that were given a wide berth by the local trawlers so as to avoid losing their gear.

One advantage of fishing from a small boat was our ability to recover tackle that got snagged on the sea bed. Hooks made fast could often be dislodged by manoeuvring the boat in a different direction and pulling some slack line from the reel. In the event of having to snap the line, it was safer to wrap the nylon around a wooden priest for grip – failure to do this could give a very deep cut to the hands, or even worse, an unplanned swim in the cold North Sea.

Seals and Sea Birds

When the fishing was slow and the weather was bad, there was always something of interest to observe on the sea. The big grey seals were a common sight along the Forth coastline and often swam close to the boat for a wee nosey at the competition. On two occasions I had fish plucked from my line by a seal as I was reeling up from the depths. Mostly the seals appeared to be creatures of leisure, and seemed happy to bob about the sea when they weren't hunting for fish.

My fishing companion James had a far less tolerant attitude towards those noble animals than I did and used some pretty colourful language whenever he saw them near the boat, wishing he had a rifle or a harpoon handy to greet them with. James's neighbours back home in Caithness had a pathological hatred of seals, being salmon fishermen: it was competition the fishermen could well do without. The inshore box nets that locals used to catch salmon with, were regularly holed and robbed by marauding seals. If my livelihood had been threatened in the same way, then I would probably have been less sympathetic towards those endearing creatures. During low water, large numbers of seals congregated on the rocky skerries to sleep and rest up above the water line. Their distant mournful howling carried for miles beyond the shore and sounded like a wolf pack.

Sea birds of all types were plentiful in the area and the Bass Rock gannet colony was a major world breeding site. We often followed the gannets when they were diving from a great height on to the shoals of whitebait and sand eels that were being pursued by mackerel. Bird activity in the area was always the best indicator of shoaling fish. Puffins, guillemots and razorbills also joined in the hunt, although they dived from the surface and swam as gracefully as penguins. We also got glimpses of rarer birds such as peregrines and shearwaters as they passed by, as well as the occasional visit to our boat by a sea-blown bee or butterfly. Our old skipper from St Abbs once had a migrating tawny owl land on his boat more than twenty miles out at sea. The exhausted bird took a rest for a few hours and then continued on its journey.

When we first began catching large numbers of fish, we gutted them on the boat, then filleted them when we got home. On one occasion I planted the stinky remains in the vegetable garden between the rows of tatties [potatoes] as fertilizer, until the local fox and her cubs decided to dig them up and disperse them around the neighbourhood. The stench of disinterred two-week-old fish was not popular with the neighbours. Another down side to this soil-enriching method is the potential harm that could result from the large, needle-sharp bones that would remain in the soil for several years. For gardeners who liked to feel the soil between their fingers, those bony relics could cause a serious health risk from a contaminated puncture wound. Dumping the fish heads and tails in the bucket for the council to remove wasn't an ideal solution either, because swarms of bluebottles were attracted to the buckets and a three-day wait in summer was far too long for these scraps to be lying about before removal.

Eventually we started processing all the fish on the boat at the end of the day. Using a sharp knife on a rolling boat outside the harbour was a useful skill. James was the expert and I was happy to let him prove it; when my hands got cold, I was not safe working with a filleting knife. There was a resident elderly bull seal that patrolled the area around the harbour at Dunbar looking for easy pickings. He was an enormous size with a head like a Labrador dog and was probably finding hunting swift-moving fish too much of a challenge. We dropped scraps over the side into the shallow water and could see the old fellow grabbing them from the sandy bottom. They were slim pickings but he seemed to appreciate them.

A Close Encounter

On one of our fishing trips to the south of Dunbar near Torness, we had an unexpected close encounter on a calm, sunny midsummer morning with hardly a ripple on the sea. The fishing was slow, the kind of day for lying in the boat with a rod over the side waiting for fish to find us as we motored slowly, parallel to the shore, trying to find a good fishing mark.

While I was dozing, James suddenly called out, 'Jeez! You just missed something!' I sat upright immediately to see what he was so excited about. James said something huge had just passed under the boat. I was wondering if he was winding me up because I wasn't trying very seriously to catch a fish that day. But now that I was fully awake and alert, I got ready to put some fresh bait on the hooks and leaned over the bow for a glimpse into the clear water.

I got a real fright. Only inches below the surface, riding the bow wave, was the head of a very large bottle-nosed dolphin and as I watched it, two others came up on either side, flanking it in a very precise triangular formation. I could see their blow holes and their eyes.

When I had recovered from the initial shock and the primaeval fear of large animals that were bigger than our small boat, I felt that common human urge to make physical contact with them. I rolled up my sleeves and reached down into the water to try and touch the middle one. The creature swam fractionally deeper, and maintained the same distance away from my outstretched fingertips.

What followed next could have been a choreographed circus show. We counted twenty dolphins, including a baby not much bigger than a porpoise. They leapt on either side of the boat, hurling themselves clear of the water, twisting and turning and crashing down on their backs causing great splashes. Seven of them leapt in the air, evenly spaced and perfectly synchronized. They stayed with us for about ten minutes. It was a joyous experience, causing the hairs on the back of my neck to tingle; even James, not the most emotional person I knew, was clearly touched by the experience. We both smiled, aware that the rest of the day was probably going to be an anti-climax.

Back at the harbour we spoke to a scuba diver, who had also had a close encounter with this roving band of dolphins, although on a less dramatic scale. He was manning a black inflatable dinghy while his chums were diving below on the sea bed. He was lying stretched out in the dinghy with his head propped on the side taking a snooze when he felt a gentle nudge from underneath. He assumed that it was one of the divers surfacing, but looked round to see the head of a dolphin looking into the boat.

It was gone in seconds and the divers below had not seen it, or any of the other dolphins. He was glad of our confirmation because his mates seemed sceptical about his story. The Firth of Forth wasn't a common place to see dolphins and the group that we saw may have been taking a trip down from the Moray Firth where they normally resided.

Sharing Nature's Bounty

Whenever we came home with a sizeable catch of mackerel, I hot-smoked several batches of fish in the garden using a metal box heated underneath by metholated spirits. Beech or oak dust produced the best results. The smoker had a capacity for ten medium fillets at a time and required the removal of the cooked fish every forty minutes to replace them with a fresh batch from the brine solution. The correct salting of the fillets overnight was important in getting the best flavour.

I made sure our neighbours didn't have any washing hanging outside during this process and most of them got a taste from the smokery. It was interesting how they suddenly appeared in their gardens whenever the first batch of golden brown, juicy fillets was being removed from the smoker. The flavour of those home-smoked delicacies was exquisite, very 'more-ish' and they were delicious eaten warm with buttered bread. It was good being able to share nature's bounty with our neighbours in the street and occasionally I received some fresh scones or a couple of cans of beer in return. Oily fish, smoked or otherwise, never tasted its best after more than a couple of months in the freezer.

A Hunting Trip without a Weapon

A friend and I took a trip down to Lindisfarne Island, in Northumberland, one weekend. Maldwyn had a VW camper van that was ideal for an overnight stay on the island, as amongst the clutter of his three young children's discarded clothes and toys were two single beds in the back. The vehicle was used as a den when it was parked in the garden at home, but fortunately the kids were staying at home with their mother that weekend, and not going with us.

It was only a few hours' drive down to Northumberland, where access to the island was only possible across a causeway at low tide. There were horror stories about foolhardy tourists taking a chance of getting their vehicles across at a risky stage of the tide and having to abandon them to the mercy of the sea and apparently this still happened. Holy Island is surrounded by dunes, mudflats and salt marshes. A monastery was founded there in the seventh century by St Aidan, but was destroyed by the Vikings in 793. Four hundred years later a Benedictine priory was established, but this was in turn destroyed by Henry VIII in the sixteenth century. The stones from the priory were used to build Lindisfarne Castle, which is still standing.

What was more interesting to us was the winery in the centre of the village, the home of the world famous Lindisfarne mead. There was a free sample of the fortified wine for visitors and a range of bottles that made attractive gifts for the folks back home. A generous slug of that sweetish nectar was the ideal nightcap for a good night's sleep; or so we thought. We found a quiet spot on the island to park the camper where we were unlikely to be disturbed and climbed into our bunks and dozed off, with the sound of the waves lapping at the shore.

Half an hour later we were rudely awakened by an electronic alarm signal from somewhere inside the vehicle. This irritating high-pitched 'beep, beep, beep' was emanating from behind one of the side panels inside the van and could not be reached by us. Maldwyn told me it was one of his children's Disney character watches that had been mislaid. Eventually the alarm went silent, peace was restored and we managed to get back to sleep again. One hour later the alarm sounded again and this time it didn't seem quite so funny; Mickey Mouse or Donald Duck was in for a serious stomping when we did find whose face was on the junior timepiece. Our sleep was disturbed several more times throughout the night and when the sun came up it was a relief to get outside the camper, which had turned into a sleep-deprivation torture chamber for us.

My friend said we would feel much better after a fried breakfast and a pot of fresh coffee, so while the bacon was sizzling in the pan, I went to get some fresh water from a crystal-clear burn nearby. Eventually the boiling water from the kettle was poured on to the coffee grounds, producing a delicious aroma which made our mouths water in anticipation of the full Scottish breakfast in the open air and a warm sun on our faces. We raised our coffee mugs, toasted the new day and took a sip. Simultaneously we spat it out in disgust. The foul taste of salt was a shock to the system. The gin-clear water in the burn was in fact filtered sea water seeping through the ground below; if only I had thought to taste it first. After a sleepless night we were in need of a little comfort on this holiest of islands.

Later we did find a tap on the island that was connected to a fresh spring. I wondered how many other pilgrims had been unpleasantly surprised over the centuries.

After fully exploring the small island we drove back to the mainland and set off for the border on the River Tweed where England and Scotland are divided by the river. As we walked along the bank I noticed a solitary ash tree in the middle of a ploughed field. The tree had been struck by lightning at some time in the past and was hollow inside. Curiosity got the better of me and I jumped over the fence to take a look inside the hole at the foot of the tree. I could see a hessian sack, tied at the top with a piece of baler twine. I opened the sack and discovered a large, freshly caught salmon with a gaff wound in its side. Maldwyn was looking over my shoulder. When he was a student he had worked on a salmon fishing station on the River Tay during the holidays.

'It's definitely a poacher's stash,' he told me.

'What shall we do with it?' I asked.

'Well, we could take it to a police station on the Scottish side here, or we could drive over that bridge into England and have a think about it.'

I swung the damp sack over my shoulder and we headed back to the camper van parked on the bridge, proceeding rather furtively with the occasional glance behind us. Once the booty was safely concealed in the back of the camper we drove across the bridge and away from the scene of the crime. Somehow we felt safer across the border and away from anyone who may have seen us in the Kingdom of Scotland. We thought it appropriate to stop at the first English pub we came to and have a celebratory drink, keeping a lookout in the rear-view mirror to see that we had not been followed. It was lunchtime as we drove into a sleepy little village with no sign of life, but there was a nice-looking pub on the village square with roses growing around the open door.

I was aware of the strong smell of salmon on my hands and was keen to wash them as soon as we got inside the pub. The only customers in the bar were three grumpy-looking middle-aged men in tweed suits who were probably either game-keepers or ghillies. We got a frosty reception as we walked in and a reluctant nod from the trio. Maldwyn went to the bar to get the pints in, while I nipped into the Gents to wash off the tell-tale aroma of the twice-poached fish. One of the tweed-clad drinkers came in as I was desperately scrubbing my hands under a scalding hot tap in a lather of soap.

'Are you here for the fishing?' he asked rather pointedly.

'No, we're just passing through,' I told him.

I felt sure he could smell the salmon on my jacket where I had carried the sack, and he seemed overly concerned about our presence there. When I joined my friend at the bar he was also aware of a hostile reaction from the tweedy crew and was anxious to make an exit before the local constabulary was summoned to inspect our vehicle. We downed our pints in record time, leaving the premises waving a cheery goodbye. We drove west, away from the pub and away from the direction of the hollow tree. When we got to the next bridge across the River Tweed, we were back in Scotland home and dry.

Our route back north took us through the Border country, passing several big shooting estates where unwary pheasants with little road sense had been whacked by passing cars. Dead birds, bumped but not squashed, were retrieved by us from the roadside verges and we arrived home that evening with one large salmon and nine bruised but lead-free pheasants. I never did like picking lead shot out of pheasant meat on the dinner plate. It seemed a wonderful thing, to be able to fill the freezer after a hunting trip without the aid of a weapon. I did wonder about the person who must have returned to the hollow tree to pick up his ill-gotten goods and could only imagine his disappointment. Many years later I was to become the victim of a similar heist, involving a deer; but more about that later.

Ferreting Further Afield

Dougie, one of my old fishing buddies, phoned me one evening to ask me if we still had ferrets. When I told him that we did, he asked me if my friend Jack and I would like to assist on a rabbit shoot up in Perthshire. One of Dougie's pals had permission to shoot over a large arable farm where the wheat crop was being seriously damaged by rabbits from a neighbouring property. Dougie's pal was an East German refugee called Garfreid, formerly a butcher but now a wine importer and a man with an interesting past.

We were given detailed instructions to get to the farm and found it without too much difficulty. When we arrived, Garfreid was dressed to kill and eager to start. One glance at his attire confirmed that he was a success in his new business venture as a major importer of German wines. He was wearing traditional German shooting clothes, had a German shotgun and rifle and was driving a top-of-the-range Mercedes Benz. He was a stocky chap with square peasant features and very direct manner that could have been misconstrued as rude to those unfamiliar with his country and his hand shake was between firm and painful.

The purpose of the hunt was to kill as many rabbits as we possibly could, in an effort to save the farmer from a seriously depleted harvest. The wheat field we were shown looked as though a combine harvester had already been through half the crop at ground level; it was the month of August and the wheat was still unripe. Garfreid had his twelve-year-old son Kurt with him and each of us had a twelve bore shotgun.

It was essential to use ferrets to flush out the rabbits from the big warrens amongst the gorse bushes on the neighbour's land which bordered the field. Garfreid had a very lively young Springer spaniel that could flush a few rabbits out for the guns, but the rabbits were too smart to stay on the surface after the first sound of a gunshot. The dog was allowed to range freely until all the rabbits had gone to earth, and then he was put back in the car. A dog that had not been trained to hunt with ferrets was unsafe to use while the ferrets were free-ranging.

After a brief discussion on shooting etiquette and safety, we let one of our three ferrets start working the nearest warren on the side of a hill. It wasn't long before rabbits were rocketing out of the holes in all directions. Young Kurt was a little over-eager and fired at several fleeing rabbits that were not in his domain. I was expecting his father to advise him on the safety aspects of shooting in company, but the youngster was allowed to continue for the rest of the day in the same careless mode. His quick reflex blasting at anything that popped up would have been more appropriate at the O.K. Corral. Jack and I exchanged glances several times and hoped that neither of us would end up in the game bag.

We stopped for a picnic after a few hours and counted the number of rabbits we had bagged so far; there were forty-three in total. Garfreid was a restless individual and was constantly on the lookout while eating. Suddenly he put down his sandwich and ran towards his car and took a rifle from the boot. He slid the bolt back, put a round in the chamber and then crawled over to a drystane dyke where he peeped over. He looked back to us and put a finger to his lips before pointing to something in the pasture which he had seen in the distance: a roe deer was making its way along the fence line about 300 yards away. Garfreid ducked behind the dyke and started crawling along the ground in an effort to get in position for a clear shot. Dougie, however, told us that the farmer had only given permission to shoot rabbits on the farm and nothing else, so Garfreid was poaching.

As it happened, the wily deer trotted off in the general direction of the farmhouse, thereby making any attempt to shoot at it with a rifle extremely unsafe. I could just imagine the worst case scenario: a hole in the kitchen window and the farmer's wife slumped over the baking board with a gunshot wound to the head and a pool of blood increasing in size on the table. Newspaper headlines would read 'Local woman shot dead by German sniper' and we would probably never be allowed to ferret there again. Garfreid was very disappointed at missing this illegal opportunity to get some free venison and was rather grumpy for the rest of the afternoon.

The final bag at the end of the day was eighty-six rabbits lined up in neat rows on the grass. I was surprised that Garfreid had no intention of even picking a rabbit up, let alone helping us process them for removal. We discovered that the rabbits he usually shot were left lying wherever they happened to fall and he had no interest in eating them. I suppose the foxes and buzzards would benefit from his efforts, although rats would also take advantage of the rotting carcases littering the landscape. Jack and I, however, were certainly not going to waste the meat and began gutting the rabbits immediately; we both had chest freezers at home that would accommodate most of it and we also had hungry ferrets to feed.

Later, Dougie told us a bit more about Garfreid's former life in East Germany as a young man. His family were poor country people who struggled to make a living. When Garfreid left school he had worked for a butcher, and when he had finished his apprenticeship he had become a travelling slaughterman, pedalling to remote farms on a bicycle in all weathers. In those days the pigs were killed in the farmyard and butchered on the spot. The meat was usually salted down, cured and eaten by the family over the winter. His experience of cycling through snow blizzards to get to these remote farms had given him the drive to find a better life elsewhere. We never discovered how he managed to get to Scotland, but he had certainly been successful in his business ventures here and was now enjoying a good life.

10
A Lurcher in the Family

On one of our rabbit hunting trips in the Borders we met a young tinker on a country road with two lurcher dogs trotting beside him. I was impressed by the grace and elegance of those fine-looking animals and stopped for a chat. He used the dogs to catch mountain hares on the high ground where the heather was thickest – though most of the grouse moors in those parts were well keepered and caution was necessary in carrying any game that the dogs caught. My friends, Jack and Scott, both fancied getting a fast-running hunting dog, but didn't want the responsibility of owning one and considered that, as a settled family man, I should be the one to make the commitment and get one.

Certainly my wife and children had always pleaded with me to get a dog as a pet, but I wasn't too sure. As a child I hadn't been allowed to have one and so came from a dogless household and I thought that the ownership of a dog would be too life-changing for my own regular hunting activities. However, my pals were very encouraging about the prospect of me taking on the responsibility of a useful pet and kept telling me about all the advantages, like catching stuff silently without a gun. Little things like the expense of feeding it and vets' fees were never mentioned.

My First Dog

A few days later, Scott made contact with a local chap called Dave who knew someone whose lurcher bitch had recently had a litter of pups, which were for sale. We arranged to go round to Dave's house to meet the owner of the pups and have a look at them. When we got there, we were directed to a cardboard box at the back door with three pups inside. They were undeniably cute, with blunt faces, big blue eyes and brindle coats: it was a sight that made grown men go weak at the knees and start baby-talking. Robin, the owner, seemed an amiable sort of person, though he had the reputation of being a somewhat disreputable character, according to those who knew him.

I lifted one of the brindled pups from the box and cradled it; it was soft and warm, with a big belly from a recent feed. The striped markings on its coat gave it the appearance of a tiger cub. Jack and Scott were smiling encouragement and nodding at me and I was experiencing powerful silent pressure to adopt on the spot. I was thinking of all the excuses possible not to get this dog, but the best I could come up with was that I didn't have the money with me. Robin had asked for £35, which seemed a princely sum at that time. As usual Jack was prepared for any eventuality and reached into his pocket to give me an instant, credit-free, short-term loan. I was scuppered, cash changed hands and I was the owner of my first dog. All I had to worry about now was what my wife would say when I got home with the new member of the family.

I needn't have worried; from the moment I walked in through the door with the mystery box in my arms and a sheepish expression on my face, the game was up. My young daughter looked in the box, scooped out the warm, furry, sleepy puppy and hugged it as tight as she dared. As usual my son had to wait for his little sister to hand over the pup for his fleeting bonding opportunity. As far as the family was concerned it was money well spent.

There was never any question of what the dog was going to be called: he was named Bob after my own childhood hero, Black Bob the *Dandy* Wonder Dog, from the comic. As a kid I loved to read about the adventures of this highly intelligent black and white Border collie and his mythical shepherd owner, Andrew Glen from Selkirk in the Scottish Borders. Ironically, one of the stories I remembered was Black Bob and his master helping the gamekeeper to catch a gang of salmon poachers on the local river on a moonless night – but I had no intention of training my own dog to do anything similar.

I was under the mistaken impression that the new dog was going to be kept in a kennel in the back garden and that he was going to be a working dog, not a child substitute, but I was swiftly overruled on that thought by the rest of the family – and of course any other plans that I might have had as a first-time dog owner were soon to be changed. On the very first night, Bob was left in the kitchen in a big cardboard egg box with a cosy blanket over him, but I was awakened in the early hours by his mournful whimpering. He was lonely, sleeping away from his mother and siblings for the first time. I sneaked down the stairs into the kitchen and put the light on, and his big blue eyes pleaded with me to pick him up.

I sat and cradled him for a few minutes and then put him down on the linoleum floor where he did the biggest pee imaginable and flooded the floor. I knew it was unlikely that either of us were going to get much sleep that first night, so I carried him upstairs in the cardboard box and put it on the floor by the side of my bed. He then tried to scrabble up on to the bed, but I drew the line on that one. Eventually he quietened down as I stroked his back and he soon fell asleep.

The kids were up early and charged into the room to play with him. It seemed strange to be using his name all the time; 'Bob' sounded so masculine and grown up for such a little chap. But it was great fun having a pup around the house, except for the little wet puddles he left for the unwary barefooted in the kitchen and there seemed to be a constant smell of disinfectant about the place. Nevertheless he was partially house trained within a few days and had learned to whimper by the garden door when he needed to go out.

We took precautions in the garden to stop him slipping through the fence into the neighbour's property, where there were two large cats that were bigger than he was. Once the gaps were blocked along the fence the pup was free to roam around his new territory and explore his leafy domain. Any plans I had of maintaining a neat flower garden were put on hold after he made some doggy improvements to the herbaceous borders in the form of dens of flattened leaves. But I was surprised at how quickly he learned to obey basic commands such as 'sit', 'stay' and 'lie down' and he soon learned that he was never allowed to climb on the furniture or beg at the table when we were eating.

Early Training

It was fun taking Bob to the park, meeting other dog owners and making new friends. Being a part of the canine fraternity increased our social life and made life a lot more interesting. Bob quickly got bigger and faster and had the look of a whippet except for his head, which had a broader skull like a collie and the potential for a bigger brain inside it, like his namesake in the *Dandy* comic. I had decided his training was to be firm and fair, just like bringing up children. Consistency seemed to be the key element in bringing up a well-balanced, obedient dog, according to most experts in the field and as far as I was concerned, this early training was going to be very important and mainly my responsibility.

I made a very painful mistake after reading a useful tip in a doggy book from the local library. The author of this training manual suggested a method that would encourage the dog to react immediately to a voice command outdoors. The idea was to take the dog into an open area and have him on a long lead. The next step was to throw an object like a stick or a ball and send the dog after it and then call the dog's name. The trainer was supposed to keep a firm grip on his end of the lead and pull the dog up after calling his name.

The theory of this exercise seemed plausible and straightforward; the problem for me was that I didn't have a suitable long lead and had to make do with about thirty yards of parcel string tied to the dog's broad collar. At the time it had seemed like a good idea to put a slip knot at my end around my finger and a couple of loops around the hand for grip. Of course the young dog was as keen as mustard to play any game that involved retrieving a moving object, so I threw the ball and away he went like a greyhound from a trap. But he was at the end of his tether before I was able to call his name and I fell forwards face down, with the slip knot pulled tightly around my index finger, which rapidly swelled up and started turning blue.

I began to panic when my efforts to loose the knot failed and the swelling and pain increased. There was no one else in the field, so no chance of assistance from any passer-by. Eventually I managed to get my key ring out of my pocket and used the smallest key to loosen the noose; my finger was throbbing for about half an hour afterwards and there was a white line where the string had been. I wasn't quite ready to quit, however and thought I might as well try something else.

I found a short, stout stick with suitable dimensions to anchor the looped string at the middle. The pup seemed to be having a great time anticipating another game. I set the stick on the ground with my foot on the string and threw the ball for the dog. Once again Bob went like the clappers in racing mode, reaching the end of the string in seconds. The force of the stick suddenly flying forwards took my feet from under me and I landed flat on my back with the wind knocked right out of me. To add insult to injury I noticed a chap watching from the hill above with a pair of binoculars. Then and there I decided on more conventional methods for any future training.

Our weekends and evenings began to centre on the dog and walks along the seashore and through the woods seemed much more interesting when small mammals and birds were flushed from their hiding places by a hound with a keen sense of smell. The large number of grey squirrels in the woods provided some exciting sprints for the pup, who raced after them and watched them disappear into the tall trees where they chattered their defiance from the safety of an overhead branch.

Bob turned out to be an affectionate and biddable hound with a real sense of fun. His acceleration and running speed on open ground was very impressive and few other local dogs were able to keep up with him. When he was only about six months old he injured a toe and had his first visit to the vets for treatment. It was a spiral fracture, not uncommon in racing dogs that turned quickly at speed. The size of the vet's bill came as a bit of a shock and we quickly took out an insurance policy against any future injuries. Bob made a rapid recovery and was soon racing around the park again doing his victory laps.

We succeeded in training the pup to ignore domestic livestock. In the countryside, sheep were the biggest worry, because they often stampeded at the slightest disturbance and there were always flocks grazing in the surrounding hills. Eventually we were able to walk with the dog off the lead in the knowledge that he was trustworthy and reliable and would not chase anything he wasn't supposed to. Chasing hares and rabbits was another matter; we had every intention of encouraging the hound to catch meat for the pot. Young dogs tended to be very enthusiastic in the pursuit of ground game but lacking in experience and were often outfoxed by their prey who led them on a merry chase, twisting and turning at every opportunity. A hare on its own territory knew every nook and cranny and chose its escape route wisely.

An Early Demise

Eventually Bob caught his very first rabbit after an impressive chase one summer's evening, through a large warren on a steep heathery hillside. My friend Jack the Ferret was a witness and we both made a real fuss of the dog when we caught up with him and celebrated the success with a pint when we got home. Teaching the dog to retrieve would be the next step in his education. However, that rabbit was to be Bob's first and his last, because within a couple of weeks the poor dog was dead. He was only ten months old.

I still find the thought extremely sad, nearly thirty years after the event; I cried bitter tears when we lost him. He was one of the family and my first dog. We discovered later that the other pups from his litter had also died prematurely after suffering from fits and collapsing. The only pup to survive was one that had been taken away from its mother early and hand reared. Whatever the pups had died of, seems to have been a mystery, although Robin, the bitch's owner, had a reputation for neglecting his dogs. We never really knew for sure, but my family was devastated by the death of the pup.

Fox

We decided that we would get another dog as soon as possible; the house was so empty without one and we were missing Bob's company. Eventually we saw an advert in the pet section of a national newspaper advertising lurcher pups for sale. The seller lived near Lockerbie, a town that was later to become one of the most infamous places in the world after the terrorist bombing of Pan Am flight 103.

It was a long drive from Edinburgh to see the pup, but well worth the effort. The breeder lived in a cottage with plenty of space for the pups to run wild and exercise and he was a real countryman with a wide experience of lurcher dogs. There were three pups, but only two for us to choose from; the other had already been claimed. The two pups that were available were very similar in appearance, both black with a white blaze on the chest; we chose the one that didn't have a white tip on the tail – at the time it struck me that ours would be slightly better camouflaged for hunting without the white warning flag. The pups were three-quarter greyhound and one quarter Border collie: the father was a very large, brindle racing greyhound from Ireland and the mother was a black and white first cross collie/greyhound. Once again the price for the pup was £35.

It was an exciting drive home with the new pup on board and we had a lengthy debate about what he was going to be called. The problem was solved as we neared home and were passing our local park by moonlight when a fox ran across the road in front of the car and into a garden opposite. It seemed like an omen and the new pup was duly christened Fox following a unanimous decision. Bringing a second puppy up was much easier than the first one because we had learned from some of our mistakes; we also had the lead, collar, bowls and quite a lot of food left over. Fox was a smart dog who learned quickly and was very biddable. I suspected that his Border collie genes made him a willing and easy dog to train. Many lurcher dogs had the black and white collie markings and thick coats of their cross-bred parents, even though they were mostly greyhound in shape.

We registered the pup with the local vet and took out an insurance policy to cover any canine health issues that we might have in the future. The vet was enthusiastic about the pup's conformation and general condition and we were advised that he was probably going to a big dog like his father.

Fox showed a keen interest in hunting from a very early age, by chasing flies and bees in the garden. He also liked to sneak up on butterflies when they settled on the flowers, attempting to pounce on them like a cat. We made a point of introducing him to the postman at the first opportunity so he established an early bond with the Royal Mail representative. As he grew in size, the pup's smooth black coat grew longer and rougher, giving him the look of a bearded deerhound. It was obvious from his play fights with us that he was going to be a powerful dog. Fortunately he was also very gentle and good with children, which was just as well because there were several small children living on our street.

It was interesting comparing the personalities of our two dogs; they were very different. Fox had a certain reserve and didn't seem to enjoy being petted by strangers; there was an aloof quality about him as he matured into an adult. He often took avoiding action when an unfamiliar person approached him and I felt happy about this because it would have made him more difficult to steal; we had been advised by other lurcher owners that dog theft was not unusual.

When we got Fox as a pup we had one surviving female ferret, an active hunter that was still catching rabbits. Her name was Bramble 2 and she lived in a large cage at the bottom of the garden, although she was regularly brought into the house to play with the children and exercise. On washing days she liked to run about the basement floor and hide under the clothing that was about to go into the washer. It was good to see the ferret in play mode, full of the joys of life, weaving in and out of the socks, shirts and sheets.

Initially the pup was very wary of her and dodged about the kitchen to avoid being nipped on the heels. Bramble was fearless in her pursuit of the dancing dog and not intimidated by his large size; one bite from Fox would have secured a permanent resting place for her in the back garden. The relationship soon settled down and both animals seemed content to be around each other, although the ferret appeared to be the dominant partner. Later they made an excellent hunting team at the big warrens and enabled us to catch rabbits without using nets.

Fox's first 'kill' was a white hare, which he caught after a speedy chase in the Pentland hills while there was still snow on the ground. Young dogs often caught and held their prey without biting and it was up to the owner to dispatch the animal humanely. With experience the dog learned to bite a rabbit or hare just behind the shoulder, across the rib cage, making a clean kill.

Most books on hunting with hounds and lurchers warned about the dangers of overtaxing a keen young dog before it was fully developed and had enough muscle power and stamina for what might be a long chase. A young dog could suffer permanent damage to heart, lungs and limbs if it was allowed to chase a greatly superior quarry. Eighteen months was the age that a male lurcher was considered adult and fit for the chase. It was also considered an advantage to hunt with an older dog that had experience and could show a pup how things were done in the field.

Hunting in the Borders

I contacted my new friend Dave in the Borders who had regularly hunted with lurcher dogs; his father and grandfather had hunted those same hills before him and he had a very detailed knowledge of every hill and gully. At first Dave was a little wary about involving an outsider on one of his hunting expeditions until he felt able to trust me; Border men can be reserved until you get to know them. But I must have seemed kosher to Dave because I was invited on a hunt with a pre-dawn rendezvous the following weekend. Dave had a very fast sleek black lurcher bitch called Spey and two beardie crosses called Meg and Ben. From Dave's cottage, we were on the hill after only a ten-minute walk and kept the dogs on their leads. Unfortunately Spey had a bad cut on her paw and had to be left at home.

There were a few blackface sheep about on the hill, but the dogs showed no interest in them. These hounds were working animals and ignored any domestic stock as a matter of course. My own dog was excited to be on new territory and one of the small pack; he was the tallest dog in the group. It was a cold November day with a strong wind that kept the rain off. A white hare got up well ahead and gave the dogs the slip as it circled back over the next hill without being spotted by its pursuers. We hiked along a boundary fence on the top of a very exposed ridge, and then down through rough broken ground, all gullies and rank heather.

A large, pure white hare sprang from the heather and was chased by Fox, closely followed by the two collies. My dog made a quick kill and immediately chased another hare that popped up nearby and started running for the summit. Fox killed the second hare within thirty seconds of the first. I was amazed to see my young dog in serious hunting mode, running across rough ground at high speed. We did a wide sweep of the next hill, putting up another hare that the dogs didn't see; it went splashing through a bog and disappeared amongst the rough heather uphill. We stopped for a rest and Dave produced two bottles of beer from his rucksack, which we swigged as we admired the distant views of the Eildon Hills to the south-east. The westerly wind was blowing hard and there were patches of blue sky above.

We heard a distant squeal far behind us and turned to see Fox with a third hare which he had flushed and caught while we were not paying attention. I had never succeeded in getting Fox to retrieve, so it was a long slog downhill to pick up the hare and bring it back. There was a brief scuffle when Ben went over to check out the hare that Fox had just killed. Fox was uncharacteristically aggressive in defence of his kill and I was surprised to see him baring his teeth like a snarling wolf.

On the way back to Walkerburn we saw another hare running down a steep scree slope near a shepherd's cottage. Fox was after it in a flash and had a hard chase for more than a hundred yards before he caught up with it and made a clean kill. When we finally started home along a narrow farm track we put the dogs on the lead – just in time, before a Land Rover came into view. Fortunately the driver was friendly and gave us a wave; besides, Dave's collies looked more like sheepdogs than poacher's dogs.

On the lower fields we saw plenty of rabbits stampeding towards the forestry at our approach; Fox managed to overtake one before it reached the plantation and caught it just short of the boundary fence. As we approached the last field before the road, in the failing light, we saw a large brown hare sitting bolt upright in the middle of the pasture. Fox also saw it and gave chase with the hare about fifty yards ahead of him. The hare first went downhill and then doubled back, with the dog only a few feet behind; they passed between Dave and myself within inches and headed towards a five-bar gate – the hare went under and the dog jumped over. I could see that Fox was keen but exhausted and I called him back and put him on the lead. He had done quite enough for one day and deserved a well-earned rest.

We stopped at the local pub for a pint and watched the three dogs sprawl at our feet and fall fast asleep. It had been a great day and I was rightly pleased with my black Fox.

The Subject of Trespass

About a month later, I invited Dave to hunt on my hills to the south of Edinburgh; I was keen to show him the land that I was familiar with. I arranged to meet him early in the morning near the local golf course, which was a good place to leave our vehicles. When Dave turned up late, in an old van with his brother-in-law and another friend, I was concerned. He also had his dog Spey and three pups; I was with my wife and our one dog. The expression 'mob-handed' came to mind. We had to walk past the local gamekeeper's cottage to get on to the hill, which wasn't a good start to the day.

We put the dogs on the lead and walked along the track past a stand of trees and across a burn, glancing back for any sign of movement near the cottage. When we felt we were far enough away from the keeper's abode, we let the dogs off to have a sniff about in the heather on the hillside; there were no sheep on the high ground. A white hare started running up the nearest hill, while the dogs were still hunting for scent down below. A shout from us directed their attention towards the fleeing prey and Fox, Spey and a pup called Mitzie set off in hot pursuit. Fox caught the hare and Spey picked it up and carried it back down and gave it to Dave. We continued walking away from the general direction of the cottage, which was now a couple of miles away and out of sight.

As we took a rest, we noticed a Land Rover in the distance heading our way at a steady pace. We put all the dogs on their leads and headed towards the boggiest ground we could find, which was alongside the public right of way and not the ideal place for a motor vehicle, even a Landrover. The vehicle had to stop on the high ground at a place called Muckle Knock and a solitary figure got out and headed in our direction walking at a brisk pace. There was no doubt we were heading for an altercation with this chap, whoever he was. We split up, with Dave and my wife walking downhill to hide the white hare we had just caught, under a peaty bank and out of sight. We wandered away from the man who was now pursuing us with the utmost urgency and gaining on us.

'Halt!' he bawled after us. We ignored him and continued walking in the same direction. He was forced to follow us into the bog and eventually caught up with us in a very angry mood with a red face. He was dressed in a smart green tweed suit with plus fours and a pair of expensive brogues on his feet; we were all wearing wellies. He was a man of middle age with a cut-glass accent and gold-rimmed half-moon spectacles perched on the tip of his nose.

'Why didn't you stop when I told you to?' he shouted in our faces. I was tempted to tell him to piss off, but asked him who he was. There was something ex-army in his attitude, a man who was used to being obeyed without question. I had stopped being intimidated by people like that the day I left school. We soon discovered that this chap was the owner of the extensive grouse moor on which we were now standing; he gave us his name, but we declined the offer to give our names in return. We were legally entitled to be on this land, on what was an ancient right of way; of course the dogs had to be under control and they were, as far as we were concerned – besides which there were no sheep on the hill.

A big debate followed on the subject of trespass and when it became apparent to the landowner that he was not going to get his own way by removing us from the moor, he threatened us with the police. I tackled him about the short-eared owl that we had found shot on his land and he told us that he had given instructions to his gamekeeper not to shoot birds of prey. When I asked him whether he was happy about having the pair of peregrines on his moor, he told me they had ways of moving them on, but wouldn't elaborate. He then stormed off in the direction of his Land Rover.

After this unpleasant altercation we were in no mood for spending the whole day on the hill. We were also concerned about what might happen to our vehicles if the gamekeeper became involved and took the law into his own hands, as he appeared to have done with the local raptors. We knew that it would be too risky to pick up the dead hare and get caught red-handed, so we left it where it was. For me it was a bad deed to kill a creature and waste that life. The irony was, that grouse shooters often shot white hares for sport and left them lying where they fell; they were not considered good eating by many people. I liked to mince the meat and mix it with onions, garlic and ginger for hareburgers, which my family were fond of.

When we got back to our vehicles there was a police car parked beside them awaiting our return. As we approached the police car a young constable got out in a very slow and deliberate manner, putting his hat on and walked towards us with a serious expression on his face.

'Good morning, I've had a complaint from the local landowner, he told me that you had threatened him,' he said. 'Have you anything to say?' We were speechless for a few seconds and thought it was a joke. Fortunately the policeman asked us for our version of events and was soon convinced that we were not a gang of thugs who had done what we had been accused of. Obviously there had been something in the landowner's statement that had not been entirely convincing to the policeman and he gave us the benefit of the doubt. Our only secret was the hidden hare, which would probably provide an easy meal for a passing fox.

The policeman was a keen ornithologist and well aware of the unlawful practices that gamekeepers used for controlling raptor numbers, namely by shooting and poisoning. It seemed that landowners were not slow in coming forward to quote the law at others, while they chose to ignore the law when it didn't suit them. I had often found pole traps set to kill birds of prey on keepered estates.

For every season of the year, a landowner could find some excuse for preventing public access and on this moor it was either tupping, lambing or grouse shooting. The grouse shooting season was relatively short and I had no problem with that activity, but the claims by keepers that hill walkers frightened the birds away from their natural haunts were nonsense. I had observed grouse behaviour for many years and knew this claim to be a lie.

We parted company with the policeman on good terms; he said he would have a word with Mr 'M', the landowner, later. On the way back home we stopped for a drink at the local pub and thawed out beside a roaring log fire; the day hadn't been a total disaster.

Lurcher Tales

I made many new acquaintances when I was out walking the dog. Lurcher owners came from a wide range of social groups and were often keen to stop and ask about the breeding of Fox; he could almost have passed for a deerhound, except that his coat was soft to touch. The occasional person could be self-opinionated and 'expert' in identifying a dog whose bloodline they had no background knowledge of at all. I had seen both of Fox's parents and had photographs of them. Very often lurcher pups in the same litter bore no resemblance to each other and it was virtually impossible to identify with any certainty the ancestors of a dog by sight alone. On several occasions I just agreed with an individual who told me, with absolute conviction, what my dog's parentage was; it just wasn't worth the bother of arguing with someone who thought they knew better.

A Horrific Experience

I met a man in Edinburgh who told me a sad story about his own lurcher. The man was employed in the oil industry and worked offshore from Aberdeen, three weeks on and three weeks off; he was on an oil drilling platform in the North Sea. Because he was away from home and family for regular intervals, his dog was sometimes taken out for long walks by his neighbour's sons, who were aged twelve and thirteen.

One day the boys had taken a packed lunch and headed for the Pentland Hills for a hike. It was the month of August and the grouse shooting season. The boys had walked round the side of a steep hill and a mountain hare had sprung from the heather, running away with the dog following close behind. Further round the hill was a line of guns waiting for the beaters to drive the grouse over the butts where the shooters were concealed.

As the hare and the dog passed the butts, the gamekeeper gave the order to shoot the dog. The boys told the dog's owner that all the men with guns had fired at the dog as it ran in front of them and that it had died in agony, full of bird shot. The boys were understandably hysterical and were told to clear off before the keeper called the police. The poor dog was left where he fell and the boys wandered home with heavy hearts, scared stiff about breaking the bad news to the dog owner's wife.

When her husband came home from Aberdeen, he went to the keeper's cottage to have words with him. He was seething with anger and worried about what he was going to do when he got there. The gamekeeper denied all knowledge of the incident; the dog's body had been disposed of, leaving no proof, and going to the police would have been a waste of time.

Life-Threatening Behaviour

There was a similar but more serious incident related to me by a young man I met in Edinburgh. He had been visiting a friend in Perthshire with his lurcher dog, which was more of a pet than a hunter. He and his chum had been walking along a quiet country lane with hawthorn hedges on both sides of the road and had spotted a big brown hare sitting in the middle of a field about fifty yards back from the road. There were no sheep or cattle in the field and very little traffic on the road. The dog had also seen the hare so they slipped his lead and let him through a gap in the hedge.

When the hare saw the dog, away it went at full speed up the hill. The chase only lasted a few minutes and the hare escaped through a small gap in the fence at the top of the field where the dog was unable to follow. The owner whistled the dog and he came back down to the road through the same hole in the fence and was put on the lead again. The friends walked along the road for a short distance and then heard a shout from the field. When they looked round, they saw a man approaching them on the opposite side of the hedge. He was wearing tweeds and carrying a rifle. He shouted for them to stop.

They rightly assumed that he was a gamekeeper and thought best to keep on walking because they were on the public highway and had no intention of being apprehended by the landowner for the dog's brief incursion into the field. The keeper ran ahead to where there was a gap in the hedge and the lurcher owner pulled his dog close beside him as they got nearer. As they got level with the keeper, he shot the dog from a distance of only fifteen feet; it died instantly. Its owner couldn't believe what had just happened. The keeper stormed off, back up the hill and left the two shocked friends standing beside the dog lying in a pool of blood, his limbs still twitching.

The dog owner stayed with his dead pet while his friend ran back along the road to where he had left his car. The friends put the dead dog in the boot of the car and drove immediately to the nearest police station in the town of Perth. They spoke to the desk sergeant and described what had just happened. To their utter amazement the policeman told them that what had happened had been their own fault, ignoring the fact that a firearm had been discharged recklessly on the public highway.

'You lads shouldn't have been poaching,' was all he said. Of course they were furious at the callous response by the policeman in favour of the gamekeeper. It seemed to them that the landowner lived by his own laws and had the freedom to do whatever he wanted. Apparently feudalism was still being practised in rural Perthshire.

However, the friends had no intention of letting the matter drop and drove directly to the Lothian and Borders Police Headquarters in Edinburgh. The police in Edinburgh took a very different view of the incident and treated the complaint seriously: they had the evidence, two witnesses and proof of what had happened. Eventually the keeper was charged for his reckless, life-threatening behaviour, receiving a severe rebuke from the Sheriff and a fine of £500, which at the time was a substantial sum of money. He also had his firearms certificate revoked, which would not have helped his future job prospects; furthermore he was lucky not to have received a custodial sentence.

An Uncanny Resemblance

Not all lurcher owners that I met had horror stories to tell; some experiences that I heard about were quite funny. One summer evening I was walking through the city with my dog Fox and saw a man coming towards me with an identical-looking dog trotting alongside him. As we approached each other we both said 'Snap!' and laughed. The resemblance between our two animals was uncanny.

The chap introduced himself: he was also called Bob and like me, had his roots in Ireland on his father's side. He came from a travelling family with a famous relative who had been a champion boxer in the post-war years. Bob was about sixty years of age with blue eyes and shoulder-length blonde hair; he also had a full beard and there was the look of a Viking about him. He had been born in a 'varda' – a traditional horse-drawn gypsy caravan with a barrel-shaped roof.

We became friends after this first meeting and I was invited down to his tiny cottage in the Scottish Borders for a splendid meal.

Bob had two convictions for poaching. Early one morning he had gone out with a crossbow and killed a couple of pheasants for the pot. What he hadn't realized was that he had been spotted by a passing policeman, who had seen him go into the field and had waited for him to come back carrying his illegally obtained game. Bob had backed out of the field through a thorn hedge to avoid getting his face scratched and was carrying a bird in each hand. His crossbow had been dismantled and was inside his jacket.

As he turned to face the road, there was the policeman standing directly in front of him with a smile on his face and his hands in his pockets. Bob lifted up one of birds and suggested they had a pheasant each. 'I don't think so' said the copper; 'You're nicked!' Bob was summoned to appear in court and received a relatively small fine, but his weapon was confiscated.

His second conviction was rather more serious and involved a curious assault. He had gaffed a salmon on the River Tweed during the hours of darkness and was on his way home along the river bank. His gaff had been hidden amongst the tree roots and he was carrying the fish by the tail so he could dump it in a hurry if necessary. Unfortunately a water bailiff had lain in wait for him and had ambushed him from a concealed position behind a large beech tree next to the path. In an effort to escape, Bob had struck the bailiff with the fish. At the Sheriff Court he was charged with poaching the fish and using it as a weapon against the bailiff. Apparently some members of the court did see the humour in the incident.

Like several other members of his extended family, Bob had joined the Merchant Navy in his late teens to 'see the world'. He had been employed as a ship's cook and enjoyed his sea voyages to foreign lands. He got left behind in Australia on one occasion when he missed his boat by two days after a trip into the interior.

On one of his trips to America he landed at the port of Mobile in Alabama with a couple of days off duty to explore inland, while the ship was being unloaded. Racial segregation was strictly enforced at the time and the civil rights movement was still in its infancy. Bob had been travelling on a crowded bus one day and had given up his seat to a heavily pregnant black woman who was carrying bags of shopping. When he got off the bus several stops later, he was followed from the bus by two white men, who set about him and gave him a severe beating on the pavement in full public view; they then got back on the bus. The bus driver sat and watched and did nothing. Bob had reported the assault to a traffic cop and was told that he was wasting his time, as he had provoked the incident himself by his actions.

Bob showed me some old faded dog-eared black and white photographs of his family that he kept in a cardboard box on the mantelpiece. One of the photos was of the family varda, parked on a grass verge at the side of a country road with a horse tethered nearby and a handsome young woman holding an infant in her arms. The baby was Bob with his mother. Another photograph showed a very good-looking young man in his teens with a wide smile and perfect teeth. I discovered that this was Bob's younger brother James, who had been murdered at the age of twenty-one.

James had been involved in a 'square go' with another traveller of a similar age; there had been a dispute between the two young men and a fist fight was the usual way of settling an argument. But James's opponent was getting the worst of the scrap and produced a knife, stabbing James in the chest; he died almost immediately from his wounds. I asked Bob if the killer was charged with murder or manslaughter. His reply was chilling: 'We took care of it and the police were not involved. It was an eye for an eye and a tooth for a tooth.'

I visited Bob several times and we let our dogs run together in the fields around his cottage. There were a few rabbits about but we didn't catch many, unless they were myxie ones that weren't quick enough to get to the boundary. When I first met Bob he had five mallard ducks, which provided him with fresh eggs, but they started to disappear one by one from his back yard. On one of my return visits he had only two ducks left and one of those was lame. He told me what had happened.

One night he had heard a commotion in the back yard and opened the door to see a fox in the garden with one of the ducks still flapping in its jaws. It made a hasty retreat, followed by Bob's lurcher Juckel hot on its heels. They jumped the garden fence and the dog caught the duck thief before it crossed the road. The fox was killed by the dog in a matter of seconds and the lucky duck was rescued with only a broken leg, which Bob later mended with a splint and bandage.

Bob never liked guns and said that he didn't need one; his dogs provided him with fresh meat for the pot. The local farmer was pleased when he learned about the demise of the fox. Bob was philosophic about the incident, and justice had been done. Normally he wouldn't harm an animal that he couldn't eat, but fox was definitely off the menu.

Bob liked a drink now and again and it was a long way to the nearest pub, with a poor bus service operating only every two hours. Late one frosty winter's night he missed the last bus and had to walk home from the pub with his dog, along the narrow country road. He had had a few too many beers and must have staggered much of the way, before he fell down and lay beside a five-bar gate on a bend in the road. A passing motorist spotted his legs sticking out from the gate, toes pointing towards the starry sky and pulled over to investigate, thinking that the body lying there must have been the victim of a hit-and-run driver. Juckel was standing guard over his master's body and snarled at the Good Samaritan as she approached. The woman thought better of trying to get too close and phoned for police assistance. When the police arrived at the scene, Bob woke up and got to his feet.

There was relief all round and Bob got a lift home in the back of the police car with the faithful hound beside him. The bemused policeman was impressed by the dog's behaviour and considered him an excellent bodyguard.

One day Bob disappeared and I never saw him again. When I stopped by the cottage a couple of years later, there were new tenants and no sign of ducks in the yard.

One of the Family

Fox was becoming a great asset to the family by keeping us well supplied with fresh meat, although sometimes his table manners needed to be reinforced. One day I was home from work for lunch and my wife had made a salad with half a pork pie each, set on our plates on the kitchen table. We went through to the living room for a few minutes to look at something in the garden and when we came back, the dog was wandering guiltily about the kitchen staring at the ceiling and avoiding eye contact. We guessed he had been up to mischief and checked the plates on the table, to find that mine was now a vegetarian platter: the pie had disappeared. The dog vanished quickly into the other room when I glanced in his direction.

We divided the remaining half pie into half again and tried to see the funny side of the incident. Some lurcher men believed that thieving was a sign of intelligence in a dog and Fox had another little quirk that seemed to indicate that he was a crafty hound. We never allowed our dogs to lie on the sofa or the beds and were very strict about this rule, right from the time they were small pups – but Fox had discovered a clever way of making himself more comfortable when we settled down for the evening to watch television. He would stand in front of the sofa and reverse very slowly until his backside was lodged on the edge of seat, but his four feet were still on the floor. He always did this in a slow, deliberate fashion, and seemed to think that nobody had noticed his crafty trick. Of course we never prevented him doing this; after all, he was one of the family.

One weekend we took him to a country park and as we walked through an old pine plantation, a roe deer crossed the path in front of us and went bounding into the trees. The woodland was littered with fallen timber and looked more like an obstacle course. The dog gave chase and disappeared into the trees – but within minutes we heard an excruciating yelp of pain echoing through the woods. We ran like hell to see what had happen to him, but it was five minutes before we spotted him limping towards us with blood pouring from a gaping wound on the inside of his thigh. The dog was clearly in distress and could hardly walk.

We got him back to the car with some difficulty and drove directly to our vet in Edinburgh, hoping that he wasn't going to bleed to death before we got there. The vet confirmed that his condition was potentially life-threatening, as the wooden 'spear' wound had just missed the main artery. The dog had impaled himself on the jagged tip of a side branch on a fallen tree that had been blocking his path, having failed to jump over it cleanly. Fox remained at the vets for several days and made a good recovery, having had the large piece of wood several inches long removed from deep inside his muscle. His youth and fitness had been a major factor in his speedy convalescence.

Several weeks later he was back to normal – or so we thought. He was catching hares and rabbits again and running well. But after one day's hunting on the hill I noticed that Fox was licking at the scar tissue where the stitches had been and the old wound was beginning to weep again. We took him back to the vet where he was X-rayed and the vet decided to keep him overnight under observation – which was just as well, because a piece of wood an inch long was discovered still lodged inside his thigh muscle. This remaining fragment hadn't been detected during the first operation. After further treatment and a course of antibiotics, the dog was back to normal – and happily the insurance company paid out for the hefty vet's bill.

I was amazed at the dog's ability to recover physically and mentally and at his determination to continue jumping fences and gates when he was hunting. I once saw him clear a deer fence that was seven feet high, his hind feet brushing the top strand as he sailed over with the grace of an antelope.

11
Hunting with a Lurcher

Deer in the Forestry

I arranged to meet my friend Dave in the Borders for a day out with the dogs in the month of December. We had to change our original planned walk because there was a pheasant shoot taking place on the nearby estate – although it was sometimes an advantage knowing where the keeper was on such a day, because then it was possible to avoid him. We had three dogs with us, Fox, Spey and Ben. As we crossed the river on a narrow footbridge, Dave pointed down below to two plastic bottles bobbing about in a deep pool beside the bank. The makeshift buoys were supporting a mono-film gill net to snare any unsuspecting salmon that might be headed upstream. Dave was not impressed with the set-up and made a scathing remark about the stupidity of the net setter: 'That guy deserves to get caught,' he said.

We managed to get into the forestry without being seen and followed the track that gave us fleeting glimpses of the distant shooters in the fields below. Spey leapt the dyke pursuing something in the field that we hadn't seen and it was a worrying moment; but fortunately she came back when Dave whistled her, without being spotted by the shooters. Deeper into the woods, Spey went in pursuit of a rabbit and disappeared for about ten minutes; she hadn't been hunting for quite a while and was raring to go. As we came to the edge of the wood we watched a well dressed couple with a black Labrador climb into a Land Rover parked in the field below. We were anxious not to be seen, so we hid amongst the trees for a while after they drove off in the direction of the shooting party.

It was a long uphill slog through the forest to the far boundary where a dyke separated the trees from the open hillside. Fox picked up a strong scent on the ground and ran forwards like a bloodhound into the trees. Something was moving deeper into the wood but we were unable to see what it was. Fox returned from the thick undergrowth, seeming to have lost interest in the chase; but two hundred yards on, he picked up the scent again, this time on the opposite side of the path.

He was following something in a wide circle, coming out of the woods and crossing the path a second time. Dave slipped Spey and she raced downhill along the track and into the trees; seconds later we saw a roe deer coming towards us at the gallop with Fox about thirty yards behind and closing the gap. The deer stumbled momentarily and went down for a second before regaining its balance and running headlong into the trees where it disappeared with both dogs, now close behind.

After about five minutes Fox came back panting heavily and lay down on the mossy banking with his tongue hanging out. Several minutes later we heard a sharp bark from down below and Fox and Ben ran along the ride towards the boundary to investigate. When we reached the dyke we saw Spey sitting on the ground breathing heavily, with a roe buck lying beside her. The deer was in shock and died soon afterwards. The two younger dogs were showing a keen interest, excited by the kill, but Spey guarded her prize from the other dogs by showing her teeth. She was most definitely the dominant member of the pack.

We carried the deer carcass downhill to a swift-running burn, where we skinned and butchered it. Dave had a sharp knife and plastic bags to pack the meat in. He was also carrying a rucksack big enough to accommodate the whole animal. We buried the skin, guts and all the loose hair we could find, in a pit amongst the trees. No doubt they would have been dug up that same night by a passing fox, but at least the evidence of the deed was concealed from any casual observer. We divided the venison equally between us and considered that we had had a very successful day's hunting alongside the big pheasant shoot on the estate.

Rabbiting in the Snow

On 2 January I walked from the house into the Pentland Hills. Being a public holiday there were no buses running and I was keen to be out with the dog in an effort catch something for the pot. The snowdrifts in the hills were several feet deep in places and made for difficult walking. Fox made an awkward jump over a barbed wire fence leaving some of his black belly fur on the top strand. The icy ground was not the ideal launching pad for steeplechasing and he was lucky not to have been badly ripped. There were a few sheep sheltering from the cold wind alongside a pine wood, understandably reluctant to move at our approach and on the higher ground close to the summit of the hill were several grouse conspicuous against the snow watching our slow progress. They seemed happy to stay put, too. The dog found hare tracks in the snow and was following them with his nose to the ground; any white hare sitting in this landscape would have been impossible to see.

As we rounded the side of a steep hill we came across a youth in summer camouflage gear, which didn't provide him much concealment in that Arctic environment. The youth had a guilty expression on his face and appeared worried as to who I might be. About fifty yards further on were two of his companions, also wearing camouflage jackets, kneeling on the ground, lifting purse nets from a small rabbit warren. I stood watching them for about ten minutes without saying a word and they looked nervous. Fox was always reserved near strangers and stood quietly beside me. He was well acquainted with ferreting procedures and was watching the action with a professional interest. The boys had two young polecat ferrets, a male and a female and were having difficulty retrieving them from the burrows. I knew the frustration of hanging about some freezing hillside waiting for a wayward ferret having fun and games, popping its head out of a rabbit hole and then diving down again before it could be bagged. Young animals were the worst culprits and didn't seem to understand the rules of the game.

Suddenly a rabbit bolted from one of the holes and sprinted through the snow, making a beeline for the fence. Fox was away in a flash and caught it before it had got more than forty yards. I took the rabbit from the dog and handed it to one of the boys; they were relieved when they discovered I was not the landowner. We chatted about hunting with ferrets and used the freshly killed rabbit to entice theirs from the warren and back into their carrying case, which was an ex-army ammunition box stuffed with straw.

We walked on, stopping at another warren further up the hill and watched a buzzard circling overhead, riding the wind; this time only one ferret was slipped into the warren, and without using the nets. Rabbits are more likely to bolt if there are no obstructions at the exits and especially if there was snow on the ground. One rabbit did bolt and the dog went after it, but the bunny managed to get under a fence dividing the open field, zig zagging along it, giving the dog the slip and reaching the safety of a well placed emergency burrow. As I looked down the hill, I saw a man with a dog watching us. Our hunting activities had been observed and the man was heading our way in a very determined manner. We managed to walk away from him and got over the summit of the hill, leaving him far behind.

The walk home was a long hard slog and the poor dog was shattered.

The following week we had an exceptionally heavy snowfall in Edinburgh and Blackford Hill became a totally white hill; even the gorse bushes were covered. I noticed signs of rabbit activity on the hill, with fresh tracks at a couple of the old warrens on the steep north side, so late one night I took the dog and the ferret up the hill, towing one of the children's sledges behind me. There was a full moon, with wonderfully clear views across the city. There wasn't another soul about and very few vehicles on the sodium-lit streets below. The silence that a blanket of snow brings is one of nature's wonders and the snow tweaked under the heels of my boots.

I let the ferret wander about the hill, playing in the snow, allowing her to find her own way to the entrance of the warren. In less than ten minutes I had three rabbits in the bag; it was almost too easy for the dog. The deep soft snow made escape for the rabbits difficult. There was plenty of meat on them and they had beautiful thick winter coats, which I kept and cured; my wife sometimes made mittens from them.

It was a surreal experience, sledging back down the hill with my ferret in the creel, the rabbits in the bag and my black dog running alongside, enjoying the game. I thought there was very little chance of being apprehended by the local constabulary for this particular contravention of the city park by-laws.

A Cottage in the Country

Eric, a neighbour of ours, rented a primitive country cottage about twenty miles to the south of Edinburgh. The property had been a shepherd's house owned by the estate and its situation was far from other human habitation, in glorious isolation on a lonely hillside with only grazing sheep for company and the warbling sound of curlews.

Eric had renovated the dilapidated property with his own hands and now paid a nominal rent for the use of the place. Inside the cottage were the basics: a cooker, a table, several chairs and a couple of beds. The focal point of the interior was a lovely old stone fireplace at the gable end and there was always a good supply of sawn logs for burning, kept in a toolshed outside. The water supply to the house was pumped from a bog nearby and filtered through a makeshift well. Boiling the water before drinking was advised because of liver fluke in the sheep; apparently there was a link between sheep and water snails in passing on the parasitic fluke to humans. To the rear of the house was a vegetable plot that produced good potatoes, beans and soft fruits and the isolated location of the garden meant that it was free of the usual pests that town gardeners suffered from.

We spent occasional weekends at the cottage, ferreting in the area with the permission of one of the estate's tenant farmers. Rabbits on the estate were a serious problem and on a summer's evening they could be counted in their hundreds on the surrounding hillsides, sitting beside their warrens amongst the bracken and the heather.

One weekend we took the dog and ferret on a rabbit hunt without bothering with nets. Fox had a good working relationship with the ferret and they both knew their jobs. The great advantage of operating without nets was the speed with which a warren could be worked; laying out nets on a large warren, carefully and quietly, was time-consuming. A few rabbits did escape, but the dog was able to get most of the ones that bolted. We always slipped the ferret into the hole furthest downwind at a warren, then waited quietly until the dog heard rumblings underground. Fox would mark the hole, cock his head to one side, listening and wait patiently for the fleeing occupant to appear like an express train from a tunnel. The chase was short and decisive and not many rabbits escaped the dog unless they dived immediately into another hole. It wasn't unusual to catch a dozen rabbits in this way and it was a struggle carrying them back to the cottage.

One rabbit we caught had no ears. I had only seen this phenomenon once before and phoned our vet to see if he knew the cause. I was told that sometimes a mother rabbit that was under stress might nibble its young ones' ears and in extreme cases might actually eat its young. Another possible explanation was that the earless rabbits were the result of a genetic disorder – but whatever the reason, a wild rabbit without ears must have been at a serious disadvantage from predators. I suppose the one advantage that the earless animal might have, would be a smaller profile against the skyline.

A few miles above the cottage on the neighbouring land, owned by a knight of the realm, there was a new plantation of Sitka spruce. The young trees had been planted with no regard for the sparkling trout burn that flowed through it and were growing only inches away from its banks. When this kind of unsympathetic planting occurred, the sunlight was excluded from the burn and it became devoid of life, a drain with no flowers or grasses on its banks and no fish in the water. I felt vexed about the doomed future of the wild trout stock and spent a couple of hours with my Swiss army knife, sawing away at the trees nearest the water.

As I walked along the fence line I found a newly cast, three-point roe antler with fresh blood still on the socket end; the tip of the antler was needle sharp.

One of the few improvements for wildlife with the sprawling forestry plantations was the increase in numbers of the black grouse in the hills; but before one new plantation I knew was fenced off, hundreds of white hares had been shot by gamekeepers and landowners to protect the young trees. I was told by a forestry worker that the dead hares were just left on the hill because there was no market for them. It seemed ironic that a man could be charged with poaching hares when the landowner had no use for them.

Lamping for Rabbits

I sent away for a powerful lamp that I had seen advertised in *Shooting Times*. The hand-held lamp was powered by a heavy motorcycle battery and was popular with farmers for checking stock at night. Gamekeepers also used them for shooting foxes and rabbits. For a lurcher owner like myself, lamping rabbits in city parks at night seemed much safer than using a gun.

I knew nothing about lamping and it took me a while to figure out the best way of doing it. One of the most important tips I learned was to use the light sparingly to conserve the battery; carrying a spare was out of the question due to the weight. I rigged up my hefty battery so that I could carry it on a broad leather belt and distribute the weight on my hips; carrying it over the shoulder and having constantly to swing it around the back was a nuisance. The tungsten lamp itself was light in weight and I wore it on a clip swivel around my neck, which left both hands free when needed. A flimsy electrical wire joined the lamp to the battery and care was needed to avoid breaking the connection at the plug junction.

The dog and I were both new to the game and we learned by trial and error. On the first lamping expedition I walked around Blackford Hill with the dog beside me off the lead as I scanned the hillside on a dark, moonless night. The beam illuminated the 'pink' eyes of several grazing rabbits about seventy yards distant and Fox was after them in a flash. He was unsuccessful in his first pursuit, but continued to quarter the hill looking for other rabbits.

I soon discovered that the dog's freelance activities were unhelpful in bagging rabbits because any that were further round the hill must have stampeded to the safety of their burrows unseen by me with my lamp and there was no point in me attempting to stalk rabbits if the dog had already cleared the hill before I got anywhere near them. I realized that I would need to train the dog on a slip lead and get him to come back quickly after each short chase if I was to be successful.

Our first attempt at night hunting with the lamp was therefore not a great success and we went home empty handed, but I had learned something that would give us a better chance the next time. I also noted that there were always more rabbits about on the hill on a windy night and that it was possible to get much nearer to them with the lamp. I made a special leather lead for the dog that was fixed to my wrist at one end and with a loop for my two fingers at the other. The strap then looped through the dog's collar and could be released by straightening the fingers and drawing the hand back.

My next attempt was rather more successful. The dog got very excited when he saw me assembling my lamping gear after supper one night; he quickly associated the equipment with a fun night out. I made it a rule not to feed him before he went hunting, in case of any digestive complications, such as a twisted gut. I always made a route round the hill taking into account which way the wind was blowing. I preferred a westerly wind, which enabled me to stalk the rabbits over a wider area.

Once on the hill I flicked the lamp on and did a quick sweep of the slope before switching the light off again. I could see that there were three rabbits grazing, the nearest one being less than fifty yards away. The dog had also seen them and was straining at the lead. I started walking slowly in the general direction of the nearest rabbit before I switched the lamp on again. The rabbit ran and I slipped the dog. This time I kept the lamp on the fleeing rabbit and it was only seconds before the dog also appeared in the beam. The two of them snaked around the hill twisting and turning before the dog caught up with the rabbit. There was a squeal and I switched off the lamp, hurrying towards the kill.

The chase had probably lasted no longer than ten seconds and it seemed a humane way of hunting to me, far better that setting snares and causing a lingering death. I bagged the rabbit and put the dog back on the lead. He wasn't even out of breath. I made a big fuss of him and told him what a clever boy he was.

He was keen to go again and so was I. We got to the top of the hill before we spotted any more rabbits and I had to take into account the dog's low vantage point. Often when I was able to see something myself, it wasn't always possible for the dog to see what I was looking at. The next chase was more bizarre, because a fleeing rabbit ran away from me with the dog close behind it and then doubled back and ran straight towards me. It was an unnerving experience as the rabbit ran literally across my boots. The pursuing hound crashed into my legs, blinded by the light and chipped one of his teeth. I found myself on my back with the lamp sending a beam of light skywards – but at least I didn't go home empty-handed at the end of the night.

Local knowledge was essential in being a successful lamper; luck only played a part in the game. Even though rabbits were creatures of habit, they could always surprise you with their unexpected survival skills. The clever rabbits lived to run another day and the less gifted ones ended up in one of my curries.

Mr Tod has the Last Laugh

It wasn't always rabbits that found themselves in the beam of my lamp in the city parks and golf courses; I also had a tawny owl, a woodcock and the occasional covey of partridges unexpectedly illuminated. On one memorable winter's evening I caught a fox in the beam, its eyes showing up yellow, unlike the pinkish eyes of the rabbits that I was used to seeing on the hill. What *was* strange was that the fox came running *towards* us instead of running away and my dog, black Fox, watched the red fox's approach with interest. When the inquisitive red fox realized it was in danger, it did a U-turn and accelerated along the side of the hill with the dog in pursuit. The dog caught the fox after a fifty yard dash and pinned him to the ground by the scruff of his neck.

I ran as fast as I could to prevent harm being done to either party. I had no problem with foxes: if they didn't bother me, I didn't bother them. Fortunately when I reached the pair I was able to pin the fox down with my foot to allow the dog to make a safe release. A frightened fox could do serious damage to a dog with its teeth. The dog was reluctant to let his prize go and didn't seem to appreciate my kindly reprieve. It took several repeated commands before the dog realized that Mr Reynard was not going home with us in the game bag.

Unbelievably, the very next night, we met the same fox in the very same place. This time he ran for his life at the first flicker of the lamp, but the dog overtook him and bowled him over at high speed. The poor fox somersaulted down the hill but appeared unhurt, except for his pride. The dog seemed to have realized that fox was off the menu.

A couple of weeks later the wily fox got his revenge when I was out lamping one starry cloudless night and hardly needed the lamp to see what was on the hill. The dog got an immediate chase and I knew he had caught a rabbit when I heard the squeal; it was a still night, and the death cry must have carried a great distance. The rabbit was heavy and I didn't want to carry it with me, so I hung it 'safely' in the fork of a young birch tree at the edge of a gorse thicket, planning to retrieve it on the return journey. When I returned half an hour later to collect my prize, the rabbit had gone. Ironically, I had often made a squealing noise with a blade of grass to bring a fox towards me for my own amusement, but this time it appeared that it was Mr Tod who had had the last laugh.

The Hunter Hunted

Sometimes I went lamping further afield around some of the golf courses within the city limits, but I was always worried about the possibility of the dog running headlong into a wire fence in the heat of the chase. I tried to hunt in places that were relatively safe from hidden obstructions; concealed rabbit holes in the long grass were another concern because a dog could easily break a leg stumbling into one.

I was walking slowly through a field one dark moonless night and got the feeling that I was being watched. When I looked round, there were three horses quietly following me in single file. The nearest one began to nuzzle the back of my neck each time I stopped and it continued like that all the way round the field. I felt that we were part of a very odd team and tried to ignore their company, continuing to sweep the field with the beam of light.

There were lots of rabbits that stampeded from the field, leading the dog a merry chase but without success, leaving him panting for breath, lying in the grass. The three horses circled around the exhausted dog, sniffing at him and I expected him to leap up in panic and run for his life because he had always been a little nervous around horses. I was utterly amazed when he just lay there, allowing one of the horses to lick his side as though it were grooming one of its companions. I had never seen such a thing before.

Blackford Hill was my preferred hunting ground with the lamp because of its close proximity to my house, only a ten-minute walk away. One night I saw someone else lamping on the Braid Hills about one mile to the south. We were both aware of each other and flicked our lamps in recognition a couple of times. He seemed to be getting more chases than me, judging from the activity of his light.

I hunted on the hill most windy nights and on one occasion it was me that became the hunted. I was spotted by a police patrol car that had come along the service road from the car park with its lights out. They must have seen me using the light and came up to investigate. I wasn't too keen on being interviewed and took evasive action by lying down in the long grass near the top of the hill; the dog had been trained to lie beside me automatically. I thought it was unlikely that the police would drive over the hill in their vehicle, but I was wrong. They came struggling up the steep slope in a low gear and passed me within about ten yards. I did think there was a real possibility of being run over by them. Fortunately for me, they were too lazy to get out of their car and search on foot; otherwise they would probably have seen me. Remaining still was almost always the best method of concealment.

Lamping for rabbits was pretty successful between the months of June and October, but when the grass died back it was always harder to find rabbits and they seemed to be more wary. The ones that survived the winter were the smart ones; they seemed to associate the lamp with danger and didn't hang about.

Two-Legged Quarry

After an unsuccessful lamping expedition on the hill one dark night, I walked home along the tree-lined street, passing the allotment gardens that bordered the end of our quiet cul-de-sac. The allotments sloped down to an overgrown railway embankment with a burn running along the near side of it. As I walked towards the top corner where the gate was, I spotted a shadowy figure peeping around the corner of a neighbour's garden wall. The man, dressed all in black, was inside the allotment but leaning out across the gate to see if the coast was clear and hadn't noticed me approaching from his left. I assumed that he was up to no good; my next door neighbour had recently been burgled. When the prowler did see me, he turned away quickly and sprinted down the hill along the narrow path towards the railway line.

I ran up to the closed gate and flicked the lamp on, catching him in the beam of light as he was half way down the hill. Instinctively the dog jumped the gate and went after him. Fox pursued him out of the light and into the bushes and brambles, where I lost sight of them both. I could hear the sound of splashing water and breaking branches as the fleeing intruder risked life and limb to escape from my hound from hell. The dog came back after a couple of minutes and I gave him great praise for his plucky action. He seemed to know that he had done a good thing. I suspected that the man in black had rearranged his schedule for the rest of the evening.

A Chance Encounter

On our country walks we often came across roe deer quite by chance in the most unexpected places. These small deer have multiplied at an alarming rate with the increase of the big forestry plantations all over Scotland and they are now being forced into marginal areas where they were less secure. My dog Fox had always been steady with domestic livestock, but when it came to wild deer it was a different matter. Most dogs seemed inclined to chase deer on impulse and can sometimes catch them when conditions are favourable. And once a dog has caught a deer, it seems to develop a taste for the chase and pursues them with the utmost vigour at every opportunity. I suppose that the dog's wolf ancestor would have been responsible for keeping down the deer numbers.

On the second day of January, following a boozy Auld Year's Night with the neighbours, my wife and I went for a dog walk in the Pentland Hills to clear our heads. I had an upset stomach and the last thing I had on my mind was hunting, so we were quite unprepared. We parked the car on a quiet country road next to a footpath that led up into the hills and walked for about a mile until we came to a young fir plantation. My stomach had been churning over and I was desperate to find a place with a bit of privacy where I could relieve myself. I climbed gingerly over the barbed wire fence and the dog leapt after me, while my wife waited on the open hillside. I squatted amongst the trees and the dog wandered a little further into deep cover. A minute later I heard a yelp, then a bark, and was aware that the dog had probably caught something close by. I made my way as quickly as possible through the densely planted trees, where I found the dog standing beside a deer lying flat on its side in the grass alongside a ditch; it was dead.

My problem was, how to get the deer back to the car without being seen, because there was no way that we were going to leave it. We decided that my wife should go first and that I would follow about a hundred yards behind her, carrying the deer over my shoulders. She would make a pre-arranged signal if she saw anyone coming the other way by putting a hand on top of her head and I would tip the deer in the ditch, hopefully before I was spotted. Fortunately we got back to my wife's car just before a battered old Land Rover came round the bend with the local shepherd at the wheel. It seemed a good way to start the New Year.

The following month my sister Ruth gave me her old car to use before the MOT ran out, an old gas-guzzling Triumph 2000 on its last legs. I took a couple of days off work to go exploring while I still had the use of the vehicle, which was the first car that I ever owned. I only learned to drive at the age of forty. I drove south along the minor roads that meandered through the Pentland Hills. It was liberating, driving aimlessly through the countryside with no final destination in mind, discovering new places that I had never seen before. I had the dog with me, and my old heavy Russian camera with a modest zoom lens, which I used for photographing wildlife when I could get close enough.

I drove through a monotonous flat landscape along a straight narrow road passing a large Sitka plantation with trees no higher than five feet tall. Beyond the plantation the road sloped down to a reservoir with two stone cottages beside it.

The lane was a cul-de-sac and I parked my vehicle at the road end and took the dog for a walk along the edge of the reservoir. It was an exposed area with no shelter from the icy breeze and not much of interest for man or dog, so I climbed up the banking and over the fence into the plantation nearby. We walked along a ride between the small trees, enjoying the low winter sunlight and shelter from the cold wind. I had my camera at the ready for anything of interest and didn't have to wait too long for something to catch my eye.

About seventy yards away, I saw movement in the grass, just a flicker. I stood still and watched; the wind was in my favour. Instinctively I crouched down and pre-focused the lens on the camera. The movement that I had seen turned out to be the long ears of a deer that was sitting between two rows of trees. I stood up and walked slowly forwards, looking through the lens of my camera and refocusing as I went, hoping to get a good shot of the deer when it leapt up and made its move.

Suddenly my dog appeared in the viewfinder running straight at the deer, which got up and lurched into the cover of the trees. The pair disappeared from sight and I followed as fast as I could go. I heard the deer bark, with the guttural sound that they make as an alarm call. When I caught up with the dog he was holding the deer down on the ground by its shoulder. The poor beast had a broken foreleg and was in a state of shock. It was an act of mercy dispatching it.

I had no bag, and now had to figure out how to get the carcass back to the car without being spotted. I knew there was no point in carrying it back to where I had parked the vehicle because it was overlooked by the cottages and I would most certainly have been seen by someone. I decided to hike through the young plantation and find the road that I had driven along to get to the reservoir, then hide the deer inside the fence, where I would be able to collect it in the car on the route out.

It was a distance of about a mile to the hiding place and it was hard going over rough ground, so I kept stopping to take a rest. When I did finally get to within sight of the road, I heard voices and ducked down, letting the deer slide down beside me. The dog crouched by my side, and we lay motionless for several minutes before we saw two men walking towards us, carrying a blue plastic sack. I was able to observe them without being seen myself. They wandered into the young trees nearby, to where there was a pheasant feeder made from an old oil drum, mounted on a wooden frame. They took the lid off the top of the feeder and poured some grain into the drum from the plastic sack. At least I felt that their appearance in the plantation was nothing to do with me and just a coincidence. However, we were not out of the woods yet and I knew that I was going to have to be very cautious when there was an active gamekeeper in the vicinity. When the men had finished replenishing the pheasant feeder they headed back towards the road and I kept them in sight by crawling forwards on my belly and watching their every move. They clambered over the perimeter fence, got into a Land Rover and drove off in the direction of the reservoir where my car had been parked.

I lay in the grass for about half an hour before I got the deer up on to my shoulders again and headed for the road. I stashed the body just inside the boundary fence, concealing it with dead bracken. The long straight road there was relatively featureless so I snapped a branch from one of the small trees and placed it at the side of the road to use as a marker to indicate the exact spot and which could be easily seen when I drove past. I then doubled back across the plantation to get to the car.

Fortunately there was no sign of any human activity when I got back to the reservoir, but it was a relief to get away from the place. The dog went on to the back seat and I cleared a space in the boot for the deer, then drove back along the forestry road until I saw my marker branch. I checked my rear-view mirror, pulled over and got out of the car. I walked round to the boot and fiddled with the key to get the damn thing open; the lock was faulty and unreliable, and I spent an anxious few minutes looking over my shoulder for approaching vehicles. It was a struggle hauling the deer over the fence and manhandling it into the boot of the car, but I drove away reasonably certain that there had been no witnesses to my crime.

When I got home, I gralloched the beast in the garden and suspended the carcass from the door frame by the hind legs on two hooks that had once supported a child's swing and which were ideal for hanging large game. As I skinned the animal, I was able to inspect the broken foreleg and saw that it was an old wound which hadn't healed; the shoulder muscle was wasted, so the animal must have been struggling around on three legs for more than a week. A .22 calibre bullet had passed through one leg snapping it and had then lodged in the inside of the other foreleg in the tendon, where it had fragmented. The poor animal must have been in agony since the wounding. I wondered if the gamekeepers I had seen were responsible for wounding it. Deer were not popular in young fir plantations where they browsed on the saplings, stunting their growth.

12
That Sinking Feeling

We had a friend, an elderly academic, who had a timeshare cabin on Loch Eck on the west coast. My wife and I spent a very pleasant long weekend there with the professor and his wife in the month of March. There was a two-man sailing dinghy that came with the cabin for general use and on the Sunday I was invited to go sailing with the prof, a novice sailor with very little experience, who had only ever sailed the dinghy with a qualified person on board. It was his birthday, however and he was anxious to take command of the vessel for the first time and I was game for a voyage around the loch and jumped at the chance. There was a strong fresh breeze that day so we were unlikely to get becalmed.

I knew nothing about sailing, but watched with some concern as the prof made ready to cast off from the shingle beach. He had run up the sail while we were still on the beach and the little craft was rocking violently from side to side, with the sail flapping like a mad thing and the keel scraping sideways against the pebbles. Somehow we climbed aboard, and got away from the shore with the wind fully behind us at an impressive rate of knots and still upright. We dropped the retractable keel, which stabilized the dinghy, in the nick of time.

Everything was fine until we got to the other side of the loch where the wind became gale force and the surface was choppy like the sea. The sensation of speed as we skipped across the waves was very enjoyable. But my companion soon realized that we were in a dangerous situation sailing in those conditions and when we had to 'come about' and head back down the loch, we made a very clumsy manoeuvre which swamped the dinghy, almost capsizing it. Neither of us was wearing life jackets and the water was extremely cold. Fortunately we had a plastic container on board and were able to bale out most of the water before we got into serious difficulties.

Getting back to our starting point was a real hair-raiser. We were sailing against the wind with the sail in a fixed position because the ropes – or 'sheets' – holding it up were tied in granny knots instead of quick release ones. As we came head-on to the shore at full speed in shallow water, we narrowly missed two boulders by inches as we sailed between them and landed our vessel high and dry on the shingle. I had just enough time to pull up the drop keel before it snapped on the beach. If we had hit the boulders we would probably have split the fibreglass hull.

One Man and His Dog

About two years after this incident we had an invitation to stay at the cabin again, though this time by ourselves because our friends had made other holiday arrangements. On this occasion we took our dog Fox with us and a friend called Paul. It was a great place for walking and there were interesting trails in the forestry that snaked up into the hills, with fine views from the clearings. It was late summer and the midges were particularly bad, so we kept away from the loch, which was the worst place for them. There was very little breeze and those tiny bloodsuckers were having a field day at our expense; even the dog was suffering.

On the final hot sunny day of our visit, I was keen to explore further afield and asked Paul and my wife if they fancied taking the dinghy to the other side of the loch to the foot of a mountain that was inaccessible by road. I had no intention of even attempting to sail that dinghy and had already hauled out the oars that were stowed under the cabin's foundations. The surface of the loch was like a mirror and the only disturbance was caused by rising trout taking flies, leaving ever-increasing circles on the glassy surface. I didn't get a very positive response from the others, so it looked like it was going to be one man and his dog in the boat. I fished out the key marked 'boat' from the drawer in the kitchen table, grabbed my rucksack and Swiss army knife and shouldered the heavy oars down to where the boat was kept at the loch side.

The dog had looked quite enthusiastic as we had set off, but seemed to change his mood when we got to the shore and watched me examining the boat. The white dinghy was upturned under an alder tree, secured by a heavy chain with a rusty padlock; I tried the key, which fitted okay, but it wouldn't turn because the padlock appeared to have seized up on the inside. I was fumbling with the key for about ten minutes without success, when one of the locals came past, an elderly man with an ancient border collie beside him. He asked me what the problem was so I showed him the key, whereupon he, too, tried to get the padlock to open, but was also unsuccessful.

'I think that you will need to saw through one of the links on the chain, the padlock is too rusty to work,' he said. 'I'll go and get my hacksaw from the shed and something to grip the chain.'

He was back in about fifteen minutes with the tools, a junior eclipse saw and a massive pair of pliers. I got to work immediately and started sawing away at the link nearest the padlock. It took an age to get through it and it had to be sawed from both sides because it was too strong to bend open. By the time I had finished I was sweating like a pig and had cramp in my wrist. The poor dog had been waiting patiently, tethered under the shade of the alder tree. I thanked the old man for the loan of his tools and we turned the boat the right way up and put the rowlocks and oars into position. He wished me a good day and disappeared along the loch side.

My next problem was getting the dog into the boat: he was most uncooperative in getting on board and I had to wrestle him into the bow and tie him to the thwart by his lead. Fortunately it only took me about twenty minutes to row across the loch and get back on to terra firma.

The far bank was peaceful and secluded, with plenty of vegetation where the sheep had been fenced out. The shingle beach had birch and alder trees growing right down to the water's edge. I dragged the boat up on to the shingle and tied the boat rope to an exposed tree root. The midges were flitting about in their thousands and biting into my scalp and eyelids. I was being eaten alive. I was hoping that once we got up on to the higher ground the midge menace would diminish and struck out uphill with the dog trotting beside me, much happier now that he had his four paws on dry land.

The first part of the walk was up a narrow forestry track alongside a mature spruce plantation which was surrounded by a high deer fence. The open side of the track was rough grassland with a few patches of heather sloping down into a gully with a burn running along the bottom. As we breasted the first hill I saw the rear ends of three red deer hinds, their tails flicking to keep the flies at bay. I was no more that fifty yards away from them and hadn't been spotted, but when the dog ran ahead of me the game was up and the animals ran uphill, out of my line of vision.

I struggled up that steep hill pouring with sweat to get a vantage point where I could see the action, but the top of the hill turned out to be a false summit and I had to keep going to see over the next one. I was worried about the dog taking on one of those large red deer; they were big and strong and had a considerable weight advantage over him. There was nothing to see from the next hill, but I did hear a distant bark from a plantation across the other side of the burn down below. About fifteen minutes had lapsed since I had last seen the dog.

Eventually my eye picked out a black shape in the distance, next to the deer fence: it was the dog and he was lying on his side in the long grass. I hurried over there to see if he had been injured. As I got near to him I could hear him panting for breath and saw blood on his chest; I had a moment of panic and wondered how I could get him back to the boat. It took me a few seconds to make out a dead roe deer lying in a peaty ditch only a few feet away; there was blood on its throat. I could only guess what had happened, which is the dog must have switched his pursuit from the red deer to the roe and chased it along the fence line where it was caught and killed.

I dragged the deer along to a narrow burn that had cut deep into the peat. I was wearing a white T-shirt, so I stripped to the waist. I was able to butcher the roe and get all the meat neatly packed into my rucksack. I had enough polybags to wrap all the joints individually; the sharp saw attachment on the knife enabled me to separate the hind quarters from the spine. The worst part of the job was the constant attack by midges – they were all over me and every time I rubbed my head, face and arms with my hands, I smeared blood all over myself. After I had bagged up the venison, I buried the skin and entrails in a shallow hole for the foxes to sniff out later and then washed myself in the icy water to get all the blood off – I was shivering in the hot sun. As my arms became clean again I could see that I had been bitten hundreds of times by the midges; there was hardly a place without a red blotch. There were a few bloody specks on my T-shirt, but I wasn't too worried about meeting anyone on the way back to the cabin.

When I got back to the boat, I had a struggle with the dog to get him back on board; his long legs put him at a great disadvantage in the confined space and he was panicky. However, after I tied him in the bow alongside the rucksack, he seemed to calm down a little. The boat was not very well balanced, with far too much weight at the sharp end and rowing back across the loch was slow going; I could see two fly fishermen on the opposite bank next to my landing place, watching my clumsy progress. I tried to look casual as I stopped rowing and let the overburdened dingy glide the last few feet on to the shingle beach. I was sweating heavily and the blood on my white T-shirt now seemed rather obvious. The anglers were observing my every move and had only nodded reluctantly when I had wished them 'Good afternoon'; as I released the dog and hauled the boat out of the water, it occurred to me that they may have been off-duty policemen.

I lifted the heavy rucksack from the bow, unshipped the oars, then hauled the boat up on to the shingle beach and flipped it over, back under the alder tree. I looped the broken chain through the forward boat seat and then around the tree, concealing the rusty padlock on the blind side. Carrying the heavy rucksack and the oars was hard going and it was a real struggle getting up the steep path towards the cabin. I looked back and saw that the two men were still watching my slow progress from the shore.

Back at the cabin my wife and friend had been wondering what had happened to me; I had been away for much longer than I had thought. However, the bag of fresh meat was a nice bonus on the last day of our holiday.

When we got back to Edinburgh I went round to see the professor with a shoulder of venison to thank him for the use of his cabin. He was pleased that we had enjoyed ourselves and thanked me for the meat.

'Oh, by the way, I'm afraid you'll need to get a new padlock for the boat. I had to saw through the chain to get use of the dinghy,' I told him.

He gave me a puzzled look. 'We don't have a dinghy. Ours was wrecked in that big storm last year and we never replaced it.'

I was speechless. Piracy could now be added to the crime of deer poaching. Fortunately, the prof thought the whole incident was hilarious and swore to keep our little secret.

A Near-Death Experience

One of our favourite country walks was around the castle not far from Dalkeith. This attractive, ruined, pinkish-golden sandstone building was set in a splendid landscape, largely unchanged, since the castle had been built in the sixteenth century. The historic building commanded a fine view of a wide, dish-shaped valley below, with a clear, swift-flowing burn, lined with alder trees, running through it. The marshy ground on the valley bottom was surrounded by low hills covered by indigenous woodland, the trees mainly ash, oak, hazel, birch and blackthorn.

Beyond the upper valley rim were arable fields that attracted great numbers of greylag geese in the late autumn before the stubble was ploughed in; it was also a good place to see peregrine falcons when the woodpigeons were feeding on those fields. I saw high-flying falcons stooping from a great height on to the unsuspecting pigeons passing beneath them over the valley, which seemed a timeless sort of place. It was a good area to find wild mushrooms and hazel sticks for making shepherd's crooks and walking sticks. There were rabbits, hares and roe deer inhabiting the woods and fields, as well as pheasants reared for shooting on the neighbouring estates. One day Fox managed to catch a woodpigeon in mid-air as it took off, heavy with grain, from the ripe corn at the edge of a field; it was at least six feet above the ground when he snapped his jaws round it.

We flushed a roebuck from the woods on the far side of the valley and the dog chased it down across the marshland over the burn and up into the woodland on the opposite side. We lost sight of the pair as they ran up the hill amongst the trees several hundred yards away and it took me at least fifteen minutes to reach the spot where we had last seen them. I stood and whistled and called Fox's name until I was hoarse. I guessed that he was somewhere close by a thorny thicket where the ground was covered in bracken and brambles and impossible to force a way through.

Eventually the dog appeared from the undergrowth breathing heavily with his tongue hanging out, then right behind him the roebuck leapt up and went crashing off in the opposite direction. It was only then that I realized the dog had caught up with the roe and had probably been holding on to it amongst the brambles where I was unable to see them. Fox had eventually released his grip on the deer and come running, leaving his hard-earned prize to escape and run another day. I could see that the dog was desperately in need of a drink and led him down the hill to the burn, but before we got there I saw him drinking from a stagnant pool at the foot of the slope. I called him off and we continued towards the burn.

That night the dog did not settle. He normally slept soundly in his bed in the corner of our bedroom, but on this occasion he whined and padded about the room all night, keeping us awake. I attempted to let him out into the garden because I thought he needed a pee, but he wouldn't leave the room; he was obviously in distress and in a great deal of pain. The area for concern seemed to be his lower back and I was wondering if he had slipped a disc. In the morning we phoned the vet and arranged to take him in immediately; he was in a bad way and had to be lifted into the car. We left him with the vet where he could be examined, x-rayed and kept under close observation.

The vet phoned several hours later and gave us the bad news: Fox had been poisoned and his kidneys had swollen to almost twice their normal size. The only way that he might survive would be with major surgery and the success rate was only fifty/fifty. We were stunned. I had to return to the vets to sign the papers and accept any risk involved in the operation.

It was three days before we finally got the news that Fox was likely to pull through and it was a great feeling going up to collect him. He was groggy from the painkillers and he had a scar the full length of his belly, but he still managed to wag his tail when he saw us. The vet told us that his successful recovery was largely due to his exceptional physical fitness and strong heart; apparently he had a remarkably slow pulse rate, the sign of a true athlete.

The vet could only guess about the ingested poison and told us that even a decomposing mouse in a stagnant pool could be enough to poison a dog. The other possibility might have been agricultural chemical run-off from the arable fields above the valley.

This near-death experience gave us an even stronger bond with our faithful hound. It was hard to imagine life without him.

Clever Hares

When Fox was chasing hares, he was in his element. His muscular build and strong legs were a great advantage when hunting over rough upland ground such as grouse moors; a finer made dog would have been more susceptible to injuries on those heather-clad hillsides where the soft peat had eroded and formed ditches, hags and bogs. Being able to jump fences was also useful when he was in pursuit of a fleet-footed hare that was running for its life and knew its own territory intimately.

A Tall Story?

Some of the best chases I ever witnessed were unsuccessful in regards of a kill, but marvellous in terms of the skill and nerve demonstrated by the fleeing hare in escaping the dog. I remember one cold winter's afternoon when we took Fox into the Pentland Hills for a brisk hike through the snowy landscape; we were walking from Balerno along a well known track that eventually came out at Penicuik to the east, when quite unexpectedly a white hare leapt out from under our feet and started running towards the distant slopes. The chase started in a flat valley, with very little cover for a hare to take advantage of and the outcome appeared to be a forgone conclusion; we stood and watched as the black dog pursued the white hare across the flat plain, the distance between them narrowing in spite of the hare's efforts to shake off the dog by twisting and turning.

Then to my utter amazement, the hare made a beeline towards a solitary figure in the distance. It was a hill walker heading our way, the only other person we had seen that day. As the hare got nearer to him, the man stood still and the hare then ran twice round the man, with the dog following close behind. This desperate but crafty move enabled the hare to escape from the jaws of death because the dog was unable to make up the ground that he lost in those few vital seconds, eventually being obliged to slow down and watch his prey reach the safety of the upland slopes at a steady canter.

We never passed the man near enough to make any comment on the incident, but hoped that his friends would believe his account of what might have seemed to them to be a tall story.

Harriers

Then the following year in the month of August, we were walking along one of the Pentland ridges when we met a large number of hill runners coming the other way; there were about fifty or sixty of them in single file, strung out along a narrow sheep track through the heather. A mountain hare in its brown summer coat had been disturbed by the runners and was heading in our direction. It hadn't seen the dog and ran past us within a few yards into the rushes at the edge of a bog.

Fox went after the hare and the pair of them snaked through the reeds before breaking cover again and heading uphill towards the runners. Incredibly, the hare joined them and wove in and out of the line with the dog following close behind. There were shouts of encouragement from the runners, some for the hare and some for the dog and the dog seemed to give up the chase rather prematurely on that occasion. I felt that he was probably embarrassed by all the attention.

A Cool Nerve

Sometimes the mountain hares were at a great disadvantage when they changed the colour of their coat but it didn't match the changing season. Some years we got no snow on the hills, but the poor mountain hares still turned white and therefore lacked the camouflage they needed for their winter survival. They often bedded down in deep cover amongst the thick heather on the hillsides, but some-times the dog was able to sniff them out from a considerable distance, if the wind was in the right direction.

One cold winter's morning I was out on the hill with a friend; we had two dogs with us and there were still a few surviving strips of snow on the north side of the hills where the deep drifts had not been melted by the low winter sun. As we sat and rested before climbing up a steep south-facing slope, we noticed that the dogs were staring fixedly at something high on the hill. I could see a small white object on the bare grassy hillside and thought it was a piece of litter by its movement. It took a while before we realized that we were watching a stoat in full white winter coat and black-tipped tail, hurrying down the steep hill, following every nook and cranny, sniffing at every rock and molehill and quartering the ground like a Springer spaniel. Both the excited dogs needed to be restrained as the stoat got nearer to us. Eventually it disappeared into a drystane dyke.

We continued with our walk, rounding the hill to the shadowy side where a few long strips of snow remained – and a white hare jumped up from the heather and sprinted towards the nearest snowdrift, about a hundred yards long but only nine feet or so wide. What followed next was like a Tom and Jerry cartoon, because the hare, with its furry non-slip paws, was able to race along the length of the slippery, ice-coated snowdrift with ease, while the pursuing dogs skidded all over the place and could hardly stand, let alone run. The hare showed a remarkably cool nerve by remaining on the ice and loping from one end to the other while the dogs raced alongside it on the dead grass, unable or unwilling to try the slippery icy surface again.

We walked away from the scene empty-handed and promised to drink a toast to the clever hare when we got to the pub in the village.

Live and Let Live

A couple of years later we experienced another noteworthy incident involving our dog Fox and a mountain hare. It was in the month of March and my wife, myself and my friend Paul took a trip down to the Borders to explore an area new to us in the hills. We walked past a reservoir, putting up hundreds of wild mallard ducks, teal, curlew, lapwings and a few oyster catchers. A large brown hare also got up in front of us from the rough grass and splashed into a burn almost on top of a mallard that had been hiding under the bank. The hare then swam to the other side and ran slowly uphill through a newly seeded field and disappeared over the skyline while the dog was straining at the lead. We couldn't let him off because there were sheep in the field and there were two houses in the distance which commanded a view across the whole valley.

We followed the burn into the hills, flushing even more mallards. A heron flapped slowly away upstream and grouse exploded from the heather as we reached the higher ground. There were also a few pheasants and a couple of black-cock amongst the stunted birch trees along the burn – but not a single hare stirred on the upper slopes. We circled back round along one of the high ridges and followed a downhill track until we spotted a white blob in the heather below, which got smaller as we got nearer. I slipped the dog off the lead and sent him away in the general direction of the hidden white hare, which he hadn't yet seen.

When the hare left its hiding place, the dog chased it downhill towards the valley bottom, crossing the burn then through the heather, where he began to catch up with it. The hare began to jink and turned the dog six times, leaving him struggling to keep up. Once the hare got into its stride on the open hillside, the gap between the pair grew wider and it became obvious that the hare was going to live and run another day.

I whistled the dog and he came back towards us at a slow trot with his tongue hanging out. As he came near to his original starting place, a fresh hare got up directly in front of him and there was a second chase. The second hare chose a different escape route to the first hare and led the dog directly towards us for a few yards, before turning and heading downhill into the valley with the small birch wood, where both animals disappeared from sight. We waited anxiously on the high ground for any sign of the continuing chase several hundred yards below, but there was no movement and after about fifteen minutes I was beginning to get concerned.

I whistled and waited: still nothing. Fox was rarely ever out of sight for more than ten minutes, even after a long chase and always came running when he heard my whistle. The three of us then began searching for him; we spread out and headed downhill in a line abreast about fifty yards apart. I was hoping that he had not been caught in a gamekeeper's fox snare, or was stuck on a barbed-wire fence in some remote place. That kind of fate was not unknown for shepherd's dogs in upland areas.

I climbed over the drystane dyke that ran at right angles to the burn in the valley bottom and spotted something black alongside it, several hundred yards away. It was the dog. I whistled, but he wouldn't come to me. Then I shouted, but he still wouldn't move. Then I saw a dead sheep, not more than thirty yards away from him and felt a pang of horror. Fox had been trained from a very young age to ignore sheep; as a pup he had been severely thrashed for chasing one and I thought he had grown up with an aversion to them.

I ran all the way down the steep hill to look at the dead sheep, lying on its side in the rushes near to the dyke. On closer inspection I saw that it had been dead for more than a week, the eyes pecked out by the crows and was greatly relieved – but wondered why Fox had still not moved. I thought maybe he had been injured and went to check him over, but he was okay and sound of limb. I did notice he had been digging beside the wall.

The mystery was soon solved when I realized what Fox was looking at inside the dyke: that plump white hare had managed to get itself into a place of safety from the pursuing hound and was sitting quietly, absolutely still and hardly breathing, *inside* the dyke – it was exactly in the middle and looked like just another stone in the wall.

I knelt on the ground for a closer look: we were eyeball to eyeball. It seemed a miracle that the creature could have squeezed into such a tight space. I was barely able to slide my hand between the narrow gaps in the stones and could only reach in by rolling up my sleeve, badly grazing my elbow in the process.

I managed to get my hand on to the hare's warm, white, furry back and stroked it, wondering how I was going to extricate it without loosening any stones.

While I was pondering this little puzzle, I saw my wife's face on the other side of the dyke. She had observed the hare, my groping hand and the dog's nose, and gave me this ultimatum:

'If you kill that poor hare, I'll never speak to you again. If it was smart enough to get in there and escape the dog, then it deserves to live and breed other clever hares.'

Of course she was right. I could be quite cold-blooded when I was hunting for food, but we were unlikely to starve if we let this one go. The dog was not so easily persuaded, however, and I had to put his lead on and drag him away from his prize; all four paws were planted firmly on the ground and I could only describe his doggy expression as furious. We put up a woodcock on the way back and four more hares, but went home empty-handed.

New Hunting Grounds

My wife and I took a drive into the Lammermuir hills to explore new hunting territory. The narrow, single-track road that linked Duns with Gifford snaked through the hills, which were mainly grouse moors. At the foot of the hills was a shepherd's cottage just below the heather line and it was necessary to slow down to drive across a cattle grid next to the gate. A few hundred yards past the house we passed the shepherd coming down the hill in his tractor; from his high seat he had a clear view of the dog on the back seat of our Mini Cooper, but he gave us a friendly wave.

Saved by an Owl

We continued along the road for several miles until we found a likely-looking spot, parking the car safely off the road. There was no sign of traffic and we were able to get on to the hill without being seen. After a few miles plodding along a rough track towards the summit, we stopped to have a bite to eat and a hot drink from the thermos, sitting beside a dyke on the hillside about fifty yards from the track.

Within minutes we heard the sound of a Land Rover labouring up the hill towards us along the track. As it got level it came to a halt. The driver had spotted us. He climbed out slowly and gave us a wave. We were sitting quietly sipping our tea with the dog beside us. The man strolled across and the dog trotted over to greet him with his head down and his tail wagging. 'Good morning,' said the man. He was friendly, but I had to think fast because I guessed what was coming next. 'What brings you to these parts?' he asked.

I had a card in my pocket relating to a short-eared owl survey that was being conducted by Edinburgh University. I told him about the survey and showed him the card, complete with university logo. It came as no surprise to discover that the man was the local gamekeeper with a professional interest in birds of prey. He seemed happy with our explanation about our visit to his grouse moor and told us that he had seen a rough-legged buzzard in the area, which was unusual in those parts.

'I got a phone call from the shepherd this morning; he told me he'd seen a couple in a red Mini with a greyhound on the back seat and assumed you might be coursing hares on the hill,' he told us.

We laughed at the very idea; fortunately the dog was well behaved and the gamekeeper made a big fuss of him. We collected our things together and scrambled back over to the track to where the Land Rover was parked. The keeper waved as he turned his vehicle around and drove back down the hill.

Then to my absolute horror a white hare got up in front of us, and the dog chased it up the hill. I was praying that the gamekeeper was paying attention to the rough track ahead of him and not checking his rear-view mirror. It was a great relief when the Land Rover disappeared around the side of the hill. Fox failed to catch the fleeing hare and we walked several miles over rough terrain without seeing another one. We thought it best to try another place to avoid meeting the keeper again under less favourable circumstances.

A Productive Evening

It was a relief to get back to the Mini and move on. We drove south past Longformacus to the reservoir where there were usually plenty of white hares in the surrounding hills. The reservoir had parking facilities for trout fishermen and a parked vehicle there attracted less attention from the local landowners and shepherds. It was late afternoon and we still had a few of hours of daylight left for hunting. I always carried a compass with me in the hills, as it was easy to get lost on moorland in poor light and my ordnance survey map was out of date; new forestry plantations had sprouted up everywhere on previously bare hillsides.

We heard the sound of gunshots; a grouse shoot was taking place in the vicinity, so we chose a route in the opposite direction. The shooters must have been on the same ground earlier because there were fresh spent cartridges and grouse feathers littering the heather within thirty yards of the butts.

It was only a matter of minutes before a rabbit got up in front of the dog and gave him a run for his money; it jinked like a hare and escaped with only inches to spare into a hole in the peat under a clump of heather. Ten minutes later a white hare sprang from the rushes and raced across a flat patch of partially burnt heather where it landed on top of a concealed grouse. The indignant bird got airborne making a noisy protest and flew low above the ground towards the hill above. The equally surprised hare stumbled for a second and then doubled back towards us, turning the dog about ten times before Fox got close enough to nudge it and get a mouthful of white fur. Miraculously the hare escaped.

A second hare ran before us, but this time we kept the dog on the lead because there were sheep nearby; any sudden movement of sheep on the hill attracted unwanted attention. Twenty minutes later Fox did catch a hare after a hundred yard dash and we caught another two on the return journey; the rucksack was beginning to feel heavy. As we were heading back towards the car at the dam side of the reservoir, the dog chased a white hare along the road. The hare ran nimbly across a cattlegrid, followed by Fox who cleared the grid in one great leap. My heart was in my mouth, because if the dog had landed short, he would most certainly have broken his legs.

We had walked about six miles over rough ground and it was heavy work carrying four hares. After this fourth kill the dog was immediately put on the lead in case he added to my burden in the last few hundred yards: he still seemed keen to hunt, but it was dark by the time we got back to the car.

A Question of Morality

When I was walking my dog through the park in Edinburgh one afternoon, I met an attractive young woman with an elderly, partially toothed whippet called Sadie. Fox took an instant liking to the old bitch and I got into conversation with her owner. I discovered that the young lady was a postgraduate student from Edinburgh University Veterinary School. Erica was a vegetarian on moral grounds, objecting to factory farming methods because the system imprisoned animals and gave them a miserable life; but she was inquisitive about hunting with dogs and didn't seem to have any scruples about pursuing wild animals for food in their natural habitat. I told her that hunting hares with a fast-running dog was a lot more humane than shooting them with shotguns; a chase rarely lasted more than five minutes and the quarry was either killed quickly or escaped unharmed. An old countryman once told me that a hare in its prime was seldom killed by a hound.

I met Erica on several occasions before I suggested that she might like to accompany me into the hills and make up her own mind about hare hunting. She agreed and brought Sadie with her for the walk. We chose a bright, sunny November day without a cloud in the sky, when there was still frost on the north side of the hills. The route we took was between two reservoirs in the Pentland hills. As we crossed a flat boggy area, a large white hare got up about twenty feet in front of Fox and he was after it in a flash, zigzagging through the sedges.

The hare took the dog on a long chase, twisting and turning at every opportunity, and gaining ground once it got on to the nearby hill. The pair raced past a small flock of sheep which stood their ground and watched them go by. The hare jumped a dyke and the dog followed, closing the gap all the time – but the hare gave him the slip somewhere along the dyke and the dog finally gave up and lay panting in the dead grass on the side of the hill.

I whistled him back and he flushed out a snipe on the way over. After a short rest, he went after a second hare, which led him up a hill and back down again before vanishing in the rough ground and escaping to run another day. Often a hare would change direction when it was momentarily out of sight and double back to elude its pursuer.

We walked on past a derelict shepherd's cottage and had a long rest overlooking the reservoir, which looked beautiful, glistening in the low afternoon sunlight. A skein of greylag geese passed high overhead, honking as they went. The air was crystal clear and we could see for miles. We continued our walk to the top of the hill, then down the other side where we flushed a woodcock that flapped away downhill. Fox had been hunting along the bottom of the hill and had sniffed out several grouse, flushing them from the deep heather.

While he was down below us another white hare ran before us on a narrow sheep track before turning downhill towards the dog, which it hadn't yet seen. Fox gave chase when he spotted the hare coming towards him and the pair ran along the side of the hill for about a hundred yards. The dog accelerated after the hare, caught it and made a clean kill. It was then that Sadie made her move and trotted over to Fox to examine his handywork, but Fox was not pleased with the intrusion and snapped at her to keep her at a respectable distance from his prize. We called it a day, the dogs had had plenty of exercise and so had we.

When we got back home, I made the mistake of laying the hare down on the kitchen floor and when Sadie tried to get a sniff of it, Fox snapped at her again, sending her whimpering under the kitchen table. Erica told me that she had enjoyed her day out, and hadn't considered the hunt to have been cruel in any way. We kept in touch during her final year in Edinburgh and said our goodbyes when she moved south to take up employment at a veterinary practice in Cheshire.

13
Brown Hares and White Hares

I've heard some lurchermen describe the hunting of white hares as being like chasing cats. Anyone who has spent significant time in the hills chasing these fleet-footed animals would know what a nonsense that idea is. Some of the most remarkable chases that I have seen in the last twenty-five years have involved white hares in their upland kingdoms.

In Scotland, white hares are often referred to as blue hares and the brown hares as red hares, to differentiate between the two species. During the summer months the white hares are of a chocolate colour and their coats change colour gradually with the end of the autumn. Whenever the hunting season started we would catch hares in various stages of this seasonal colour transformation and the mixture of brown and white hairs in their coats did give them a bluish-grey tinge.

In the summer, a hare that had been feeding and had a full belly was at a definite disadvantage when it was being chased, but in the winter months when the grazing was sparse those hungry animals could run like the wind.

Out-Foxed

In the month of January we took the dog south, for a hunt on the hills on the way to Moffat; there was a gale-force wind blowing that day. We stopped en route to pick up a freshly killed brown hare that had been bumped by a car; there was very little damage to the poor creature. I sometimes used to stop for squashed hares and take the ears, as the short soft fur was good for making trout flies. We parked the car in a layby at the heights, and walked uphill along the sheep track, passing a solitary hiker on the way down; he told us, 'It's wild on the top!'

Further on, a pair of mallard flew from a deep pool in a burn where the wind was blowing back the waterfall below, over the rocks in a large spray. Our route took us around the hillside and up along the ridge to the trig point on the heights. It was almost impossible to stand upright in those conditions and we soon moved down the lee side for shelter. The sheep that were already sheltering there were easily spooked and ran downhill in the direction of a distant cottage. Fox put up a white hare, dashing after it in the direction of the cottage. We didn't know if the place was inhabited and were not keen on being seen by the occupants.

The hare ran downhill for several hundred yards, crossed a burn, went under a fence at the bottom, through a green field alongside to the house, then back round again under the fence and back into the heather. The dog leapt the fence easily both ways and continued with the chase, but eventually lost ground on the uphill stretch. The hare never really looked in danger of being caught and continued its run to safety over the top of the hill where the chase had begun. The dog was totally pooped and flopped down in the heather for a well earned rest. We were glad to see the hare making its way to freedom after such a marathon run. I wondered if the strong gale had worked to the advantage of the hare, which would have had less wind resistance than the dog.

Fox was exhausted and didn't look as though he had much energy left for any further action that day. However, he spotted another white hare sitting upright like a little snowman in a patch of short dark heather about seventy yards above us. He went after it and closed the gap very quickly; the hare came down the hill and crossed the same burn that the first hare had done. The chase continued up the other hill and the hare led the dog over to a ring-dyke sheep-pen, which it ran twice around; at the third circling, the dog stood still and waited for the hare to come round to him. It was a comedy moment as the pair almost collided, but the hare was smart and led the dog across the burn again, where it turned the dog six times at the vital moment, on a steep embankment, before escaping with the dog flagging behind.

It had been a beautiful chase; the hare had used every trick in the book and had proved his superiority. Fox had been outclassed. We had a three-mile walk back to the car, but at least we had nothing to carry.

Hunting with a Camera

I sometimes carried a camera with me when we were hunting and managed to get a few decent shots when conditions were favourable. Good reflexes were essential and also the ability to guess where the chase was going to lead. Once the camera was set up for shutter speed and light conditions, the only thing left to concentrate on was focusing the lens on swiftly moving objects, often passing surprisingly close to the photographer.

Wild Swans

On a cold sunny winter's afternoon we took the dog for a walk along the River Tweed following a narrow, little used angler's path upstream from Bellspool. The river was high and fast flowing, with recent signs of flooding high above the banks. We saw three well preserved dead salmon at the water's edge, bobbing in the gentle current where their journey had come to an end. The flat plain beside the river was boggy in places, with long deep pools surrounded by sedges and reeds. Beyond the wet area were arable fields on slightly higher ground that stretched about a quarter of a mile towards the road that ran roughly parallel to the river.

We kept close to the river on the marshy ground and flushed flocks of mallard and teal as we passed the pools along the way. The ducks circled overhead before heading downstream. There were three white domestic geese along the river, far from human habitation. The rabbit holes in the sandy river banks had been vacated before the floodwaters had reached them. Our walk upstream terminated near the village of Drumelzier, where there was an old manse close to the river. It was second nature to us to avoid being seen when we were hunting and we doubled back to cover the ground we had not quartered on the way up.

Two swans were holding court on a long, narrow strip of water surrounded by reeds; it was the perfect photographic opportunity and I had my camera with me. It seemed likely that the birds would make a speedy exit when they saw the dog approaching. The length of run needed on that narrow waterway for the birds to get airborne gave me plenty of time to focus the camera on the swans as they flapped and splashed the length of the pool. The spray from their feet glistened in the bright sunlight against the dramatic backdrop of hill and sky and I got my picture of a pair of wild swans on the point of take-off.

The dog raced below this pair of low-flying giants and stumbled, landing upside down in the soft mud with four legs flailing in the air – but we didn't have to worry about cleaning him because he misjudged his next jump across a deep pool, and became fully submerged in the icy cold water. By the time he managed to get out of the pool again he was clean, but shivering with the cold. A cold, wet dog is a frisky dog and he was on racing form after his unexpected dip. Further on we flushed a snipe that left a white streak of guano in the air as it zigzagged away from us.

A Memorable Chase

As we got to the last field before the car, the dog began to quarter the ground and put up a big brown hare from a clump of sedge grass in the middle of the field. I was ready with my camera, which had now become a reflex reaction and managed to get a snapshot of the dog only six feet behind the hare as they passed close by. The chase was a difficult one and the hare turned the dog more than a dozen times. Fox began to bark in frustration and I thought he had no chance of catching his fleeing prey; however, he pressed on, bringing the hare down in the open and somersaulting at the moment he connected with it. It was a memorable chase and only one hundred yards from where the car was parked.

A Moral Dilemma

The most difficult chase that I ever witnessed any dog make was in the month of September the following year. I was walking a section of the Southern Upland Way with a neighbour of mine from the street. We took Fox with us on the bus down to Moffat and planned to take three days to walk part of the route heading east from that Border town. We limited the stuff we had to carry to the absolute essentials, although I had the additional burden of carrying food for the dog. Of course there was always the chance of catching something along the way to replenish our rations.

Any rabbits that we did see at the start of our journey were usually in close proximity to grazing sheep, so that was a non-starter. On the second day we saw a fine-looking brown hare sunning itself half way up the hillside, watching us pass by. The dog also noticed it and stopped to gaze at the creature with great interest, rooted to the spot. Every so often the hare would twitch its ears almost like semaphore and the dog would let out a little whimper. When the hare decided to make a move from its seat, I let the dog go after it.

The hare had about eighty yards start and seemed in no hurry to get away from the dog. For the first part of the chase the hare seemed to canter effortlessly up towards the summit of the hill, with the dog following at full gallop and slowly closing the gap between them. Then the hare made a right turn and ran alongside the hill, maintaining the same distance from the dog. When the dog did start gaining on the hare, the hare changed its tack more frequently and began to jink at every opportunity. They ran up hill then down hill, covering some of the same ground they had been before.

This pattern continued for ten whole minutes and the chase became slower and slower. The pair were evenly matched, but I was convinced the dog would be the loser: the dog was running for his supper whilst the hare was running for its life. Then to my utter amazement the hare just suddenly stopped and sat still on the bare ground. The dog caught up with it and lay down beside it gasping for breath, unable to go any further. They were lying only two feet apart and had run themselves to a standstill.

I dumped my rucksack and ran uphill towards them, expecting the hare to recover and start running before I managed to reach the spot. It was a hot day and I was exhausted by the time I reached them. Neither the hare nor the dog moved; both were panting in the heat. I picked up the hare and quickly broke its neck, but I would be a liar if I said the deed hadn't bothered me. It was a moral dilemma: we had several pounds of fresh meat, but it seemed a dishonourable way of obtaining it.

A Painful Lesson

There was one particular location in the Pentland Hills where the white hares were numerous during the breeding season in the early spring. We never hunted them at that time of year but liked to watch them cavorting with each other, racing and chasing, still in their winter coats; sometimes we counted as many as twenty. The place was a smooth, rounded glacial valley between two steep, scree-sided hills. Anyone who had ever watched a dog chase a hare across a scree slope knew what a waste of effort the exercise was, because the dog would most likely slip and slide on the jagged stones and cut its feet badly. The hares were aware of these convenient escape routes and used them quite deliberately, benefiting from their lighter weight and well padded, furry feet.

It was a cold winter's day when I took the bus out to Balerno for some hare hunting with the dog in the hills. I had a couple of hours of daylight left before the sun went down and always enjoyed being in the hills by myself, often forgetting to tell anyone at home where I was going.

It was a long uphill slog after departing from the footpath and climbing up on to the tops to find where the hares were lying. On a windy day they could usually be found sheltering on the lee side of the hill in deep heather. I stopped to watch four kestrels hovering in a straight line alongside the first hill. I assumed that either two or three of them were getting flying lessons from a parent bird. I watched them through my field glasses and followed one of them down on to a clump of heather where it perched rather unsteadily.

Enter stage left, a red grouse: it appeared in my line of vision and knocked the little falcon clean off its perch. There were several other grouse concealed in the heather making a noisy racket with their 'go-back go-back go-back' calls. They had objected to the intrusion from above by the raptor family and were having none of it. One of the hovering kestrels stooped elegantly several times over the spot while its winded companion recovered and got airborne again and the four hawks drifted off around the blind side of the hill to find a safer place to hunt.

It didn't take long to get a few chases and I bagged two hares before the light began to fade. I was quite satisfied to call it a day and set off home. It was a long, tedious hike back down the hill to civilization and public transport; I was exhausted after striding through so much deep heather and took the most direct route down the biggest hill, down a steep, deep, scree-lined gully. This route turned out to be a big mistake; it would have been easier and safer to have followed one of the narrow sheep tracks that traversed the side of the hill to the bottom. I stumbled much of the way down and my legs gave way several times. The weight of the two hares in the rucksack didn't help my clumsy progress. I was anxious to get down off the hill before complete darkness, when I wouldn't be able to see where I was placing my feet.

Then I managed to get my lower leg stuck between two boulders and fell sideways; I was expecting to hear the sound of my leg snapping. The weight of the bag twisted my body around so that I fell forwards, hitting my chest against a sharp pointed rock. Agony would be the best description of the physical sensation that followed: the pain was almost unbearable. My knee was twisted and every breath that I took hurt my ribcage. I knew that I had cracked a couple of ribs. I managed to get the rucksack off my back and hauled my leg out from the fissure between the rocks. I lay on the ground gritting my teeth; my eyes were watering and tears were streaming down my face. The dog began to lick my salty face, and I was unable to move for about half an hour.

When I did get up, it was dark with no moon to see by. I was in a bad situation with a long way still to go. It would have been sensible to have dumped the hares and lightened my load, but for me that was not an option after all the effort the dog and I had gone to obtain them. The last few miles getting back to the town were murder and I was glad that I had the dog with me for company; he seemed to know that I was in distress. I had to take very short breaths to reduce the inflation of my lungs and the painful movement of my cracked ribs.

When I did finally get home late that evening I was advised by my better half to let her know where I was going on any future trips in case she had to organize a search for my lifeless body – but at least I hadn't returned from the hill empty-handed. I had to take a week off work to recover from my injuries.

Over the years I had experienced plenty of other painful injuries on my hunting trips, the commonest one being a sprained ankle when stalking game over rough uneven ground; nasty cuts to hands and legs from rusty barbed wire was another hazard. When I was out at night, hunting along the hedgerows, I always walked slowly with one hand extended in front of my face in case I got a thorn in the eye. One dark night I stooped beneath a spruce tree to pick up a woodpigeon that I had just shot from its roost and impaled myself just below the eye on a jagged upturned branch. I was lucky not to have been permanently blinded.

Skullduggery

We had an acquaintance who rented out a small cottage in the Highlands; the place was ideally positioned for walking and fishing and for our purposes, hunting with the dog. The immediate area was Forestry Commission land on both sides of the River Spey and the neighbouring landowners on the higher ground ran well keepered sporting estates for deer stalking and grouse shooting.

A Distinctive Head

One of our favourite walks was along the riverside through the birch and alder groves; the trees were relatively sparse, but provided us with sufficient cover and concealment from prying eyes. There were a few rabbits and hares inhabiting that stony ground and no sheep to worry about. As we made our way along the footpath we spotted a pair of roe deer grazing below a large, twin alder tree in the corner of a field next to the river bank. We saw them before they saw us and crouched down. The dog had also seen the pair. The distance from the tree was about seventy yards. I had my camera with me and guessed which way the deer were likely to run when they did see us. I pre-focused the camera on a spot about thirty yards away.

The dog ran forwards, almost reaching the grazing deer before they saw him. The two deer split up and ran in opposite directions and Fox followed the buck, which came towards us. I panned the camera and caught the action with a fast, pre-set shutter speed. The chase was short and the roebuck managed to give the dog the slip by weaving in and out of the trees before disappearing into a thicket. I was happy to capture the image on film and pleased with the photograph when I saw the result. The antlers on the buck were very distinctive and unlike any others that I had seen previously, being exceptionally long, curved and evenly matched.

By a strange coincidence we returned to the same spot the following year in the same month and after a short chase the dog did catch what could only have been the same buck in almost exactly the same place. We gralloched and skinned the deer beside the river and sent the offal floating downstream for the foxes to find on some shingle bank downriver in the shallows. There was little doubt in confirming that the buck was the same one, when we compared the skull to the photograph taken of the buck the previous year.

I was never interested in hunting for trophies to put on the wall, but I did have a small collection of animal and bird skulls that had been found over the years. Once I found a freshly killed badger, which had been killed by a car on a quiet country road. I hauled the unfortunate creature over to a nearby ditch and left it there, using a distinctive tree to mark the spot. About a year later I went back to retrieve what was a reasonably clean skull after letting nature to do the work for me.

An Evil-Smelling Prize

The largest mammal skull in my natural history collection was a little more problematic in obtaining. One weekend in the month of March we had a family outing to the seaside at Aberlady. The sun was shining and there was a mild southerly breeze with skylarks singing overhead. We stumbled across a large, dead grey seal marooned high on the sands. Downwind, the smell from this decaying monster was atrocious and overpowered the senses. I used a piece of driftwood to lever the jaw open and inspect the worn yellow teeth. This animal appeared to have lived a long natural life and had been ready to meet its maker.

I was keen on obtaining the skull for my collection, but I was with my wife and mother-in-law and the only cutting tool that I had with me was a miniature Swiss Army knife on a key ring, more appropriate for use as a tool for a manicure. The wind was blowing the sand in our faces and the stench from the decomposing flesh held together by tough, impenetrable sealskin was too much to bear and I had to admit defeat. I noticed that my mother-in-law didn't look too downhearted at the prospect of losing an opportunity to share her car with a grisly cadaver.

However, I couldn't sleep that night for thinking about the prize awaiting me on the shoreline.

Two days passed by and I knew I had to go back to that beach with the right tools for the job. I phoned my fishing pal and asked him about the state of the tides in relation to where the dead seal might be a couple of days later. He made a quick calculation from his tide timetable and told me where he thought the body might be. I took the day off work and went back to Aberlady on the bus with Fox. In my rucksack was a long-shafted hedging knife with a very sharp 10in blade, as well as a plastic bucket and several polythene bin bags.

My friend's estimate of where the animal was likely to be found was spot on. It was less than half a mile from its original resting place, but wedged amongst the rocks in a tangle of seaweed and flotsam and jetsam. The swollen body had breeched and it was difficult to tell the head from the tail. It took me half an hour's beachcombing to find a piece of timber that enabled me to lever the carcass out of the water, where I could work on the head. The stench was still foul, but at least the flesh came away from the skull much more easily than I had expected. I cleaned the skull as well as I could by rolling it in and out of the water. Next, I triple-bagged the head and put it into the plastic bucket; the smelly knife was also multi-wrapped and put back in the rucksack.

I hiked off the beach through the nature reserve, over the slippery wooden bridge and back to the bus stop. The bus coming from North Berwick was there in less than five minutes and I was soon on my way back to Edinburgh with my prize. I was very pleased with myself for a job well done and sat at the back of the bus stretched out. It was only then that I noticed the awful smell emanating from the bucket wedged between my feet; it was truly evil. Two passengers sitting in front of me, muttered to each other and moved away, further up the bus. I opened both windows nearest to me and sat rather uncomfortably for the rest of the journey, expecting to be ejected from the bus. When I got home I placed the bucket at the bottom of the garden at the furthest point from the house.

In the morning I phoned the Department of Zoology at Edinburgh University and asked for advice about cleaning the seal skull. The woman I spoke to was very helpful and told me that my enquiry was very well timed as the department had just received the gift of a hind leg from a recently deceased brown bear at the zoo. The departmental technician was already making preparations to boil the leg down in the car park at the rear of their building. Later that afternoon I hung the smelly bucket containing the seal's head from the handlebars of my bike and cycled up to the zoology department, where I had arranged to meet one of the lecturers.

Long before I got there, I could smell the wonderful scent of cooked meat on the wind; initially I assumed it was coming from the kitchen behind the refectory, but when I arrived at the car park I saw a huge steaming metal cauldron suspended on bricks with a gas fire underneath it. There were two people standing nearby so I walked over to introduce myself. Pat, the lecturer, whom I had spoken to on the phone, was a tall, handsome, dark-haired woman with a firm handshake. She introduced me to 'Wee Jimmy' the technician, who was attending to the boiling of the bear bones. 'Why don't you pop the skull in with the bear?' suggested Pat. I was happy to oblige. Jimmy flipped the hinged lid over, and I slipped the head from the polybag into the bubbling stew.

It was a couple of days before the skull was ready for collection and I was advised to bleach it for about a week to remove all traces of the remaining unpleasant oily fragrance that was still lingering in the bone. I was very grateful to Wee Jimmy and gave him a few cans of beer for his trouble.

More Hares

My friend Dave, from the Borders, got himself a new lurcher bitch called Moss. She was a twelve-month-old, racy-looking dark brindle with white forelegs. We arranged a hunting trip in the hills for our dogs to get acquainted with each other. The first hare got up in front of the dogs and Fox seemed content to stay behind Moss as they gave chase. Moss caught the hare, making a very nice pick-up, and retrieved to Dave's hand. This was her first kill and Dave was very pleased with her.

I couldn't figure out if Fox was being an officer and a gentleman or whether he was interested in staying behind the young bitch for other reasons. However, Fox's mood didn't last long because he took the next two rabbits and then the next two hares. The second hare, Moss had been chasing first, but then Fox joined in and barged into her, giving her a 'dead' leg, leaving her whimpering and out of the action. Fox turned that fleeing hare half a dozen times and made a clean kill. We found two fresh peregrine kills, both woodpigeons; one of them was plucked clean and headless, but the breast meat was still intact.

As we headed back, we walked along a short section of the Southern Upland Way and stopped at the Twin Law Cairns to take a rest. Inside one of the cairns was an old biscuit tin that contained a visitor's book full of names and comments from long-distance hikers who were walking from coast to coast. The most recent name in the book was a neighbour of Dave's from Innerleithen, who had passed that way on the very same day. Many rude comments and witticisms in the book were aimed at the television personality Jimmy McGregor, who had done a series of programmes about his walk from 'sea to shining sea'. Several hikers had made references to their suspicions that Jimmy had done most of his journey in a BBC helicopter.

14
A Very Black Day

Diary Extract

30th August, Edinburgh.

Fox was killed last night during the Festival Firework Display. The poor dog had begun to show a terrible fear that had increased with age, whenever he heard distant shots or loud bangs and was afraid of fireworks, even in the safety of the house with the family around him and the radio turned up. I decided to take him out of town to the ski slope at Hillend for the duration of the firework display. I drove up the hill about 10.30 and parked in the car park at the top and walked over the hill to the T-Wood on the golf course. Fox was quite perky, scenting downwind of the trees where the rabbit warrens were. It was the kind of still cold night that sound carried. There was a loud boom from the distant castle esplanade to signal the start of the display and Fox ran off into the darkness towards the wood. I assumed that the frightened dog had instinctively run for cover amongst the trees. The firework display continued for about half an hour and I whistled to let him know that I was still in the same place to reassure him. When everything went quiet, I expected him to come running back to me as he had always done in the past. I could hear a dog barking somewhere high in the hills and it sounded like Fox. I continued whistling for more than half an hour before I began to feel a sick feeling in the pit of my stomach. He had never done this before. I went back to the car in case he was waiting for me there, then I paced round the hill shouting his name and whistling, until my lips were numb and by that time mine was the only vehicle left in the car park.

About 1 a.m. I watched the headlights of a car making its way slowly up the hill towards me. It parked nearby and a young couple got out. I went over to them.

'Have you seen a black dog around here?' I asked the man.

'Yes, we have,' he told me.

The young woman held up a dog collar. I recognised it.

My heart sank. I knew that instant that my dog was dead.

They had found Fox lying on the road near Howgate which was three miles away. He had been hit by a car and had died instantly. The young man had already phoned my wife from his mobile at the roadside, after seeing our home number on the dog tag, so my wife knew about the dog's fate before I did. She told them where I could be found. The young couple took me back to where they had left the dog on a grassy bank beside the road. There was a pool of blood and broken glass in the middle of the road and the vehicle that had been involved in the collision had not stopped, which seemed a bit callous to me, but I suppose the driver must have been in shock. I had prepared myself on the short drive to the accident scene for what I was going to see. It made me feel sick when I saw Fox; his head was undamaged but his body was missing a lot of hair around the rib cage, which was bloody. He appeared to have extensive internal injuries and there seemed little doubt that he had been killed instantly, which gave me some relief. His spirit seemed to have left his body. He looked unfamiliar when I looked into his open eyes. The young couple asked me if I wanted to take the dog home with me but I decided against it. The three of us lifted his body, which was surprisingly heavy and carried it into a nearby wood to lay it to rest and let nature take its course. It seemed an appropriate resting place for our faithful hound. He was nine years of age. The drive back home was a blur for me and anyone who has ever lost a dog knows the pain and anguish that is left behind. The sudden unexpected death of a relatively young and very fit dog compounded the grief. It was difficult afterwards seeing Fox's collar and lead hanging from the hook in the kitchen. The house was so empty without him and the well meaning remarks from friends and neighbours gave me a lump in the throat while I was coming to terms with our loss. Whenever I went out for a walk alone in the woods, I could sense the ghost of the dog beside me.

As I wrote to my friend Dave, the following day with the sad news, my watering eyes stained the ink on the page.

Life Goes On...

My solitary walks in the favourite places where I had hunted with Fox over the past nine years were bittersweet. In the month of November I went to the nearby ruined castle to collect some fruit from the blackthorn bushes for making sloe gin. The ground was frozen and very slippery, but the trip was well worth it. I had never seen so much fruit before and I got all I needed from one single thorny bush. There were fresh roe tracks on the softer ground near the burn.

Fierce Little Hunters

On my way back to the castle on the north slope I heard a rabbit screaming in terror amongst the undergrowth close to the path. There were a few minutes silence and then the screaming started again. I came across the victim, a large rabbit with a stoat attached to the back of its neck. Every time the rabbit moved, the stoat bit harder and the rabbit began to scream again, rolling over and over but unable to escape. I was standing only twenty feet away, downwind and didn't want to interfere. As the rabbit lay still, paralysed by fear, the stoat released its grip and used its front paw to remove the rabbit fur from its mouth. It then gripped its victim's neck again and the screaming continued.

The drama lasted for about ten minutes until I could stand it no longer. I clapped my hands and the stoat withdrew very slowly, looking back at the rabbit, which was lying on its side, very still but still breathing. Eventually the stoat disappeared into a hole at the base of an ash tree and I killed the rabbit with a single blow from my stick. It was a myxie one and was slightly underweight.

I had seen something similar before, many years previously, on an old drove road in the Border hills above Peebles and on that occasion the poor rabbit had already had half of its neck muscle eaten by a stoat and was still alive. The stoat fled from its victim when it saw me approaching and watched from the safety of a nearby dyke where it weaved in and out of the stones, peeping out with its beady eyes. I killed the rabbit and took its hindquarters for my own supper, leaving the rest for the hungry stoat. Sometimes it was hard not to interfere when you witnessed how cruel nature could be in the raw.

Later that same day, I walked along the banks of the River Tweed below the Manor Bridge and spotted a sleeping duck downstream at a bend in the river. The bird was on a strip of sand below the overhanging bank and I thought that it might be fun to stalk it from above; I succeeded in getting directly above the bird without waking it. The duck was a beautiful female goosander, sleeping with its beak under its wing and oblivious to any danger. I slid from the bank, landing with my feet astride the bird and grabbed it with both hands. The duck awoke and appeared quite calm under the circumstances.

I noticed a small metal swivel in the side of its beak, attached to a length of fishing line and a large trout hook, which had penetrated the lower bill at the tip. The duck's tongue had been trapped by the line and looked very dry. I managed to cut the line free with my penknife and discovered that its tongue had been almost severed by the fine nylon line. The bird was underweight with a prominent keelbone, but otherwise its plumage and general condition seemed to be okay. The brown head was particularly beautiful, with a punk-style tuft at the back, above a long and elegant neck. The goosander's eyes had a soft, gentle look about them and remained focused on the river as I carried her downstream. After about ten minutes she appeared to regain strength and began to struggle.

It seemed like a good idea to let her take her chances on the river, so I put her down in the long grass beside the water on an easy slope and watched her waddle down into the river. She began to preen herself, splashing water over her back with flapping wings and then swam for the far bank with her outstretched neck flat upon the water. On reaching the far bank, she stopped in a pool where the slow current was eddying backwards and tucked her head under her wing and slept for twenty minutes. On waking, she swam into the main current and started to fish.

Guerilla Warfare

I was missing the companionship of the dog and walks in the country were not the same without him. I was pretty much addicted to hunting as a way of life so I went back to using my rifle to obtain fresh meat. When I had the use of a car I drove around the quiet roads in the Borders in the early morning and did reconnaissance. There were many well keepered shooting estates in the region and there was always the risk of being caught when shooting pheasants from the vehicle.

The best time for potting pheasants illegally was just before the official shooting season opened when their numbers were at a maximum. The birds hadn't yet experienced the beaters thrashing through the woods and the salvos of lead shot from the line of guns waiting for them as they broke cover from what had been a safe haven only the day before. On the down side, landowners and gamekeepers were especially diligent at that time of year and extreme caution was needed to lessen the risk of being caught. Luck was also a factor. Given a choice I shot the cock birds because the white ring on their necks gave a clearer target for the open sight on my air rifle.

When shooting from the car, it was best to have the nearside front passenger's window wound down, to be able to shoot without poking the gun barrel outside the vehicle. I kept the rifle on the back seat under a rug. An ex-squaddie that I knew had cut out the back panel from his glove compartment so that he could hide his deer rifle under the bonnet; the weapon was supported by a home-made bracket which enabled him easy access. He had served in Northern Ireland and had seen the same trick used by the IRA when he himself had been the target for a sniper.

I hunted from the car quite successfully, never shooting at birds near a bend in the road or a place where I was unable to see an approaching vehicle. Between thirty and forty yards was an ideal distance for me to shoot from. Cocking the under-lever rifle was awkward whilst sitting in the driver's seat, because of the confined space. I kept the lead pellets in my top pocket for easy reach when reloading. Sometimes it was possible to shoot two pheasants in quick succession, before the second bird became aware of the danger.

I was getting less agile at that time and was unable to vault a fence with the grace and dexterity of my youth. Climbing a barbed-wire fence into a stubble field beside the road became a challenge and I was caught by the seat of my pants on several occasions. This was not an ideal situation when there was a dead bird flapping about all over the field and a vehicle might drive past at any moment.

I became a little over-confident on some of those pheasant-shooting expeditions and was lucky not to have been caught in the act.

Neighbourhood Watch

The reason I gave up on that guerrilla-style, wide-ranging hunting activity was because of an incident that occurred later in the year in the month of December, during severe weather conditions. I began to explore further south into the Border region and knew several places where pheasants presented themselves as convenient targets in sufficient numbers. On that particular morning I got a relatively late start because of the winter solstice. There had been plenty of snow on the Lammermuir Hills, but the narrow, single-track road between Gifford and Duns was passable due to the efforts of a snow plough the day before, although there was still sheet ice where the snow had compacted and the grit had been ineffective.

I drove across the hills at a slow and careful pace, especially round the unfenced hairpin bends, where a skidding car would most likely end up on its roof in a snowdrift far below. Beyond the hills to the south, where the landscape levelled out, I began to see a few plump pheasants strutting stiffly about the snowy fields. I slowed down at the top of a small rise when I spotted four pheasants sitting equally spaced along the top of a five-bar gate, like targets in a fairground. I pulled over and stopped. The birds were only about thirty feet away, sitting ducks. I loaded the rifle and wound the passenger window down, checking the rear-view mirror to see that the road was clear.

As I put the gun to my shoulder I glanced down at the road below and saw a Land Rover approaching at a brisk pace. I put the safety catch on the rifle and quickly stuffed the gun under the rug on the back seat. I took the handbrake off the car and drove slowly down the hill towards the oncoming vehicle. I waved to the driver as we passed each other; he glowered at me and didn't return my greeting. It was a safe bet that I had been rumbled by the red-faced man in the tweed hat and drove speedily away from the area, keen to put some distance between us.

About five miles away I began pheasant-spotting again. As I drove round a bend in the road, there was a Land Rover parked on the grass verge with two men standing beside it; one of them was speaking into a two-way radio. I slowed down as I passed them and we got a good look at each other. The man who wasn't using the radio jotted something down in a notebook, which I assumed was my car registration number.

What I seemed to have blundered into that morning was a gamekeepers' 'neighbourhood watch' exercise. It was a Sunday and most certainly not a shooting day in Scotland. I realized that I was probably going to have to change my plans and abort the trip if I didn't want those tweed-clad vigilantes after me. However, temptation is a powerful thing and I wasn't quite ready to call it a day. I began to wonder if my suspicions were unfounded and that I was just being paranoid. I convinced myself that the two Land Rovers that I had seen had no connection with each other and continued on my journey, now heading north.

It was another five miles before I felt safe enough to look out for more pheasants to shoot. I came to a small hamlet at a crossroads, made a left turn and drove up towards the reservoir along a track that I knew to be a dead end. At the end of the track I got out of the car to stretch my legs and admire the snowy winter landscape and beautiful pink sky. There were hundreds of mallards on the big reservoir and the water was dead calm. But there was very little heat in the low sun and it was too cold to stand around for long.

I drove back down the track to the crossroads and noticed two Landrovers that had not been there before; they were parked beside each other and the drivers were in conversation, but they were not the same men that I had seen earlier. I waved, but they didn't wave back. I turned left at the crossroads in the direction of Gifford and drove up a long, steep, straight hill for about a mile before spotting a fine cock pheasant sitting on a dyke beside the road with its fine plumage shining like polished bronze in the sun. I managed to stop exactly level with the bird, an easy shot, less than twenty feet away. The passenger window was already down and I took careful aim.

The pellet snapped its neck and the bird somersaulted backwards over the dyke. In my haste to retrieve the pheasant, I left the rifle jammed upright against the passenger seat and got out of the car, leaving the driver's door open. I could hear the bird flapping behind the dyke. When I looked back down the road I saw one of the Land Rovers approaching, less than a hundred yards away.

A Desperate Situation

I was in a bad situation. I knew the bird would have to be abandoned and that I would need to be quick to get back into the car and conceal the rifle, with only seconds to spare. The Land Rover overtook my stationary vehicle and pulled in front of me; I was sitting with the engine running and both windows down. The driver, a big middle-aged man in tweeds, climbed out of his vehicle and came striding towards me very aggressively, leaving his door wide open, partially blocking the narrow road ahead. He had an angry expression on his face. I could still hear the pheasant flapping in its death throes behind the dyke, and realized that he would also be able to hear it unless he was totally deaf.

I decided in that split second to make my escape. I revved the engine and swerved round the man, driving up the steep grassy banking on the right-hand side of the road. My nearside wing mirror brushed against his open door and flipped back without breaking, and I was on my way, but it was a long haul up that hill. I watched the man in my rear-view mirror as he got back into his Land Rover and came after me. I drove as fast as I dared with so much ice on the road, and left him way behind, feeling some relief at the increasing distance between us. I was desperate to escape and was prepared to take more risks than he was, in his efforts to catch me. As I neared the summit of the Lammermuir Hills, I could see no sign of my pursuer behind me and was convinced that he had given up.

I slowed down and began to drive at a less life-threatening pace, more appropriate to the icy conditions. That morning I had not seen any other vehicle in those hills, but half a mile ahead I did see one, a family saloon, driving in the same direction as me, towards Gifford. It was driving ridiculously slowly, even allowing for the poor road conditions. I assumed that the driver was probably an elderly person who was perhaps being over-cautious. However, when I did manage to get a look at the driver, it was my turn to be concerned. He looked like a pub bouncer, and there was a second man, ducked down in the back seat using a two-way radio.

It seemed likely that I had been under observation, and the vehicle now in front of me was effectively boxing me in until the Land Rover behind me was able to catch up. I knew the road ahead well, and there was only one possible place that I was going to be able to overtake that car without the driver's cooperation, and I was going to have to force my way past him at the earliest opportunity. The driver was watching me constantly in his rear-view mirror.

When we got to a high point on the moor where the road was marked by a five-bar gate beside a cattlegrid, I put my foot down on the accelerator and squeezed past the car in front by bumping up a peat banking that was covered with snow. Fortunately I didn't get bogged down and managed to maintain traction without skidding into the fence post.

The driver of the other car certainly hadn't expected me to get past him, and came after me, driving much faster than he had been previously. I took off at speed towards Gifford, and it was a white-knuckle ride on some of those bends. The car behind me was unable to keep up and I lost sight of him after about a mile. I thought there was a good chance of being caught on the Gifford road by other parties involved in this *Crimewatch* operation, so I turned south again at a fork in the road which led towards the reservoir; it seemed like a safer bet to try the Abbey St Bathans road where I was able to turn east along a narrow farm road that came out on the A1 near Dunbar.

I had considered stopping and hiding the rifle somewhere along the way, but the snow on the ground would have made the place obvious. It would also have meant a return journey to the scene of the crime. The drive through the hills along the narrow winding road passing the farms was less suicidal and I didn't see any other vehicle until I joined the traffic on the busy main road; then I watched a police car with flashing lights coming the other way, indicating to turn right on the farm road that I had just left.

That was the last time that I ever shot pheasants from a car.

Good News

Several months later I got a call from my friend Dave. Spey, his black lurcher bitch, was pregnant. We had always intended to breed from Fox and Spey and keep the bloodline going because they were both exceptional hunters. Unfortunately we left it too late and missed a golden opportunity to produce some fine pups. However, Dave was enthusiastic about Spey's forthcoming litter and was quite right about my keenness to adopt one of her pups.

The sire was a brindle lurcher dog called Paddy, who had a fairly relaxed attitude when coupling with Spey. The mating had taken place in the road in full view of the local residents, including the kids who were playing in the street. Apparently Paddy was keen as mustard and had mounted the bitch immediately with no qualms about waiting for a formal introduction. When he had finished his job he took a short break and scoffed a few chips from a greasy newspaper poke that had been discarded in the street. After his well earned snack he mounted Spey a second time, demonstrating his prowess as a canine stud.

Dave invited us down to his house to see the pups when they were just a couple of days old. They were kept in a comfortable purpose-built heated shed in the back garden in a big nest of golden straw. There were nine pups in total; three were brindles and the rest black with some white marks on them, mainly on their chests. Three were males. Before they were even born Dave had told me that I could have the pick of the litter. He knew that I had been devastated by the death of Fox. I wanted a male pup and I preferred a dark brindle, which was just about the best camouflage in any terrain.

A New Pup

Eight weeks passed before we returned to Dave's place to choose our pup and take him home with us. I had already decided on the name when I had first been informed of Spey's pregnancy. The pup was to be called Finn. I had tried out the name for sound by shouting it out loud from a hilltop during a solitary walk in the Borders after making sure I was alone except for the sheep. It was a familiar name in Ireland.

We watched the pups cavorting about the garden and noticed that one of the brindled males seemed to prefer his own company, isolating himself in a den under the garden hedge. It was most certainly not from a lack of self-confidence, because he saw off any of his brothers or sisters who attempted to disturb his peace. The pup seemed to be demonstrating the character of an alpha male. After about an hour of watching the pups at play, we decided that the little brindle dog in the hedge would be going home with us.

Finn turned out to be an independent little chap and spent the first night alone in his box bed in the kitchen without waking us up. Of course the family were up bright and early to mop the floor, play with the pup and give him his breakfast. We introduced him to the postman on that very first morning and ensured a swift bonding with the Royal Mail. Once he had had the appropriate jabs from the vet we took him out to meet all the other pooches on the hill. He was a confident young dog and didn't seem to be fazed by much.

It was fun observing Finn's exploration of his increasing new world. The neighbours in our street made a fuss of him whenever we took him out and he socialized very quickly. One morning we led him up the street and approached Jinx, an elderly tabby cat, who was enjoying a snooze on the pavement in front of her house in the warm sun. The pup strained at the lead and made a beeline for the sleeping cat, barking as loud as he could, to exert his authority. The cat slowly raised her sleepy head and gave the insolent pup a look of utter contempt. The dog barked again, failing once more to intimidate that regal moggie.

As Finn approached the cat even closer, with his nose just inches from her body, he received what could only be described as a punch on the nose. The cat's claws had not been extended and it was just a warning to the cocky young pup that she had no intention of letting a whippersnapper like him intimidate her in what was her kingdom. I have to say that I did admire that cat for her cool demeanour in the face of adversity, however junior her would-be assailant.

Strange to say, the pair became very fond of each other and remained friends for life, much to the relief of both their owners. The dog's fondness for felines did not extend to any of the other cats living on the street and he pursued them at every opportunity with the utmost vigour.

The Pup Becomes a Hunter

Finn made his first contribution to the meat larder when he was just ten months old. His early success in the hunting field was witnessed by my young friend Scott, who was now a father himself, with his two-year-old toddler called Sam in tow. The place we chose to hunt was a great place for rabbits and ideal for a keen young pup to try out his skills. The chasing zone was an overgrown weedy plateau about five hundred yards square, above an in-filled quarry, which was where most of the warrens were situated. The rough cover provided the rabbits with some security from predators such as foxes and buzzards, so the trick was to ambush them in the open, giving the dog an opportunity to catch them before they reached cover.

Often when a young dog caught his first rabbit he was inclined to hold on to it without biting and it wasn't unusual for a rabbit to escape unharmed and live to run another day. Finn, however, seemed to be made of sterner stuff and knew instinctively how to secure a meal in the wilds. The rabbit he caught was killed with a single bite and little Sam wandered over to take a look, pointing down at its lifeless body. 'Noo Noo,' he said. I asked Scott what he meant. 'Oh, he has a toy rabbit at home instead of a teddy bear and calls it Noo Noo.' I hoped the incident wasn't going to have a detrimental effect of Sam's future development.

When Finn met his first squirrel, it was a case of the biter being bitten. As we walked through our local park, the pup raced along a wooden fence and jumped up to grab a squirrel that was running along the top rail. The nutkin was very agile and nipped the dog, leaving him yelping in pain with a bloody nose: Finn's rubbery black nose had been pierced through the septum and he was not a happy dog. The squirrel ran up the nearest tree and gave forth with an angry chatter from a safe perch.

Following that traumatic event, the dog began to hunt squirrels with a vengeance; he seemed to pursue them with a pathological hatred. Whenever he did catch up with one, he grabbed it and shook it, like a terrier with a rat and I never saw him bitten again. I wasn't concerned about his squirrel-hunting activities unless some unsuspecting woodland walker reacted badly to the shocking spectacle. Many cat owners that I knew excused their pets for killing songbirds, by telling me that it was only nature taking its course.

From a practical stance, thinning out the destructive grey squirrel was providing a service to the community. Their numbers had increased to such an extent that city houses were being damaged by their nesting activities, as well as the plants and bulbs in the gardens. One of my friends had two resident squirrels in his attic, which caused serious damage to the fabric of the house. They had removed slates and chewed timbers to gain access to the roof space and then made a cosy nest from the insulation material between the cross-beams. Many of the young sycamore trees in the local woods had been severely ring barked and were in a sorry state. Nesting birds also suffered from squirrel predation, and their numbers were being seriously depleted by them. At least I was still able to sell the squirrel tails that I collected, to the fishing shop for fly tying.

Finn Earns His Keep

As Finn grew in size and experience, we took him further afield to hunt for his supper. We rented a cottage in the Highlands for a few days, which was on the shores of Loch Inch. On a hike above Kingussie, we took the dog up on to the high ground, scrambling across a boulder-strewn, heather-covered mountainside and within five minutes he caught two white hares. The rocky landscape there seemed a little dangerous for chasing and we were relieved to get the dog back off the hill unscathed and undetected.

On our route back down the hill we had to pass a gamekeeper's cottage and we had no idea if our hunting activities had been observed by anyone from the estate. My wife walked about half a mile ahead carrying the game in her rucksack, leaving the dog with me, to attract less attention to herself. Anyone who saw her would hopefully assume that she was a solitary walker and I was happy to follow behind and stroll innocently past the keeper's cottage with nothing to declare if I was stopped and searched.

When we got back home to Edinburgh I made a big hare curry and invited friends round for a meal the following day. It took me most of the evening to prepare the curry from scratch and I simmered it for three hours. There was a delicious spicy aroma permeating the house and a taste of the sauce assured me that it was a good one. Just before midnight, I removed the big pan from the cooker and left it on the draining board by the sink to cool overnight. The dog had been fed and was curled up fast asleep in his bed next to the radiator in the kitchen. I went to bed happy with a job well done and slept like a log.

In the morning, I wandered downstairs for a leisurely breakfast and as I walked into the kitchen, the dog walked out, glancing upwards towards the ceiling. There was a strange smell in the room: it was gassy, blue and farty. I went over to check my curry in the pan by the sink: it was empty, all gone, except for a ring of sauce around the inside at the bottom. That vanished meal had been intended to feed ten people.

There was only one suspect and he had just left the scene of the crime. I followed him into the living room to where he was hiding under the table and hauled him out. His stomach was swollen and rock hard. What amazed me was the dog's capacity to eat all that spicy meat following his own huge supper. I wondered if he had scoffed it all in one go, or had done it in stages.

His preference for spicy foods remained undiminished by the experience. Chips were another favourite food of Finn's, a taste I imagine he had inherited through his father's genes.

Early Training

Whenever we got a new pup we made sure that part of its training was to discourage it from disturbing birds' nests on the ground and this extended to chicks and ducklings. Our local pond had limited nesting opportunities for ducks, and the bullying coots always seemed to secure the premium sites under willow trees around the water's edge. The moorhens were moderately successful in obtaining the secondary sites and the small island in the middle of the pond was lorded over by an aggressive pair of mute swans. The cob hunted down any ducklings on the pond and drowned them by holding them under the water. Most of the mallards had taken to nesting far away from the pond on a steep hillside under the gorse bushes, where they were at risk from foxes, weasels and stoats.

One sunny May morning I watched a mallard duck leading her eight newly hatched, day-old ducklings in single file down to the pond through a field below the woods. When she got to the bottom corner of the field, she flapped up on to the dyke and quacked repeatedly to encourage the young ones to follow her. There were no gaps in the wall and it was too high for them to get over. The ducklings were panicking and running along the bottom of the wall; some of them doubled back the way they had come.

It was one of those occasions where I felt it was necessary to intervene. I climbed into the field and with the help of the bemused dog, rounded them up into the corner, where I was able to pick each one of them up and place it on the other side of the wall. The mother duck was making a great deal of noise while this was going on. When she was reunited with her flock, she waddled down the footpath towards the pond with Finn and myself as an escort and we watched them tumble into the pond and paddle speedily away from the side.

The birds in my own garden didn't always fare so well. For three weeks I watched a tiny wren build a beautiful domed nest in the clematis beside my back door; it even took a few cotton strands from our washing line for the nest interior. As we sat in the garden the bird made discreet little flights along the fence and hedge to its feeding ground along the burn at the end of the garden. Unfortunately the bird was killed when one of those flights was intercepted by a black and white cat belonging to one of our neighbours. We didn't disturb the nest for several weeks until we were sure the victim had been our wren. The nest contained a clutch of eight cold, unhatched tiny white eggs.

Night Shooting

Within the city limits, not far from where I lived, we had unexpected visitors one late autumn. A group of fifteen pheasants had moved into the area, attracted by a turnip field in the green belt. They fed on the 'neeps' during the late afternoon until the light failed and then slowly made their way through a hedge into a sheltered glen where they flapped up to roost in the tops of the hawthorn trees. I watched them from a hill opposite and noted that their movements were timed like clockwork.

I was anxious to make use of that fresh game larder on my doorstep and started planning to bag a few birds. Using an air rifle to shoot a large bird in the dark was out of the question, as the fine mesh of twigs on a hawthorn tree could so easily deflect a single pellet aimed at a bird's neck. Heavy artillery was therefore needed for the job, and that meant a shotgun. Unfortunately the only one that I had access to at that time was a twelve bore, a very loud weapon to be using within the city and containing far too many lead pellets to be of much use at close range. My solution was to wait until conditions were right before I attempted to shoot one of the pheasants with my noisy blunderbuss.

I walked up to the roost on several evenings, without a weapon, purely to observe the birds' behaviour. I discovered that if the newly settled birds were disturbed too soon, in the grey light, they tended to panic and one would set the others off and they would explode out of the trees with the cock birds crowing blue murder. When I waited until the sky was darker but I could still just about see, the birds reacted quite differently: they were alert, following my movements below with interest, but they remained on their perches.

I waited until we had gale-force winds and driving rain before I ventured out at night with murder in my heart and timed my arrival at the roost so that the remaining light in the sky was just enough for me to see by. The dog had been keen to go with me but I had no idea how he would react to a loud gunshot close by and the memory of my late previous sadly lamented dog was still fresh in my mind. Finn had shown no distress when he had heard fireworks, but I wanted to be sure.

He was whining at the door as I set off from the house with the shotgun under my jacket in two parts. I took only one cartridge with me, in case I was tempted to fire more than one shot, I guessed it would be difficult for a person to pin-point the exact spot of an isolated bang heard in those conditions, unless they were very close. I managed to move around under several of the roost trees before deciding which bird to shoot at. I wanted a target with the head and the neck visible against the sky. I knew that if I wanted to end up with something edible after shooting a bird at such close range, then I would have to aim above the head and hope that a few pellets on the outer pattern of the spray would hit the mark.

I put the gun to my shoulder very slowly; the pheasant above was aware of my movements and I saw its head moving sideways, watching me. I squeezed the trigger and fired. The noise was deafening, louder than I had anticipated, but the bird came crashing down beside me with a thud on the ground, stone dead. I could hear the other birds nearby flying off in all directions. From what I could see of the cock pheasant in the dark, there seemed to be very little damage to the body. With the bird in the bag I sat quietly and listened; the wind was bending the bare branches on the trees, but there were no other sounds. I was concerned about walking through the park to get home in case I met anyone who had heard the shot. Sometimes there were late night dog walkers about, but I was in luck that night and got home without meeting anyone.

Finn came running to meet me when he heard the key in the door, and followed me into the kitchen poking his nose into the game bag. When I tipped out the still warm pheasant he nuzzled it with great interest. I skinned the bird and discovered that it had been hit by only three pellets, two in the head and one in the neck. At least I knew that the method of aiming was the right one.

It was a fortnight before I returned to the roost to try my luck again and this time I took the dog with me. He had become very excited when he saw me getting the gun ready and seemed anxious not to miss out. When we left the house, he strained at the lead and pulled me all the way to the park. I kept him on the leash until we got to the roost, in case he went off rabbiting by himself in the dark. The birds were still in the same trees and I positioned myself for a clear shot. Bang! Down came the bird and off went the dog in the opposite direction. Poor Finn had got a big fright when he heard the loud bang and I was worried about him. But he came back a few minutes later, approaching me very cautiously – and when he got wind of the bloody pheasant on the ground, his fear of the bang seemed to subside and he sniffed at the bird with great interest.

The following week I went back to the roost for a third time; the dog went crazy when he saw me with the gun and seemed to know where we were going. He waited at the door whining and wagging his tail furiously. Once again I got a swift tow through the park to the hunting grounds. At the roost, Finn backed off when he saw me getting ready to shoot a pheasant and stood well back. I knew he was feeling nervous about the coming bang. When I did shoot, the pheasant came down heavily at my feet – and as I stooped over to pick it up, I was knocked over by the dog as he crashed into my back to get at the bird. He picked it up and started to run around with it. This behaviour was most unusual for him and he had certainly never been an enthusiastic retriever in the past.

On the fourth visit to the roost, the dog made himself very useful, because the bird that I shot came crashing down through the branches and landed on its feet running. Finn was after it in seconds and managed to grab it before it disappeared in the darkness into a bramble thicket.

By the time the season was over, I had managed to get nine of those pheasants with just nine cartridges, before my conscience got the better of me with thoughts of conservation. Of course it was common sense to leave some breeding stock for the future. There was only one night when I had a problem and that was when the single cartridge I had taken with me turned out to be a dud and didn't fire. After that I always carried two.

I was always careful leaving the roost after shooting, sitting down for half an hour and then taking the long route home, avoiding the wooden bridge over the burn, which would have been an obvious place for an ambush by the local constabulary.

Woodcock

A bird that has always fascinated me is the woodcock. When I was a kid I came across a nest at the foot of a tree on a private estate. I marvelled at the four beautiful eggs, their points turned inwards and so well camouflaged against the brown leaves. It was only because the bird flew off directly in front of me that I found the nest.

On another occasion I witnessed another noteworthy incident: I was walking along a narrow path in a damp wood during the early summer when a woodcock flew up from under my feet, only inches away. I could see quite clearly that this bird was carrying a chick, gripped firmly in both feet. I had heard of woodcock carrying their young away from danger, but was very pleased to see the evidence for myself.

Late one summer evening I found a dead, still warm woodcock by the kerbside in an Edinburgh city street. The Grange area south of the city was a leafy suburb and provided ideal conditions for those mainly night-feeding birds. I assumed the victim had been killed by a passing vehicle as it had jinked out of one of the gardens to cross the road.

One very severe winter, when the ground had been frozen for about three days, I was walking towards the woods near to my allotment and noticed a crow sitting on a low branch in a sycamore tree not far from the path. From its behaviour I suspected mischief and went to investigate the cause. Below the tree, sitting quietly on the frozen, icy ground, was a woodcock, its camouflage quite useless.

I approached it, expecting it to fly off at any moment and was surprised to be standing only feet away. In the snow nearby I could see where the bird had unsuccessfully attempted to thrust its long beak through the snow and ice to find food, but the ground was solid. I picked it up quite easily and could feel the keelbone through its emaciated body. I wrapped my scarf around it and started home with my dog Finn, who didn't seem too happy with his shortened walk.

What to feed it on was my main concern. The compost heap was frozen solid, so I couldn't get the obvious worms and grubs that were needed. I decided on a tin of dog food mixed with egg yolk and with the help of my wife, my daughter and a single chopstick, we managed to force feed the bird and gave it plenty of water. The long beak made things difficult to begin with, but we became more confident as our patient seemed resolved to be helped. Immediately after feeding, the bird was put into a large cardboard box, with shredded newspaper and water to drink; the box was then put into a dark, cool room where it was left in peace. We fed the bird about every four hours and as late into the night as was feasible, to match its natural feeding pattern.

After two days there was a marked improvement and our frisky bird ran round the skirting board in the kitchen and along the full length of our bemused dog's back, up the tail and down the nose. Fortunately, the dog behaved well under provocation. On the third day, the bird flew up to the ceiling and round the kitchen, piercing our polyball lampshade with its slender bill. On the third evening I was happy with the woodcock's bodyweight and also with the weather, which was beginning to thaw, so I took him back up to the woods where I had found him. I placed him gently under a beech tree and left him in the darkness among the leaves.

Two days later, Finn flushed a pair of woodcock near to the release area and they circled above. One of them looked fairly dishevelled, so I suppose it could have been ours. I've always had a special affection for woodcock since that time.

15
Life is Sweet

A Highland Paradise

We had young friends that lived on the west coast of Scotland in a small cottage with magnificent views. They were surrounded by high, snow-capped mountains on three sides and overlooked a sea loch to the south where the incoming sea trout could be caught on rod and line from the shore at the flood tide. Their modest stone cottage had been built on a steep slope and was reached by a narrow, single-track road that snaked upwards to a right-hand bend, before levelling out and running parallel to the road below, along the shoreline.

There was a woodshed at the back of the house and a garden on three sides, with fruit trees, a vegetable plot and free-ranging ducks that roamed about the place, doing good work by eating the slugs and snails that preyed on the vegetables. The red and gold sunsets there were wonderful to behold, like another planet; and the stillness and silence of the place at the end of the day was truly awesome. Simon and his French wife Audrey were living in a Highland paradise. They had one child, a three-year-old boy called Silas and another on the way.

The weather was hot and sunny during our stay there in the late spring. One afternoon, my wife and I took the dog up the nearest mountain to find a shallow lochan we had heard about, on the other side of the summit where we could swim. It was a long slog to the top and well worth the effort. Most of the sheep were grazing on the lower slopes and we could hear the young lambs bleating in the distance far down below. The lochan was sheltered by steep hills on two sides and there was a soft balmy breeze barely rippling the water: a perfect day.

The water was shallow and relatively warm for the time of year and the bigger mountains we could see in the distance still had snow on their north sides. The lochan had a small rocky island in the middle with a surprising amount of flora sprouting from its stony crevices and shallow peat layers. The lush but miniature vegetation was due to the lack of grazing by sheep or the red deer that ranged in those hills. The stunted growth of mini trees and shrubs gave the impression of a Japanese bonsai garden that had been carefully tended, while the area around the lochan was heavily grazed and denuded of any wild flowers.

A pair of red-throated divers on the far side of the lochan observed us with interest. I waded into the water and swam slowly towards the birds; they appeared to be unconcerned by my trespass into their domain. It must have been obvious to them that I was low on the predator list. One of the divers flew towards me for a closer look and passed over my head within a few feet. I was quite excited by the close encounter with these beautiful, normally shy Highland birds – but there was soon still better to come. I swam around the little island for a closer look and admired the busy, buzzing insect and butterfly life at close range, then headed back to the shore for a shivery bite, where my wife was still testing the water, almost up to her knees; she was no wilderness swimmer.

A Royal Visit

As we sat by the shore having our picnic, we were indeed treated to an even more exciting experience: we heard a whistling sound above and looked up to see a golden eagle gliding above us on fixed, outstretched wings. This king of birds was so close that we could see its eye and every feather. As it banked low above the water, the sun caught its back, which shone like gold and the name for this magnificent bird of prey was truly appropriate.

A second eagle joined the first and they glided around the lochan, one following the other, effortlessly, riding the breeze and the wind whistling through their upturned pinions was clearly audible at a surprising distance. But the magic of the moment was then rudely interrupted by the sudden appearance of a bold, noisy, croaking raven, which pursued one of the eagles, dive-bombing it and almost landing on its back.

The eagle was irritated by the raven and went into full flight mode and with a few heavy, powerful flaps left its pursuer far behind. Within the space of two minutes, that magnificent giant raptor was only a speck in the sky and its mate had disappeared in the opposite direction. It was a golden moment to be remembered for life, etched into the brain.

A Life Saved

The trip back down the hill was also eventful. The dog was sniffing around in a flat, boggy area covered by a carpet of short heather and had his head thrust down a hole in the peat. I was expecting him to be scenting for mountain hares or pipits hiding in that rough ground. As we walked on, I called him to heel, but he wouldn't budge from the spot. I bawled at him again and he still remained rooted to the place. I trudged back, feeling quite irritated by Finn's disobedience, but when I got beside him I saw what was holding his attention. There was a cutting in the peat, a waterlogged, narrow drainage trench about two and a half feet deep and six inches wide and inside the bottom of the cutting was a lamb no more than a couple of weeks old.

It was cold and wet, but still breathing, but the poor thing was wedged in the trench, unable to move; it was with great difficulty that I was able to extract it without doing any damage to the unfortunate creature. Its body had formed a little dam, which had backed up the cold water under it. I was convinced that it hadn't been there very long, otherwise it would have died of hypothermia. Its tight, curly fleece was heavy with water. We squeezed it dry and rubbed its little legs to get the circulation going. It was very perky under the circumstances and showed no fear of the dog as Finn nuzzled and sniffed at it.

So where the hell was its mother? We had seen no sheep that far up the hill. My wife did a brisk reconnaissance of the area and found no desperate ewe bleating for its lost lamb. It was a mystery. We were disinclined to take the young thing with us, in case its mother was still somewhere in the vicinity, but if we did leave it there, either the eagles or foxes would kill it.

We took it with us, carrying it for a short distance and then putting it down to try its legs out. Considering its terrifying ordeal it was remarkably strong and was able to keep pace with us. It would have made a strange sight to anyone watching our steady downhill progress in single file: two humans, followed by a brindle lurcher, followed by a new lamb attempting to suckle on the poor dog's private parts. Finn was black-affronted by the lamb's attempts to nuzzle his undercarriage and quickened his pace. It must have been about a mile down that hill before we got to the nearest sheep and their lambs. Our own little lamb showed no interest in the bleating flock in the field and seemed content to stay with us. There were no other sheep in the vicinity and we were convinced that our newly rescued pet had an anxious mother somewhere in that flock.

We got as near as we could to the lamb's woolly relatives and ran away when it gambolled towards a group of lambs playing by the fence. We watched the creature searching the field, hoping that its cries would unite it with its mother. We were concerned that it might not be claimed and hurried back to the cottage where Simon phoned the local shepherd, who promised to check the field. We never did find out what happened, but hoped for the best.

Bad Luck Comes in Threes

On my next visit to the cottage the following September, I went by myself and without the dog. Most of the domestic ducks that I had seen in the garden the previous spring had been killed and eaten by a visiting otter. By then, Audrey and Simon had a new addition to the family, a beautiful baby daughter whom they had named Luana.

It was the season for wild mushrooms so we made an expedition with the children along the river and up the glen to collect chanterelles. Those apricot-scented, yoke-coloured wild mushrooms grew plentifully amongst the damp birch woods, half hidden by the mosses beneath the trees; we picked a large wicker basketful in less than an hour. I wandered about the wood to photograph the beautiful birch trees against the luminous green grass where the sun was filtering through the leaves. But as I leaned against the dead stump of an old birch tree, it gave way and I fell, head first, about nine feet down the steep embankment, landing between two boulders and scraping my forearm from wrist to elbow. Miraculously my head landed in a patch of springy moss and I didn't break my neck or my camera.

They say that bad luck comes in threes and that day was no exception. Later that afternoon back at the cottage, I scalded myself when I spilled a hot mug of coffee on the kitchen table. The third incident of the day was rather more life threatening and involved my wife's Mini Cooper, the little red car that was her pride and joy and which I had borrowed, on sufferance, for my Highland trip while she was in London.

I said goodbye to my young friends at the kitchen door and climbed into the Mini, which was parked alongside the gable end of the house, in line with the steep hill down to the shore. For some reason I thought it might be fun to take the hand brake off and freewheel silently down the hill to the road at the bottom. It was a pleasant sensation rolling down that steep gradient with the window wound down, smelling that clean country air with a tang of autumn. As I approached the first left-hand bend in the road, I pressed the brake pedal to slow down – and nothing happened. Worse, I pulled the steering wheel hard to the left and was unable to turn: the steering had locked.

'Oh s——!' I froze; it was the stuff of nightmares. The Mini left the road and ploughed straight ahead, into a boulder-strewn field with the sheep scattering before me. Directly in my path was a wooden telegraph pole with its steel supporting cable angled towards me, anchored into the ground. The runaway vehicle mounted the cable, dead centre, under the front bumper. There was no audible impact, no breaking glass and no crunching of engine parts: I was high and dry, with the front wheels in the air, staring at the bonnet. I felt as if I had just crash landed a small aircraft and survived.

I climbed out of the car and went to inspect the damage. The front number plate had been sliced neatly in half and there was only a slight dent in the bumper where it was resting on the thick steel cable. None of the boulders in the field had made contact with the low chassis and I knew that I had been extremely lucky.

Then came the embarrassing part, the slow walk back up the hill to my friend's house to seek assistance. Simon and Audrey had been unaware of my plight because of the steepness of the hill below the house. I expected them to laugh when they caught sight of the little red Mini climbing the telegraph pole in the middle of the field, but to their eternal credit they were sympathetic and kept straight faces while we recovered the vehicle and pushed it back up to the road. Simon advised me that the steering and break failure was due entirely to the ignition being switched off. He had had a similar experience in the past. I declined an offer of a cup coffee before I left the house for the second time.

My main concern was to get back home and repair the damage to the car before my wife saw it; she was due back in Edinburgh the following day, which gave me plenty of time, or so I thought. I went through *Yellow Pages* that evening and found a car accessory shop, not far from the house, which made car number plates.

I was standing outside the shop bright and early the next morning when they opened for business and was assured that the new plate would be ready to collect before noon that day. But when I returned, the shop was closed. I waited for about half an hour, but no one showed up, so I went home and then returned an hour later. The shop was open, but my new plate had not been collected from their other shop. It was four o'clock in the afternoon before I received the replacement number plate and then found there were no holes in it for fixing. I rushed home, got out my drill and made two holes for the fixing screws and disposed of the old plate.

The new plate fitted, but was slightly bowed, due to a slight misalignment with the connecting holes. I hoped that it wouldn't be noticed. I stepped back from the car for a final inspection and heard the sound of a taxi coming down the street. Phew! It was a close thing. I stuffed the screwdriver in my pocket and greeted my wife's homecoming with great relief. My secret was safe, at least until I wrote this.

A New Shooting Opportunity

One day I was in conversation with a woman at my workplace who loved dogs and had several ferrets as pets. I discovered that her husband was a shooter and had permission for rough shooting on several farms in the vicinity of Edinburgh Airport. A few days later I was introduced to Frank and invited to accompany him on one of his weekend shoots. To me, the opportunity of being able to shoot legally in broad daylight without looking over my shoulder and having to duck behind hedges and dive into wet ditches was a luxury. I was not as young and agile as I used to be and relished the opportunity of wandering about the fields in a tweed jacket with a shotgun under my arm like a country gent.

Frank was a stocky chap in his late fifties and shooting and keeping ferrets were his main interest in life. He also had a young dog that was a three-quarter bred Canadian timber wolf. Later, that dog became a cause for concern. What I noticed first about Frank was his abrupt manner, bordering on the rude. He was a somewhat self-centred individual, lacking in basic social skills and my welcome new shooting opportunities had to be measured against my concerns about my new hunting companion's unpredictable behaviour with firearms in the field.

Our first outing took a little while to get started from Frank's house. I liked to be punctual and my own hunting and fishing friends were the same. I always had everything that I needed, laid out the night before. I arrived at Frank's house at the appointed hour on the dot, but it was to be an hour and a half before we finally got started. It was extremely frustrating watching him pacing back and forth from the house to the shed, hunting for all sorts of things that he had mislaid. First it was his gloves, then his car keys, then something else that he had put down while he was looking for the car keys. I felt like calling it a day and going home to read a book about shooting.

Frank's vehicle was a 4x4 jeep, which was handy for crossing steep muddy fields. We arrived at our shooting destination, a field of potatoes that had been blighted by a bulldozer, which had flattened much of the standing crop to clear the ground for the laying of a water pipeline. I wondered if the farmer had been given short notice by the water board and what kind of compensation had been given for the damage to his 'tatties'.

We parked at the edge of the field and loaded our shotguns; Frank carried two polecat ferrets in a smart wooden box that looked more like an attaché case. We walked across the field and slipped one of the ferrets into a small warren under the thorn hedge and positioned ourselves along the hedgerow, guns at the ready and waited. Seconds later, a rabbit bolted and made a beeline for the rows of giant steel pipes that traversed the field awaiting burial. Bang! Bang! Frank loosed off both barrels at the fleeing rabbit and spattered the steel pipes with lead shot – but the rabbit was already safe inside its shell-proof bunker and escaped to run another day.

Against my Better Judgement

I had been observing my companion's shooting etiquette with interest and noticed that his gun barrel had been carelessly pointed towards me on more than one occasion. We did get another rabbit before it reached the safety of the pipes, but the soggy field was not ideal for ferreting. Beyond the hedge was a high security fence around a storage depot and the ferret slipped through the wire and went walkies on the other side. We tried everything to coax the little blighter back, but to no avail and we were forced to follow the perimeter fence around to the main gate and ask the security guard at the entrance if we could have our ferret back. The smirk on his face suggested that his mates in the pub were going to hear about this one that night. We retrieved the wayward ferret and went to try elsewhere.

The main Edinburgh/Queensferry railway line passed close by and we stopped at the embankment and looked across. 'Let's try the other side,' said Frank. This seemed like a very bad idea to me: what was the point of shooting legally on land we had permission to hunt and then trespassing on a railway line with firearms to poach on the other side? Against my better judgement I followed Frank to the other side, fully aware that someone may have been watching us and phoning the police. Later Frank mentioned that his previous shooting companions had stopped going out with him. I wondered why. The trains that passed were travelling at very high speeds and it was a relief to get back home in one piece that night.

Frank was oblivious to my safety concerns and had already made plans for future trips.

A More Successful Excursion

The following excursion turned out to be a little more successful, although getting away from Frank's house in the morning involved the same amount of faffing about to get his equipment organized. The car keys always seemed to go missing at the point of departure and while Frank was running about like the proverbial blue-assed fly, I was 'playing' with his wolf dog in the garden to pass the time.

Those games were interesting and unlike the games I played with my own dog. I noticed that when I held a stick or a ball to throw for the wolf dog, he focused on my eyes and not the object being held. He seemed less interested in retrieving and more interested in charging at me and knocking me over with his large well placed paws hitting me square in the chest. While I was on the ground he licked at my throat. I felt he was rehearsing for a real attack that was coming soon. That wolf dog was a big powerful animal with an impressive size of skull and jaws that were half again bigger than an Alsatian dog. He was an intelligent creature with a mind of his own and a powerful personality that spelled 'pack leader'.

Eventually we left the house and drove a couple of miles to a stubble field, where we set up two hides for shooting pigeons from. We made the crude but effective hides by rolling three giant bales of hay together in a triangular shape. The space within was perfect for a single person. Those massive Swiss rolls, if they were dry, could be manoeuvred relatively easily by using the slope of the field to help position them. We set the decoys down in the stubble between our hides to attract any passing pigeons to within shooting range and waited patiently.

It was quite a while before the birds began to appear and I dozed off while I waited. When I opened my eyes, the birds were directly in front of me, circling above the decoys. We downed a couple of woodpigeons and propped them up beside the plastic decoys and waited for more to appear. It wasn't a heavy bag at the end of the day, but the meat was good to eat and the carcases made good soup stock.

One of the birds I killed turned out to be a racing pigeon, with a numbered ring on its leg and a hand-written message attached to the other leg under a rubber ring. The blood-spattered, neatly folded note carried the bird owner's name and address in County Down, Northern Ireland. The date on the note was a month old, so the bird must have lost its way and gone feral. I knew the place where the bird had originated in Ireland; by a strange coincidence I had been there the previous year and had photographed two Belfast men releasing homing pigeons at Kilkeel below the mountains of Mourne.

I felt duty bound to write to the owner of the bird and make a full confession. I posted the ring back to him and included copies of the photos I had taken of the Belfast men, in case he recognized them and could give them the photos. I imagined that the pigeon racing fraternity in Northern Ireland was non-sectarian but I never did get a reply to my letter or an unexpected visit from the bird's owner.

Frank's Reckless Endangerment

Some of our shooting expeditions turned into marathons, rushing around the countryside from one small parcel of land to another. One morning we parked the jeep in a small wood behind a cottage and walked through a five-bar gate into the corner of a field. There were two small rabbits close by, and Frank emptied both barrels at them. The poor creatures were hardly worth shooting, they were so small. We walked to the top of the field hunting for bigger rabbits and ten minutes later a Land Rover appeared at the gate below and the driver got out and called us over. It was the farmer who had given Frank permission to shoot in the field.

The woman who lived in the nearby cottage had phoned the farmer with a complaint. Her young daughter had been sitting on her horse by the house when

Frank had blasted the rabbits. The sudden noise had frightened the horse, which had reared up, almost dumping its rider. Quite understandably the girl's mother had been very angry about the incident, as her child could have been seriously injured. When the farmer told Frank what had happened, Frank just shrugged his shoulders and said nothing. It was left to me to apologize for the incident and ask the farmer to speak to the mother. It seemed pretty obvious to me that our presence there in the future would not be welcomed.

In the afternoon we drove back in the direction of the airport, to a narrow strip of woodland that was full of rabbit warrens. The woods bordered a field that sloped down to a smart baronial hotel at the bottom of the hill. The hotel was a popular venue for wedding receptions.

We put the ferrets to work and began shooting at the fleeing rabbits as they raced from the woodland and into the field, in the general direction of the hotel car park. I glanced down the hill when I heard the sound of bagpipes. The bride and groom had arrived in a white Rolls Royce and were making a splendid entrance at the front of the building. A photographer was filming the event with a video camera. This wedding sequence was going to be a memorable one for the young couple, especially when they heard the soundtrack on the film. Our contribution to the movie was explosively noisy: the fusillade of shots was like something from the gunfight at the OK Corral and their ceremony had become a shotgun wedding.

A Nasty Surprise

When we got back to the jeep it was our turn for a nasty surprise: the vehicle had been broken into and the rear window smashed; there was glass all over the road. Frank's face was red with fury; I was expecting to see steam shooting out of his ears. The thief would have been unable to see anything of value in the jeep because of the heavy blanket covering the interior. I had left my air rifle in the jeep. It had been stolen, along with a nice old leather cartridge bag. Nothing else seemed to be missing. Inside the jeep, hundreds of little cubes of broken window glass littered the seats and floor. Frank spent an age picking them all up, effing and blinding continuously.

When we left the scene of the crime, our first stop was to the nearest police station. I was greatly concerned about the police reaction to leaving a gun in the unattended vehicle, which we had assumed was safe and secure. The desk sergeant at the station looked relieved when we told him that the stolen weapon was only an air rifle. The reason that I had taken the rifle with me was because a local farmer had problems with wild stock doves in his barn, and using a twelve bore shotgun in a building with a fragile roof was not an option, although Frank had tried it. This same rifle was the one that had been confiscated by the police in Selkirk when I had been caught by the gamekeeper on the local estate. Buying it back at the courtroom had been a great relief to me. The weapon certainly had a chequered history.

It was almost three months later that the police in Edinburgh contacted me to inform me that my weapon and cartridge case had been recovered. I went to Fettes to collect my property and discovered only then that the Highland Constabulary had apprehended the gun thief the day after the theft in Edinburgh! He had been spotted by a member of the public in Glencoe using my rifle butt to break into another unattended vehicle. The informant had phoned the cops with a good description of the thief and his vehicle and the police had waited for him further north and headed him off at the pass. He had confessed to his recent crimes and told the arresting officers that he was on his way to Aberdeen to attend a court appearance for other car thefts.

The police in Fettes informed me that the thief would not be charged with the firearm theft because they couldn't afford to send two Highland officers down to Edinburgh for what was a relatively petty case, but I was assured that the thief was going back to prison in Aberdeen for numerous other offences that he had been charged with. The expression 'scot free' came to mind.

The wooden stock on my rifle had been cracked on either side of the barrel when the thief had used it as a battering ram. I was able to make a reasonable repair to the stock and then sanded it down and repolished it. The wood carried numerous scars and dents from a lifetime of use. Fortunately the fine sights were undamaged and I was still able to shoot accurately with the rifle I had used since my teens.

Time to Call it a Day

Shooting with Frank turned out to be a high risk venture and each time I came back from a hunting expedition with him I felt like a survivor. On one particular trip I decided to call it a day. I was always safety conscious with guns and especially shotguns. I was in the habit of removing the cartridges from my gun whenever I came to a fence or a ditch to cross; safety was a matter of common sense if you didn't want a serious accident.

Frank, on the other hand, seemed to have absolutely no basic awareness of the dangers relating to the negligent handling of lethal weapons. I once sat in his jeep bouncing across a stubble field with his shotgun pointing at my kneecap; apparently it was loaded. One memorable morning I watched him lay his loaded shotgun down in a stubble field and walk over to a five-bar gate to bring the jeep through. I watched in disbelief as he drove into the field and directly over the stock of his gun. He seemed unconvinced of what he had done until I showed him the tyre mark on the polished wood. The ground had been soft, so there was very little damage to the gun. However, the possibility of an accidental shooting was truly alarming. I was beginning to understand why Frank's former shooting companions had looked elsewhere for their rough shooting.

Two other incidents were instrumental in convincing me that our shooting partnership should be terminated before any serious harm was done.

We had been given permission by a local farmer to shoot rabbits and pigeons next to a field of rape seed that was ready for harvesting. The large field was surrounded by woodland and we stood against the trees waiting for the birds to come over. We managed to bring down several woodpigeons as they flew above the field, but unfortunately we were unable to retrieve them all because of the thickness of the crop; rape grows high and thick and becomes impenetrable by the time it is ripe. A dog would have been useful but we didn't have one with us; Frank's untrained half wild wolf dog would have been more likely to go hunting for sheep than downed pigeons in that matted jungle.

Later in the morning a combine harvester arrived at the field. The driver gave us a friendly wave and started cutting a great swathe around the outside of the field, so we moved on to look for rabbits in the adjoining woodland. By the time we returned to the rape field a couple of hours later, much of the standing crop had been levelled. As we stood watching the combine pass by, a rabbit bolted in front of the vehicle and ran towards us. Frank let fly with both barrels in direct line with the combine harvester without any regard for the man in the cab. I was speechless. The man in the cab gave us a look that I will never forget. He stopped the combine, produced a mobile phone and made a call. To say I was embarrassed would have been a gross understatement; ashamed would have been more appropriate.

We scuttled into the wood to avoid the inevitable confrontation that would most surely follow. Less than ten minutes later we heard the sound of a speeding Land Rover circling the outside of the wood looking for us. Frank confirmed that it was the farmer who owned the field. We dodged about those woods like two escaped convicts hiding from the law. Our day's hunting activity had been cut short, but there was still one last trip that I was to make with Frank before the day was over.

A New Friend

Frank had heard about a shotgun for sale. The seller lived nearby and it was only a ten-minute drive to get over to his house and take a look. We drove along a short curved driveway with beech trees on either side, to a small stone-built lodge house. There were gundogs barking in the kennels in the garden to the rear. A stocky, grey-haired chap in his early fifties came out of the front door to meet us. He had piercing blue eyes and a confident manner about him and I guessed he was not the kind of person to suffer fools gladly. He introduced himself as George.

George was selling the gun to raise cash; he had recently been made redundant after the engineering firm where he worked had been destroyed in a fire. I had witnessed the blaze myself from the top of Blackford Hill several months earlier. The factory was not far from the shore and the black smoke pluming into the sky could be seen from miles away. The double-barrelled, twelve-bore shotgun for sale was a quality piece and in very good condition and the price was a bargain.

Frank said he wanted to try it out, so George suggested that we follow his jeep in our vehicle to a nearby stubble field to test the weapon. We drove into the field and parked both jeeps close to the fence. Frank examined the weapon to his satisfaction and then found a short plank in the field, which he leaned against the barbed wire fence. He paced out his steps at right angles away from the fence, then suddenly turned around and fired both barrels at the plank, which happened to be dangerously close to where George and I were standing beside his jeep. We looked at each other in disbelief; a stray pellet on the outside of the shot pattern could have hit either one of us. It was fortunate that we were standing close to the jeep and had some protective cover.

Frank's habit of loosing off both barrels whenever he fired a shotgun was a habit he seemed unable to lose. His second finger was constantly bandaged because of the damage caused by the recoil from the trigger guard. If he had used the first joint of his index finger to pull the trigger, then he would have had no need of the bandage – but it was pointless offering any advice to Frank, he was not one of life's listeners. If George had not been so strapped for cash, I think he would have told Frank there and then to 'F— off'. However, the deal was done and the transaction made.

Something good did come from this meeting: I recognized a fellow hunter in George as opposed to a shooter. We exchanged phone numbers when he had done the necessary paperwork for the sale of his shotgun (the police had to be informed in writing whenever a firearm changed hands).

I made the excuse to Frank that my failing physical condition was the reason that prevented me from continuing to go shooting with him. I didn't know whether he believed me or not, but I suspected that I might live longer without his company and that my name would be less likely to appear in the *Evening News* as an accidental shooting victim.

Frank mentioned to me that the farmer, who had owned the field of rape with the combine in it, had phoned him that same night and withdrawn his permission for Frank to shoot on any of his land in the future. Of course it was exactly what I had expected, but Frank seemed surprised by the farmer's response. What worried me about Frank was that he could never understand when he had done something wrong and always blamed other people.

16
Slowing Down

George phoned me soon after our meeting and invited me round for a chat. I think he may have been intrigued by my connection with the lunatic that he had just sold his gun to. George had an extensive knowledge of hunting from his own lifetime experiences and it was nice to meet someone I could relate to, with a real love of nature. Initially we were both guarded about our murky pasts. We had both hunted at night and at the dawning of the day when most respectable law-abiding citizens were still in their beds.

I discovered that George was a member of a shooting syndicate that raised its own pheasants for sporting purposes on a hill farm in the Borders. It was a case of meeting a poacher turned gamekeeper. My previous experiences of shooting pheasants had not been in company or in broad daylight with a pause for lunch and then drinks afterwards.

A New Experience

My first invitation to a 'shoot' came soon afterwards. It was to a private shoot on the land of a gentleman farmer who was an academic at Edinburgh University with agricultural interests. His modest hill farm was part arable and part livestock, with grazing for several hundred sheep and several acres of attractive mixed woodland, which was managed for shooting. The hills above the farm were topped with heather. George was attending the event in his capacity as a dog handler for the purpose of retrieving fallen birds. Many organized shoots seemed to rely on getting help from other shoots when their dates didn't coincide and having enough well trained dogs to do the job properly was essential. I did have some preconceived ideas about organized pheasant shooting and was pleasantly surprised by the social mix of the people taking part. It was a highly organized affair handled with military precision.

I took my camera with me so that I would be able to get a few shots in myself, and also so that I could record this new experience, which might be my one and only opportunity. I felt like a fox in a hen coop, watching the beaters driving the birds through the woods towards the line of guns waiting in the meadow below. The running birds launched themselves into the air only when the beaters and their dogs were close behind them at the fence at the edge of the wood. I lost count of the number of shots fired.

I was upset to see a tawny owl shot down as it flew towards the guns and watched one of the dog men pick it up and discreetly shove it down a deep rabbit hole with the help of his shepherd's crook. I assumed the owl had been shot by accident – its plumage wasn't too dissimilar from a hen pheasant when seen approaching from that angle – although some keepers still shot them on sight because of their predation on pheasant poults. I believed that any decent farmer would be glad to have owls around the steadings to prey on the mice and rats that did so much damage to the grain stores.

I had to admit that I enjoyed the experience of a good day out. The black and white photographs that I had taken turned out to be rather good, with a timeless quality about them. Traditional shooting attire had changed little since Victorian times and tweeds were still in vogue. I made copies of the portraits that I had taken and asked George to pass them on for me.

A Driven Shoot

Over the following two years I was invited to other driven pheasant shoots run by George's syndicate. The shoots were situated on two upland farms in the Border country to the south. During the shooting season those bare hills were open to the elements and exposed to the chill easterly winds that came from the Russian Steppes. The narrow shelter belts of spruce trees and wind-bent beech trees provided enough cover for the pheasants that were reared, driven and shot there. Often the ground was boggy or frozen, and it was hard work stumbling across the steep hillsides where the beef cattle had left a honeycomb of deep hoofprints in the earth. The drives through the thick overgrown woodland were hard going for the beaters who struggled to keep a straight line and prevent their keen dogs from wandering too far ahead. Some of the beaters got to shoot on alternate drives.

Sometimes potentially dangerous incidents occurred involving the inexperienced. One young man who was a novice on his first shoot, had been placed in the corner of a field with his equally young spaniel pup beside him. The youth had his double-barrelled shotgun crooked over his arm and was waiting anxiously for the driven birds to appear over the trees in front of him as the beaters approached. I was standing behind the young man less than twenty yards away when the birds broke cover and he swung up his gun and shot down a high-flying pheasant in fine style; the bird thudded on to the ground beside me, flapping in its death throes and the young spaniel came after it in a highly excitable state.

Unfortunately the spaniel was on a long lead and was pulling its young master close behind it; the youth was cursing at the dog and whirling round trying to keep his balance and even worse, pointing his still loaded gun in all directions. It was like a Charlie Chaplin movie, but only funny in retrospect. The dog grabbed the bird and ran with it, tripping his master in the process. Some of the other shooters in the line had heard the commotion and were looking across at the circus and it seemed unlikely that any of them would be happy standing alongside that boy for the next drive. Afterwards, George gave him some useful tips in shooting etiquette and gun safety for the future.

The banter in the smoke-filled bothy after the shoot was very enjoyable, but God help anyone who had done anything to invite ridicule from the assembled company. There was an interesting cross-section of shooters around the table from various backgrounds, most speaking in broad Scots. We had farmers, roofers, pest control men, engineers and ex-gamekeepers. They were a rough and ready bunch, but good-natured and good company. We sat around the log fire in the hearth to warm our numb fingers and finished whatever food we had left; there was plenty of drink to go around and the whisky flowed freely.

Shooters who had missed easy birds in sight of the other guns were taunted mercilessly about their poor performances. One short-sighted gentleman who had failed to shoot at an overhead woodcock, thinking it was a thrush, was subjected to a tirade of jokes from the others. One wit suggested that he couldn't tell the difference between a f—ing wren and a f—ing eagle. But it seemed better not to shoot at something you were unsure about. Sharp eyes and quick reflexes were essential for successful shooting and a thick skin was useful in the bothy.

The birds that had been shot during the course of the day were tied in braces and hung in the byre next door to the bothy. Most of us took birds away and they were equally divided by those who wanted them. I was glad to see that none of them were wasted. My colleague at work had been a beater on a large estate near Sandringham in England and had witnessed hundreds of perfectly good pheasants being buried in a trench after the shoot. Gamekeepers and landowners claimed there was no market for this harvest – so how could they justify their country pursuits? It all seemed good ammunition for the anti-hunting and shooting brigade.

Woodpigeons

I got an invitation from George to go pigeon shooting on a small estate on the outskirts of Edinburgh where big flocks of 'woodies' had moved in to the area to feed on the autumn stubble and bean fields. We met the gamekeeper at the lodge house and he walked us over towards the fields where the birds were feeding. We ducked down behind a drystane dyke and peeped over the top to see more than a thousand birds forming a moving carpet in the field with their grey backs as they waddled about hunting for loose fallen grain left behind by the combine. George and I both had our double-barrelled twelve bores at the ready, but had not loaded them – and then without warning, the keeper suddenly stood up and clapped his hands.

The great flock of birds arose, flapping from the field, swarming upwards like locusts before disappearing over a line of tall beech trees on the far boundary. George gave me a knowing look: it wasn't necessary to comment, we were both thinking the same thing. Then the keeper wandered off and left us to make our own plans for the day's shoot – though we had just missed a perfect opportunity to ambush the feeding flock and bag what was likely to have been a good haul with very few cartridges.

Once the birds had been spooked we wasted several hours testing other parts of the estate where we could conceal ourselves under a useful flight path. Eventually we set up a camouflage net along a line of tall trees at the foot of a steep grassy field and settled down to make ourselves comfortable, waiting patiently for the pigeons to fly over. The gamekeeper showed up again to see how we were getting on and sat beside us rolling a cigarette. We heard the sound of a buzzard mewing above us as it circled lazily on high.

'I'm going to shoot that bastard! Pass me your gun,' the keeper exclaimed. I refused to hand over my weapon. 'It's a protected bird,' I reminded him. He laughed and said, 'I can see you're a city boy!'

He was obviously antagonized by my unwillingness to aid and abet his rural crime; however, I considered myself to be a hunter, not a shooter and didn't really fancy eating a buzzard. Within a few minutes the lofty raptor had spiralled upwards and out of range. I suspected that hawks and other predators soon disappeared in that neck of the woods. Later in the afternoon we saw a bit more action when the pigeons were on the move again, flying directly towards our concealed position in the hide and providing with us with some very fast snap shots. The bag at the end of the day was fairly modest considering the plague of pigeons we had seen on our arrival.

The humble woodpigeon must be one of the easiest birds in the world to pluck, and the breast meat is easily filleted from the bone. When I got home, I followed George's advice about using the pigeon carcasses to make a very tasty, beefy stock for soup.

Stick Dressing

George introduced me to the traditional country craft of stick dressing, after casting a critical eye over a rather clumsy walking stick that I had cobbled together from a broken elm-wood chair seat and a whittled-down broomstick. I had joined the handle to the shank with a section of copper piping and the joint was beginning to work loose with use.

I became a fellow member of the Lammermuir Stick Dressers Society under George's recommendation and guidance. The society had been formed in the nineteen-eighties at an isolated sheep farm in the Lammermuir Hills in the Scottish Borders. Crook and stick handles were made from traditional materials using ram's horn, deer antler or hardwoods and a variety of timber was used for the shanks, hazel and blackthorn being the most favoured. The society had a splendid logo featuring a black-faced ram's head above crossed shepherd's crooks.

When I joined the society they had a fully equipped workshop near the village of Athelstaneford in East Lothian and it was an interesting group of chaps that met there on Thursday evenings, including an ex-policeman, a county road worker and one American church minister. There was good-natured banter between men in the workshop as they inspected each other's creative efforts in an attempt to produce a presentable stick either as a present, or to enter in one of the competitions that took place annually at the country sports fairs.

The use of machinery was a great help to me in speeding up the process of shaping handles and drilling them for fitting to the shanks. In the past I had broken many delicate saw blades roughing out handle shapes from a piece of oak or elm wood, retrieved from a city skip. The bandsaw and the pillar drill were great assets to my new hobby and gave more time to concentrate on the finer details in producing a graceful stick handle. Stylized thistles and leaping salmon or trout were popular designs for many of the stick makers and the workshop members were always willing to help with advice for the novice, sharing their knowledge and experience.

I made several crooks with wooden handles of yew, hornbeam and burr elm, before graduating to a piece of ram's horn, which needed a lot more preparation than the wood before shaping with a file. The curved, spiralled ram's horn needed to be much larger than one would have supposed, to have enough solid material for carving purposes after the hollow section was cut away. After boiling for several hours to soften the horn, it was flattened in a press.

The process of flattening was done by degrees, and the horn had to be boiled again when it cooled, to re-soften it before it was pressed into the next mould for shaping. The object of the exercise was to reduce that bulky ram's horn into a workable flat slab of similar dimensions to the timber that we used for the handles. I learned how to taper the top of a hazel shank into a dowel to fit snugly when glued into the handle; if the joint was properly made, it was almost invisible.

Members of the society made regular trips into the countryside to harvest suitable hazel sticks for the making of crooks; these were brought back to the workshop, had the date written on them and were stored on high shelves for seasoning, which normally took about a year. The natural pattern on those smooth-barked sticks varied considerably depending on what kind of ground they had been growing on. Hazel shrubs growing close to water often produced a very beautiful mottled silvery bark.

When I began searching for hazel sticks myself, I often found stubs on trees where sticks had been cut many years before and the stump had healed over. I also found many potentially good sticks which had been badly damaged by the roebuck that liked to rake their antlers on them to help shed the velvet and to mark their territory. Those rubbing sticks were often shredded and many of them died as a result of the damage caused. Almost every hazel grove I saw had deer tracks through the trees.

Blackthorn sticks of the right dimensions were much harder to find, but I did get a good one from Blackford Hill: it was growing out of a rocky crevice and the rock had forced the root to grow sideways so the natural angled shape at the foot of the stick enabled me to carve it with a handle as a one-piece job. I chose a tawny owl to carve because it was a suitable shape and also because it was one of my favourite birds from childhood.

I carried that owl stick with me in later years when I travelled across America, and I was stopped by an Ojibwe Indian woman in the international airport at Minneapolis in Minnesota because she wanted to take a look at the carving. She told me that in most Native American cultures the owl was a symbol of impending death and if an owl landed on your lodge then it was likely that a member of your family was soon going to die. If no one passed away within a lunar month, then you would be okay until the next time. I heard the same story from both Shoshone Indians in Wyoming and Northern Cheyenne Indians in Montana.

Another popular stick pattern, favoured by society members with shooting interests, was the stout, long-shanked deer-stalker's stick topped with a section of red deer antler in the shape of a V. This stick was useful for crossing hilly and uneven ground, as well as providing a steady rest when aiming a rifle.

Deer Stalking in the Borders

I had a memorable day out with George, who took me deer stalking in the Borders area. I sat beside him on a raised platform overlooking a Sitka plantation, with a clear view along two rides that were a favourite crossing place for the ever-vigilant roe deer in the woodland. After several hours waiting patiently in the cold damp air, talking only in whispers, a buck suddenly appeared at a distance of about a hundred yards, sniffing the air and strutting cautiously around before posing side on and presenting itself as a suitable target. Neither George nor myself were wearing ear-fenders and when he took aim and fired, the muzzle of his rifle was only a couple of feet away from my head.

The bang was horrendously loud and I wasn't prepared for the impact of the explosion in that silent landscape. The pain in my right ear was excruciating and my head was ringing from the shot. The deer went down instantly on the sloping ground and out of sight. We climbed down from the platform and made our way over to where the roe had been standing. It was lying on its side in the grass with a bullet straight through its heart and was probably dead before it hit the ground. I complimented George on his marksmanship, but he just shrugged his shoulders and told me that when telescopic sights were zeroed in on a rifle, there was no excuse to miss the target.

I had a serious headache for the rest of the day and my hearing was most definitely impaired for several days afterwards.

Postscript

Old age has taken its toll on my body and I have been forced to slow down. The risk of being caught hunting on private land is that much greater, but I am still game for an opportunist chase whenever my new dog Jack flushes a rabbit or a hare during one of our slow country rambles. My present canine companion is a smallish, smooth-coated black lurcher with a keen interest in scenting out rabbits and crafty pheasants hiding in the long grass. He is the least successful hunter of all our dogs on account of lack of opportunity due to the lack of mobility on my part, but he has a great knack of making new friends for us and increasing our social circle. I named him after my old friend Jack the Ferret, who emigrated to Australia nearly thirty years ago.